THE FEMALE BODY

Psychoanalytic Ideas and Applications Series

THE FEMALE BODY
Inside and outside

Edited by

Ingrid Moeslein-Teising and Frances Thomson Salo

General Editor
Gennaro Saragnano
Psychoanalytic Ideas and Applications Series

KARNAC

First published in 2013 by
Karnac Books Ltd
118 Finchley Road
London NW3 5HT

British Library Cataloguing in Publication Data

A C.I.P. for this book is available from the British Library

ISBN-13: 978-1-78049-133-2

Typeset by V Publishing Solutions Pvt Ltd., Chennai, India

Printed in Great Britain

www.karnacbooks.com

CONTENTS

PART IV: SEXUALITY AND THE FEMALE BODY
IN THE LIFE CYCLE

ACKNOWLEDGEMENTS

I would like to take this opportunity to thank all those authors who agreed to contribute to this book, and who have in this way allowed us to reflect further on issues of the female body inside and out, and then on wider issues of femininity and female creativity.

On the behalf of the Committee on Women and Psychoanalysis, I also wish to thank the IPA Publications Committee, and particularly Leticia Glocer Fiorini, the immediate past Chair of the Publications Committee, who contributed to making possible the production of this book.

I wish to especially thank my co-editor Ingrid Moeslein-Teising whose part in the overall vision contributed to these chapters, and along with the German COWAP group helped make the possibility become a reality, and also to all those who have in any way sponsored this book, and lastly and above all to the International Psychoanalytical Association (IPA) for their ongoing commitment to the work of the Committee.

Frances Thomson Salo
Overall Chair of COWAP and co-editor

Mariam Alizade (died March 2013) was a psychiatrist and training analyst of the Argentine Psychoanalytic Association. She was a past overall Chair of the IPA Committee on Women and Psychoanalysis (2001–2005) and former COWAP Latin American co-chair (1998–2001). She had authored *Feminine Sensuality* (Karnac, 1992); *Near death: Clinical psychoanalytical studies* (Amorrortu, Buenos Aires, 1995); *Time for women* (Letra Viva, Buenos Aires, 1996); *The lone woman* (Lumen, Buenos Aires, 1999); *Positivity in Psychoanalysis* (Lumen, Buenos Aires, 2002). She was the editor of the COWAP—Karnac Series (*The Embodied Female, Studies on Femininity, Masculine Scenarios*) and of the collected papers of COWAP Latin American Intergenerational Dialogues (Lumen, Buenos Aires).

Ute Auhagen-Stephanos is a neurologist, psychiatrist, doctor for psychosomatic medicine and a psychoanalyst (member of the German Psychoanalytic Association DPV/IPA). During psychoanalytic training she worked at the Sigmund-Freud-Institute in Frankfurt/M. She is in private practice in Neu-Ulm/Bavaria and has, over the past thirty years, worked with women suffering from fertility disturbances. She wrote numerous papers about psychosomatics of infertility and the interaction of the psyche and reproductive medicine. She published two books: *Wenn die Seele nein sagt* [When the Psyche says No] (1990, 2006); *Damit mein Kind bleibt* (For my baby shall remain) (2009).

Rotraut De Clerck is a psychoanalyst in private practice in Frankfurt and a training analyst of the German Psychoanalytical Association DPV/IPA. She did post graduate training 1985–86 in Kleinian Psychoanalysis at the Tavistock Clinic and the Institute of Psychoanalysis in London. Since then she has been a long term guest of the Institute of Psychoanalysis. Her clinical interests include creativity, narcissism, trauma and paranoia, female homosexuality and the "negative" Oedipus. Her interests outside the clinical field lie in psychoanalysis and culture, psychoanalysis and literature, and psychoanalysis and art, as well as theories about the creative process and what psychoanalysis can contribute to these areas. She has lectured and published on these issues, especially on the painter, Lucian Freud. She translated and edited the *Letters of James and Alix Strachey 1924/25 (*Klett Cotta, 1995) into German. Her main publications in the field of Psychoanalysis and Culture are *Von der Unerzählbarkeit des Traumas: Der Roman ohne "e" von Georges Pérec* (Merkur 2000, Psychosozial 2004), *The penetrating glance: Sigmund Freud—Lucian Freud* (Psychosozial-Verlag, 2007), and *Trauma and Paranoia (ed.)* (Psychosozial Verlag, 2006).

Thomas Ettl, Dr.phil., is a psychologist and psychoanalyst, and member of the German Psychoanalytic Association DPV/IPA, trained at the Sigmund-Freud-Institute Frankfurt. He works in private practice. He worked on the significance of imitation and identification in Piaget and Lacan. For ten years he was a co-editor of the *Journal for Psychoanalytic Theory and Practice*. He has published essays and lectures on psychoanalysis and art, literature, education and eating disorders, such as, *Das bulimische Syndrom (The bulimic syndrome)* (Edition Discord, 2001) and *Geschönte Körper*—geschmähte Leiber (Psychoanalysis of the cult of beauty) (Edition Discord, 2006).

Claudia Frank, Priv.-Doz. Dr. med., is a training analyst of the German Psychoanalytic Association DPV/IPA, and works in private practice in Stuttgart. From 1988–2001 she worked at the Department for Psychoanalysis, Psychotherapy and Psychosomatics of the University in Tübingen, and from 1998–2001 was the Chair for Psychoanalysis, Psychotherapy and Psychosomatics. She is a guest member of the British

Psychoanalytical Society. She has published works about technique, theory and history of psychoanalysis (e.g. a monograph about Melanie Klein's first child analyses in Berlin) and papers in applied psychoanalysis. Together with L. Hermanns and H. E. Löchel, she has been an editor of *Jahrbuch der Psychoanalyse*, and with Heinz Weiß has edited various books on Kleinian psychoanalysis.

Teresa Rocha Leite Haudenschild is a training analyst and a child and adolescent analyst with the Brazilian Psychoanalytical Society of São Paulo, and a full member of the International Psychoanalytical Association. She has been working in the field of clinical psychoanalysis for thirty-eight years, particularly studying early symbolization, and the constitution of identity and of masculinity and femininity. She has published papers on these topics in Brazilian, Latin-American and European journals and collections. She studied philosophy and also worked as a journalist until she became interested in psychoanalysis. Mrs. Haudenschild is currently a representative of COWAP in the Brazilian Federation of Psychoanalysis.

Marianne Leuzinger-Bohleber is a psychologist and psychoanalyst, and a training analyst of the German Psychoanalytical Association (DPV) and the Swiss Psychoanalytical Society (SGP). She has been Professor for Psychoanalytical Psychology at the University of Kassel since 1988. Since 2002 she is the director of the Sigmund-Freud-Institute, Frankfurt a. M. From 2001–2009 she was chair of the Research Subcommittee for Clinical, Conceptual, Epistemological and Historical Research of the International Psychoanalytical Association (IPA), and since 2009 she is Vice Chair of the Research Board of the IPA. She is Visiting Professor of the University College London and Member of the Action Group "Neuropsychoanalysis". Since 2010 she has again been chair of the Research Committee of the DPV. Her research areas are clinical, conceptual and empirical research in psychoanalysis and developmental research, and she leads interdisciplinary projects with neuroscience, cognitive science, educational sciences and German literature.

Ingrid Moeslein-Teising is a psychoanalyst of the German Psychoanalytic Association (DPV/IPA), group analyst (DAGG), a doctor in psychosomatic medicine working in private practice and a senior consultant in an inpatient psychosomatic clinic (Klinik am Hainberg,

Bad Hersfeld). She teaches at the Alexander-Mitscherlich-Institute, Kassel. Her scientific interests, publications and presentations focus on the woman in psychoanalysis—her sexuality, her body, her history. Her contribution to the panel "Woman and Psychoanalysis in Germany", at the forty-fifth IPA Congress Berlin 2007, outlined "The destruction of psychoanalytical emancipation: the expulsion of women psycho-analysts under National Socialism." Her activities for COWAP include workshops on COWAP topics within DPV conferences as well as con-tributions to European COWAP conferences. She has been a Committee member for Germany in the COWAP Committee on Women and Psy-choanalysis since 2009.

Ilka Quindeau, Dr. phil. habil., psychologist, sociologist and psychoan-alyst (DPV/IPV) works in private practice and is Professor for Clinical Psychology and Psychoanalysis at the University of Applied Sciences, Frankfurt. Her research interests include psychoanalytical concepts (memory, trauma, sexuality); gender studies, individual and collective consequences of National Socialism (extreme traumatization, actual social discourses); anti-Semitism; psychoanalytical film interpretations. Recent publications are *Seduction and Desire. Sexual Theory According to Freud* (2008, Stuttgart: Klett-Cotta) and *Psychoanalysis. An Introduction for Social and Cultural Studies* (2008, UTB 2008); *Infantile Sexuality—concepts and controversies* (2011, Juventa, Weinheim); *Psychoanalysis of maleness* (in press, Stuttgart: Klett-Cotta). Her recent main research area is in traumatization in older age, the psychic aftermath of war and persecu-tion in early childhood.

Joan Raphael-Leff is a Fellow of the British Psychoanalytical Society and a Professor of Psychoanalysis and Social Psychology in academia. In 1998, she co-founded COWAP, serving as first International Chair. Her clinical practice over the past 35 years has been devoted to emotional aspects of reproduction and early parenting, resulting in numerous publications, including Psychological Processes of Child-bearing (1991/2005); *Pregnancy—the inside story* (1993/2001). *Female Experience: Four generations of British Women Psychoanalysts on work with women (co-edited with R. Jozef Perelberg) (1997/2008). Between Ses-sions and Beyond the Couch (2002). Parent-Infant Psychodynamics—Wild Things, Mirrors and Ghosts (2001/2009). Spilt Milk—Perinatal Loss and Breakdown (2000); Ethics of Psychoanalysis* (2000). She is Leader of the

University College London Academic Faculty for Psychoanalytic Research, and at the Anna Freud Centre directs training for professionals working with teenage parents. Previously she was head of UCL's MSc degree in Psycho-Analytic Developmental Psychology, and Professor of Psychoanalysis at the Centre for Psychoanalytic Studies at the University of Essex, UK. She acts as consultant to perinatal and women's projects in many high and low income countries, including South Africa, where she is Professor Extraordinary at Stellenbosch University.

Elina Reenkola (Mäenpää-Reenkola) is a training analyst of the Finnish Psychoanalytic Society in Helsinki. She is a teacher and supervisor of psychoanalysis and psychotherapy. She works in private practice. She is European COWAP co-chair. Her publications include three books on female psychology in Finnish: *Naisen verhottu sisin* (1997), also published in English, *The Veiled Female Core* (2002); *Intohimoinen nainen* (*Female desire* (2008)) and *Nainen ja viha* (*Vicissitudes of female aggression*). She has written articles on pregnancy, breastfeeding, female shame, sister fantasy and female revenge.

Frances Thomson Salo is a Member of the British Psychoanalytic Society as a child and adult psychoanalyst and is an Associate Professor of University of Melbourne. She was appointed Overall Chair of the IPA Committee of Women in Psychoanalysis by Charles Hanly in 2009. She is immediate past President of the Australian Psychoanalytical Association and a Training Analyst in private practice. She is a Consultant Infant Mental Health clinician in the Royal Women's Hospital Centre, Melbourne; Associate researcher for the Murdoch Children's Research Institute; on the teaching faculty for the University of Melbourne Graduate Diploma/Masters in Infant and Parent Mental Health. She has published in the fields of child psychoanalysis and psychotherapy, and infant mental health.

Marianne Springer-Kremser is a psychiatrist, psychotherapist, and psychoanalyst (IPA) in Vienna/Austria. She was Ordinaria of the Clinic for Psychoanalysis and Psychotherapy of the University of Vienna. She was honoured "Senator for female and gender issues" due to her dedication to gender equality. Her research interests include female psychosomatics, gender studies in psychotherapy/psychosomatics,

psychoanalytic short-term psychotherapy, and psychosomatic counselling. She has published numerous publications.

Laurie Wilson earned her undergraduate degree in art history from
Wellesley College, her master's degree in Fine Arts and Fine Arts
Education from Columbia University, and her Ph.D. in Art History
from City University of New York. She received psychoanalytic training at The NYU Psychoanalytic Institute where she is on the faculty as
Clinical Associate Professor of Psychiatry at the Psychoanalytic Institute
affiliated with NYU Medical Centre, and she practices in New York City.
She directed the Graduate Art Therapy Program at New York University
for twenty-three years and is Professor Emerita there. She has published
extensively in three fields—art therapy, art history, and psychoanalysis
and art therapy. Her book *Alberto Giacometti: Myth Magic and the Man*
was published by Yale University Press in 2003. She is currently writing
a book on Louise Nevelson.

INTRODUCTION

Ingrid Moeslein-Teising

The Ego is first and foremost a bodily Ego

—Sigmund Freud, 1923

Penis envy is not our foremost concern

—Elina Reenkola, 2002

COWAP—Committee on Women and Psychoanalysis

The Committee on Women and Psychoanalysis (COWAP) was established in 1998 as a committee within the IPA in order to provide a framework for the exploration of topics relating to women. Since 2001 it has also worked on the relations between men and women, and masculinity and femininity in our times.

The particular quality of the Committee has been the possibility to link theoretical and clinical psychoanalytical views with continuous attention to the outside world and its problems, as was already understood by Edith Jacobson (1937, 1976) in her early work. Using a psychoanalytical framework to explore these issues is not only significant from a socio-cultural viewpoint; our experience has been that it often contributes to a revision and update of psychoanalytical concepts.

One of the Committee's goals is to further psychoanalytical research concerning the complex relations between categories of sexuality and gender and their implications for psychoanalysis, and to study the cultural and historical influences on the construction of psychoanalytic theories related to men and women. In national and international conferences in all the IPA regions and in several publications, edited by Mariam Alizade (2003, 2006), Irene Matthis (2004) and Giovanna Ambrosio (2005, 2009), COWAP has contributed to these issues.

In the contributions to this book, the subject of: "The female body—inside and outside" is intensively discussed, based on knowledge and experiences which analysts are able to gather from daily work with their patients. One interesting aspect of the analytic profession is the experience continuously developed of our minds and bodies, as receptacles and containers. This is echoed in this book in four main topics, "The female body in art", "Pregnancy and motherhood", "Sexuality and the female body in the life cycle", and "The body as a scene of crime".

The theory of femininity

By the 1920s and 1930s, the psychoanalytical discourse on the theory of femininity, female sexuality and the psychic development of girls had begun. In his *Three Essays* (1905–1924) Freud formulated the foundations of a concept of femininity. As a riposte to a paper by Abraham (1921, 1922) on the female castration complex in 1920 ("Äußerungsformen des weiblichen Kastrationskomplexes", 1923), Horney opened the controversy over female sexuality in 1922 with her lecture "Zur Genese des weiblichen Kastrationskomplexes", (1923; On the genesis of the castration complex in women, 1924), on the occasion of the Seventh International Psychoanalytical Congress in Berlin.

Horney disputed the fundamental significance of penis envy for the normal female psyche and attempted to prove that its virulence rested on a particular and even pathological organisation of the Oedipus complex. This text, announcing Horney's rebellion against the established view that women felt themselves constitutionally inferior, resulted in a series of contributions in which she challenged Freudian assumptions about femininity, Freud's "dark continent" (Freud, S. 1926). The discussion was opened up and classic contributions (by Jeanne Lampl-de

Groot, Lillian Rotter, Helene Deutsch, Melanie Klein, Therese Benedek, Otto Fenichel and of course Jones and Freud himself) followed.

In a second, and later a third, wave alongside developments in society, and cultural and philosophical reforms of ideas about sexuality and sexual practice, contributors to the feminist tradition took up the conceptualizations in the discourse on femininity and developed them, which led to complex of theories and knowledge about female development from childhood to old age. Nancy Chodorow (1989), Janine Chasseguet-Smirgel (1970), Jessica Benjamin (1988), Julia Kristeva (1989) and others contributed to this discourse. Judith Kestenberg's (1968) paper, "Outside and inside, male and female", especially referring to the female body, inspired us in the title of this book.

These psychoanalytical discoveries and wisdom were, however, periodically ignored or forgotten (Bilger, 2009). A renewal of the discourse on femininity in Germany is unthinkable without the work of Margarete Mitscherlich-Nielsen (1975, 1996), nor its development without Christa Rohde-Dachser (Rohde-Dachser 1991).

The female body

Women today are aware of the primary sensual consciousness of their own sexual and generative body; their vulva, vagina, breasts, skin, the internal genitals; their primary passive and active sexual power as a potential, a secret, a veiled power—at least as powerful as the magic penis.

Our subject is the female body as defined materiality, as well as the material of fantasies. The unique characteristics of the female body are its potential for becoming fertilized, being pregnant, carrying a foetus in its womb as a part of the woman and separate, giving birth and breastfeeding; major events that only women experience (Reenkola, 2002; Pines, 1993).

Woman's deepest anxiety focuses on damage that might threaten her genitalia (and the pleasure they bring), her fertility or her baby. The loss of an illusory penis, or the lack, does not touch upon the woman's core in the same way as imaginary or real damage to her own genitals or her fertility might. The threat of feminine castration anxiety emerges as fear of the mother punishing the girl for her forbidden Oedipal desires towards the father. The universal repudiation of femininity is based on the anxiety-provoking nature of inner-genital sensations; the man can more persistently externalize these sensations and is less vulnerable than a woman to fears of injury and loss of the inside genitals as a result (Kestenberg, 1968).

The double function of woman as both mother and sexual being is shown through the breast. It is a nourishing centre as well as a centre of sexual lust (Welldon, 1988). Welldon (2006) also reminds us that the body of the woman is a receptacle for the penis as well as for a potentially foetus during pregnancy; the woman as a container in many ways.

Psychosomatics

The relationship between body and mind becomes powerfully clear through our work as psychoanalysts, especially with the psychoanalytic psychosomatic experience. A patient's body expresses feelings vividly; for example, during unbearable pain, the body is forced to act out feelings that could not be consciously known or transmitted. As words are unavailable to such patients, their emotions have to be expressed somatically and understood by an object, a mother, or, transference and countertransference at work, by an analyst. Many patients somatize (develop bodily symptoms) rather than speak. A woman's body offers her special means of avoiding conscious thought and facing psychic conflict.

The contents of the book

The female body in art

For thousands of years sexuality has been an object of art, religion, science and literature. For the cover of this book, we chose a beautiful ancient Venus (found in southern Germany), and at 40,000 years old the oldest human sculpture. It is a maternal and sexual goddess in mammoth ivory, symbolizing fertility, the mother, love and sexuality. It is a symbol of the eternal human sexuality, of humans desiring and feeling love and passion, as well as aggressiveness and destructiveness.

Laurie Wilson shows what the testimonies of the different eras of culture reveal about the concepts of femininity, about theories of birth and death and the woman's function in them. She explores the change in the relations of men, women, and social roles throughout the ages (over more than 40,000 years); the formation of ambivalence towards the woman as a godly-libidinous-pure image balanced with a dangerous-seductive-deathly being; the special relationship between mother and daughter with its ambivalence and resulting female identity. In "How deep is the skin?" Rotraud de Clerck digs below the surface, deep into Lucian Freud's female nudes. Claudia Frank investigates Alberto Giacometti's "Caress/Despite the Hands" representing and transgressing Bion's reversible perspective in the face of fertility.

Pregnancy and motherhood

Pregnancy, abortions and miscarriages are major subjects concerning the female body, and are both multidimensional and complex. The decision to become pregnant or not, consciously and unconsciously, is determined by innumerable factors and is a unique bodily experience of great impact. Consciously, a woman may become pregnant in order to have a baby, but unconsciously her ambivalence towards her pregnancy might be acted out in miscarriage or abortion. Pregnancy may be used to solve unconscious conflicts (e.g., concerning sexual identity, or other psychic difficulties such as unconscious rage against the mother), and can help to strengthen the successful achievement of a feminine sexual and gender identity. Reenkola (2002) sees in the potential ability to become pregnant the veiled female core, which influences the woman's specific anxieties and desires. Female fears do not centre around a lack, but on the potential of her veiled reproductive core.

Pregnancy offers proof of a gender identity and the visible manifestation to the outside world that the woman has had sex. Such an enormous change, both physically and emotionally, is a normal critical transitional phase and is thus accompanied by a revival of past conflicts and anxieties. The early childhood identifications with her mother are reawakened and enacted in her relationship with her own child. At the same time, her relationship to the mother may mature and old ambivalent identifications may be resolved. Pregnancy is a crisis point in the search for female identity; it is a point of no return, whether a baby is born or the pregnancy ends in abortion or miscarriage. It implies the end of the woman as an independent single unit and the beginning of the unavoidable mother-child relationship. Although the first sexual act is the first step of separation from the mother, it is at the same time the first act in motherhood (Deutsch, 1945).

The woman as a social being, as conceptualized by Jacobson and Horney, has to feel her inner world as well as her outside reality in the sense of the Anna Selbdritt phantasy; as a good and holding mother, to be able to be in "good hope" (a German expression for being pregnant), and to mother. She has to feel safe with her true core, her fertility and her child in her culture.

Medical-technical achievements have loosened the close relationship between sexuality and pregnancy. Women and men can have sex without it resulting in pregnancy; a woman can become pregnant without having intercourse. This being said, sexuality is still unconsciously connected with reproduction (Alizade, 2006). We shall further explore in this book the psychic implications of modern life, in which the primal scene is displaced into a laboratory, as well as ethical dilemmas in prenatal diagnostics.

Joan Raphael-Leff puts the body as receptacle under the spotlight and focuses on the emotional responses to fertility treatment. Marianne Leuzinger-Bohleber raises the question of ethical dilemmas in her work on "The Medea-fantasy" and asks if this is "an inevitable burden during prenatal diagnostics ", connecting "Gender, ethics and medicine in dialogue". Ute Auhagen-Stephanos discusses issues in the fate of assisted pregnancies "inside the mother's womb".

The body as a scene of crime

The female body can be used as an object to reflect intrapsychic tendencies and aggressions; it mirrors cultural dependencies and circumstances, and normative borders and restrictions. Historic and contemporary phenomena use the body as a stage. Thomas Ettl explores rage and hysteria in connection with the body in the novel *Wetlands* (*Feuchtgebiete*) by Charlotte Roche, both a literary and a cultural phenomenon. Modern pathological conflict solutions are expressed using the body and self-mutilation. Marianne Springer-Kremser discusses "The female body as cultural playground" and Elina Reenkola in her wide-ranging paper examines female revenge through body and life, exploring forms of revenge specific to women; that is, indirect revenge with her own suffering, revenge through motherhood, revenge on a man and revenge for and through her body. The vicissitudes of female revenge are shaped by her bodily reality; the feminine inner space.

Sexuality and the female body in the life cycle

The development of female sexuality beyond gender dichotomy is discussed by Ilka Quindeau in relation to the male, through a social and historical perspective. Alizade explores the developments and changes of the female body during its life cycle in its complex dimensions—in the interaction between linear and unconscious time, and suggests that this can be viewed as exciting yet vulnerable and has to be integrated. Women are deeply influenced by bodily changes throughout their lives, and cope differently with these events in line with their previous histories and ability to manage life problems. Adolescent girls, who experience the inevitable bodily changes of puberty and the emotional impact of powerful sexual urges, can either accept such changes in their bodies, or deny the move to adult femininity by becoming amenorrheic or anorexic, thereby avoiding the secondary characteristics of an adult feminine body, such as breasts. Menstruation, a monthly return of readiness for conception or not, has to be worked through psychically and integrated. Fantasies about menstruation are dependent on personality structure and unconscious conflicts, which have been explored as an important psychosomatic issue (Benedek, 1959; Deutsch, 1945).

Sexuality, passion and love in the adult woman is not self-evident but may be disturbed in many ways. Mariam Alizade shows how the deconstruction of the female human being triggers a multiplicity of psychic alternatives and avatars of identity, which question conventional shared beliefs about the stages of life. Teresa Haudenschild reminds us that facing the losses of the menopause in positive terms depends on the capacity constructed in the preceding life for working through mourning and leads us into "Menopause dreams".

I hope this publication contributes thoughts and insights to further illuminate and develop the thinking about the female body and the "dark continent".

References

Abraham, K. (1921). Äußerungsformen des weiblichen Kastrationskomplexes. *Internationale Zeitschrift für Psychoanalyse, 7*: 422.

Abraham, K. (1922). Manifestations of the female castration complex. *International Journal of Psychoanalysis, 3*: 1–29.

Alizade, M. (1999). *Feminine Sensuality*. London: Karnac.

Alizade, A.M. (Ed.) (2003). *Studies on Femininity*. London: Karnac.

Alizade, A.M. (Ed.) (2006). *Motherhood in the Twenty-First Century*. London: Karnac.

Ambrosio, G. (Ed.) (2005). *On Incest*. London: Karnac.

Ambrosio, G. (Ed.) (2009). *Transvestism, Transsexualism in the Psychoanalytic Dimension (Controversies in Psychoanalysis)*. London: Karnac.

Benedek, T. (1959). Parenthood as a developmental phase. *Journal of the American Psychoanalytic Association*, 7: 389–417.

Benjamin, J. (1988). *The Bonds of Love: Psychoanalysis, Feminism, and the Problem of Domination*. New York: Pantheon.

Bilger, A. (2009). Female Sexuality: Development of Concepts in Psychoanalysis. 46th IPA Congress, Chicago, Poster.

Chasseguet-Smirgel, J. (Ed.) (1970). *Female Sexuality: New Psychoanalytic Views*. University of Michigan Press.

Chodorow, N. (1978).*The Reproduction of Mothering*. University of California Press, Berkeley and Los Angeles.

Deutsch, H. (1945). *The Psychology of Women*. New York: Grune & Stratton.

Freud, S. (1905d). *Three Essays on the Theory of Sexuality*. Standard Edition.7: 7–122.

Freud, S. (1923a). *The Ego and the Id*. S.E.19.

Freud,S. (1926). *The Question of Lay Analyis. S.E.,. 20: 212*

Horney, K. (1923). Zur Genese des weiblichen Kastrationskomplexes. *Internationale Zeitschrift für Psychoanalyse*, 9, 12–26.

Horney, K. (1924). On the genesis of the castration complex in women. *International Journal of Psychoanalysis*, 5: 50–65.

Jacobson, E. (1937). Wege der weiblichen Über-Ich-Bildung. *Internationale Zeitschrift für Psychoanalysel*, 23: 402–412.

Jacobson, E. (1976). Ways of female superego formation and the female castration conflict. *Psychoanalytic Quarterly 45*: 525–538.

Kestenberg, J.S. (1968). Outside and inside, male and female. *Journal of the American Psychoanaytic Association*, 16: 457–520.

Kristeva, J. (1989). *Black Sun: Depression and Melancholia*. New York: Columbia University Press.

Matthis, I. (Ed.) (2004). *Dialogues on Sexuality, Gender, and Psychoanalysis*. London, Karnac.

Mitscherlich, M. (1975). Psychoanalyse und weibliche Sexualität. *Psyche, 29*: 769–788.

Mitscherlich, M. & Rohde-Dachser, Ch. (Eds.) (1996). *Psychoanalytische Diskurse über die Weiblichkeit von Freud bis heute*. Stuttgart: Internationale Psychoanalyse.

Pines, D. (1993). *A Woman's Unconscious Use of Her Body*. London: Virago.

Reenkola, E.M. (2002). *The Veiled Female Core*. New York, Other Press.

Rohde-Dachser, C. (1991). *Expedition in den dunklen Kontinent. Weiblichkeit im Diskus der Psychoanalyse*. Berlin: Springer.

Welldon, E. V. (1988). *Mother, Madonna, Whore: Idealization and Denigration of Motherhood*. London: Free Association Books.

Welldon, E. V. (2006). Why do you want to have a child? In: Alizade, A. M. (Ed.). *Motherhood in the Twenty-first Century*, pp. 59–71 London: Karnac.

PART I

THE FEMALE BODY IN ART

CHAPTER ONE

The female body in Western art: adoration, attraction and horror

Laurie Wilson

Abstract

37,000 years of art history will be examined to observe the many ways women's bodies have been experienced and portrayed in Western culture. Thoughts, feelings and fantasies about women, and especially the manner in which they are divided into absolutes and opposites (e.g. good or bad; weak or powerful, seductive or innocent) will be illustrated. Themes such as nudity, relationships, birth, and fertility will be explored. The art of Picasso, Matisse, pre-historic Egypt, Hellenistic, Roman, Medieval, Renaissance, and nineteenth and twentieth century Western European art will all be presented. Greek art uses images of females, such as Hera, Aphrodite, Athena, Demeter, Persephone and Medusa, in order to illustrate the ways women have been depicted in art for the past 2500 years. Psychoanalytic understanding of female psychology will be part of the discussion about the Greek goddesses. Idealized or ordinary depictions of women were created depending upon the civilization. The splitting of women into categories will be clearly depicted in images from more recent civilizations.

In this Chapter we are going on a journey through 37,000 years of art history to catch glimpses of the many different ways the female body has been experienced and portrayed in Western culture.[1] The themes I shall use derive from what we, as psychoanalysts, know of the thoughts, feelings and fantasies about women that come from our patients (both male and female); and from the patients, who have been seen and heard over the last hundred years by our fellow professionals, including Freud himself.

The mind frequently functions in terms of absolutes and opposites, especially when we are very young and have immature cognitive and perceptual abilities. We shall repeatedly find that women are depicted as good or bad; weak or powerful; desirable or terrifying; bearers of life or harbingers of death; the font of nurture and intimacy, or the source of deprivation, separation and abandonment.

All these themes will be visible as we proceed through the history of Western art. Sometimes our subject will be the issue of nudity. Often it will be the relationships between the goddess and her peers, and/or the goddess and her audience. At times we will jump forward in time following a particular theme and its variations. The wide range in the way women's bodies are depicted reflects the very sort of individual disparity that Chodorow (2010) urges us to recall. We also see how that variety alternates with some remarkably fixed ways of seeing.

Whilst there is much speculation about the earliest images of the female body, we know that in pre-historic times (40,000–10,000) there was an emphasis on the female figure. We also know that certain forms, namely roundness, budding, blossoming, were all equated with woman. Indeed in art-historical terms, anatomy was destiny. The most prominent anatomical features, breasts and big bellies, are seen in every cultural era and locale, from the earliest to the present. The *Venus of Willendorf* is a perfect example. (Figure 1)

Not surprisingly we find the mysterious subject of pregnancy and birth playing a dominant role in the art and architecture of earliest civilizations. The oldest known representation of the female form is the recently discovered *Venus of Hohle Fels*, a small ivory figurine with a loop on the top so that it could be worn as a pendant around the neck. (Figure 2). This *"Venus"* figurine has been dated to 35,000 BCE, and was unearthed in a cave in southwestern Germany. The bulbous shapes of "Venus" figurines found at other locales in Europe as well as in the Near East,

Figure 1. Venus of Willendorf (ca. 24,000–22,000 BCE).

with their hugely rounded breasts and bellies, carry the same message: they are fertility figures who imply the potential to be pregnant.

It may not have been clear to Paleolithic cultures that intercourse was connected to pregnancy and birth, and that ignorance could have made women appear fantastically powerful as they seemed to magically bring forth children without the help of men. In prehistory, the connection between sex, subsequent pregnancy and birth would only have been observed in agricultural societies where animals were kept.

The earliest documented image of childbirth itself was found at the Neolithic site Catal Huyuk in Anatolia 8500–5500 BC. The image is of a woman giving birth seated on a birthing chair. Her pendulous breasts hang over her bulging belly, and, between her ankles, an infant's head emerges. In prehistoric Malta, the female body illustrated fecundity in other ways; sacred buildings were created in the shape of a woman's body. The large temples on the island of Gozo, Malta, whose entrances were obviously sacral spaces located at the vagina-like openings of the buildings, were constructed from 3600–3000 BCE, approximately one thousand years before the first Egyptian pyramid.

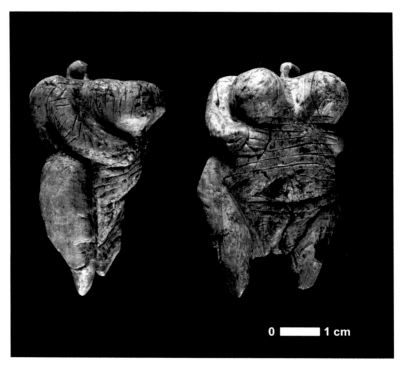

Figure 2. Venus of Hohle Fels (35,000 BCE).

Figure 3. Ggantija Temple in Xaghra (3600–3000 BCE).

Here is *Ggantija* (Giant Lady in Maltese) (Figure 3). We can only guess at the rituals and spiritual practices of the builders of such temples, but the shapes of the structures leave little doubt about the gender of the cult goddess for whom they were built. The numerous sculptures of bulging-bellied figurines that were discovered at the sites show the correlation of the sculpture to the architecture and the power the female body exerted on the artists and their audiences. Another Neolithic monument in Malta raises the subject of the link between birth and death—also understood as the link between the womb and the tomb. The *Hypogeum* (dating from 3600–3300 BCE) was an underground place of worship and a funerary crypt. It is an extraordinary large multilevel, hollowed-out architectural space with halls, chambers, and passages, in which were found rounded female figurines, human bones and various prehistoric artifacts.

While we do not have clear evidence of the links between birth and death in prehistory, we shall see that those themes are continuous in art and become more numerous over time, largely because the invisible inside of female bodies is both awe-inspiring and terrifying. In the sexual act it can provide release and pleasure and can also produce a phallus-like creature in the form of a human baby.

Attempts to draw a sweeping simple picture of earliest human activity, such as the idea of a pervasive goddess cult, have been dismissed as wishful hypotheses. Nevertheless, the preponderance of divine female figures and the nearly complete absence of male divinities strongly suggest that the earliest Mediterranean cultures, including Minoan and Cycladic, were matriarchal and matrilineal. They may have been part of a continuous network of diverse cultures, originating in and around the Mediterranean Sea, which worshipped an ancient mother goddess. As we proceed, we shall find traces of these ancient matriarchal cultures in the better-known and better-documented patriarchal cultures of Greece and Rome. Many, if not most, of the gods and goddess of those two cultures had double natures; either because the humans inventing them had recognized their own complex inner worlds, and/or because they were composites created in different regions at different periods of time.

Ancient Egypt

Egyptian culture was one of the longest lasting in the ancient world. While the dynastic realms began in 3200 BC and ended only when the Romans conquered Egypt in 31 BC, the predynastic period goes back almost two thousand years earlier. The fertile Nile valley and the relatively isolated situation of ancient Egyptian cities made this relatively stable 5000-year history possible.

The sculpted images of women with infants (from c.3000 BCE, the most ancient period of Egyptian art) are roughly in line with the prehistoric images of fertile females with large hips and bountiful breasts. Eventually a topos developed of the goddess Isis with her son Horus. The image of *Isis* seated with her suckling son, Horus, (Figure 4) would become the dominant way—if not almost the only way—in which women were depicted partially nude in Christian art. (Figure 5) Ennobled by maternity, mothers could be shown to have sexual characteristics as long as they were useful to the continuation of the human race and/or could recall for their observers the blissful moments of unity between mother and child. Here was an instance where the generalized image encouraged viewers—specifically

Figure 4. Isis and Horus (ca. 600 BCE).

young mothers—to identify with the loving care bestowed upon an
infant and to recall the lost paradise of early merging (Baxandall,
1972).

   Egyptian art tended to change gradually, and there were established
prototypes for the depiction of men and women, both separately and

Figure 5. Nino Pisano: Madonna Nursing the Child (ca. 1350 CE).

together, that codified the appreciation of female beauty and reflected the female status. Thus we find magnificent images of the wives of pharaohs dating back to the earliest dynasties and moving forward through Ptolemaic times. Women, like men, are usually depicted as they are meant to be in the afterlife—young, attractive and healthy, just as the actual bodies were embalmed to preserve their best bodily self. Without such images and preserved bodies, the soul and spirit of the deceased would not be able to continue his or her journey through everlasting life.

> The earliest preserved records from the Old Kingdom onwards suggest that the formal legal status of Egyptian women was similar to that of Egyptian men. Women could acquire property in their own names and dispose of it as they wished, and they, like their husbands, could terminate a marriage. While Egyptian women had more power than did their later Greek counterparts, their social status was still restricted largely to the home and the activities associated with childrearing. A New Kingdom literary text clearly reflected this: "A woman is asked about her husband; a man is asked about his rank." As for men, a Middle Kingdom text warned men: "Do not contend with your wife in court. Keep her from power, restrain her. Thus will you make her stay in your house". (The Instructions of Ptah-Hotep, 3580 B.C.)

When presented as a sculpted couple, the aesthetic formula, which corresponded to the legal and social status of each, was fairly strict. Men were coloured red or reddish brown to indicate their experience as outdoor or worldly beings. Women, by contrast, were painted with lighter skin, as befitted their place *inside* the home and away from the searing sun.

A seated figure of a man with his wife and son from Saqquara demonstrates another way that Egyptian artists could depict the differences between male and female, and adult and child. The father sits stolidly centred and is a large full-size figure. His wife and son, who are much smaller, are placed next to his feet and legs. The wife sweetly grasps her husband's lower limbs; and the boy's small standing body, like his mother's upper torso, is nude.

Men wore kilts, usually white, leaving their upper bodies bare, while women wore long garments, also usually white, covering them from neck to mid lower leg. But the most striking difference between the sexes appears less in the garments they wear than in what the clothing tells us about the body—and the genitals—underneath. Unrevealing garments cover a man's lower torso, such as the stiff triangular kilt of The *Stele of Kai* (Figure 6) which shows prototypical images of both a male and a female. With remarkable regularity, the phallus is symbolized as the

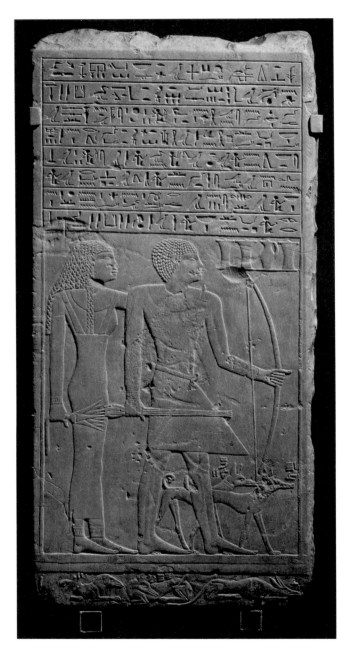

Figure 6. Stele of Kai (ca. 2000 BCE).

scabbard of a sword tucked in at the waist and aiming downwards, like a fold of fabric—or a long vertical belt or tassel hanging down from the centre of the kilt. For women, the clinging nature of their gossamer-thin garments leaves little doubt about their nudity or near nudity. In many cases, as in the *Stele of Kai*, the upper part of the woman's dress is abbreviated to a strap, showing one or both of her breasts. The nipples are usually emphasized or visible.

What can we know about the unconscious of the artists and their audiences from past millennia? Just as we can hypothesize from typical behaviours that we observe in our patients, we can cautiously speculate about patterns we see in art history, particularly when those patterns are repeated over time. The repetitions suggest that the conventions must have been known to both the artists and their audiences. I feel on reasonably safe grounds in proposing that the males presented in Egyptian art needed to have a visible displaced-phallic symbolic element. Women on the other hand, needed to be tangibly appealing, inviting the viewer to imagine touching the rounded shapes so lovingly emphasized by the linear patterns of the nearly transparent garments.

Hatshepsut, the female pharaoh who reigned in the 18th Dynasty (1508–1458), (Figure 7) was famously depicted as both male and female. However strong a ruler a woman could be in actuality at the time, Hatshepsut still needed to have masculine attributes attached to her body to justify her masculine form of leadership. Thus, she is given a phallic beard in almost all sculpted depictions. Though her face is allowed its feminine shape, her breasts are invariably reduced to an androgynous near flatness. Daughter of a pharaoh, wife/sister of another and regent for her stepson, (yet another pharaoh) this powerful female led the kingdom for approximately twenty-two years.

Kubie (1974) wrote extensively about the drive to become both sexes, positing it as a universal phenomenon, though one that both sexes mostly deny. Direct observations of children and his vast psychoanalytic experience convinced Kubie (1974, pp. 355–6) that "the unconscious drive is *not* to give up the gender to which one was born but to supplement or complement it by developing another, side by side with it—the opposite gender, thereby ending up as both." In our art historical tour we shall observe a fairly constant thread of androgynous imagery from ancient Egypt to the twentieth century.

The Akhenaten period (c.1351–c.1334 BCE) deserves special attention since it produced Egyptian art that is most sympathetic to the modern

Figure 7. Queen Hatshepsut (ca. 1475 BCE).

eye. During his brief reign, Akhenaten challenged the old order, the old gods and the old aesthetic. He encouraged his artists to depict the intimacy of his family. In a stele in Berlin depicting the royal family (from c. 1345 BCE), both he and Nefertiti are shown holding their children with a spontaneity and playfulness absent from earlier or subsequent images of Egyptian monarchs. Furthermore, Akhenhaten as well as his daughters were sometimes depicted with unsightly bulges—unsightly because it broke the pattern of several thousand years of sculptural conventions of idealized beauty. The female members of his family seem to have enlarged craniums and he is often shown with an exaggeratedly extended chin.

Especially during the period of Thutmosis, one of Akhenaten's most gifted court sculptors in whose workshop the fabulous and famous Nefertiti head was found, remarkably modern and vital depictions of individuals were created; something that was uncommon in art for many millennia. It was as though the individual could not possibly count as much as the individual's office, status or function. So lifelike were many of these works that archeologists initially thought they had found death masks. During the Amarna period, when Akhenaten's court moved to the city he created for the monotheistic worship of Aten,

Figure 8. Queen Nefertiti (ca. 1350 BCE).

there are some extraordinarily interesting and beautiful portraits of his mother Tiye, his daughter Meritaten, Akhenaten himself and his beautiful queen Nerfertiti (Figure 8).

Certainly Nefertiti is one of the earliest examples in Western art of a young woman portrayed and celebrated for her beauty. She would not be the last, and most museums in the world contain a continuous line of such portraits. All the revolutionary artistic activity during the Amarna period was almost immediately reversed after Akhenaten's death, and the more characteristic generalized style of previous dynasties continued for another few thousand years. The influence of Egypt, with its exceptionally long-lasting and relatively stable culture, is visible in the early artwork of the next few cultures that created memorable art: Classical Greek, Hellenistic and Roman.

Greek civilization

Since we are on a very long journey in a short time, I shall condense the Greek story and focus largely on the classical period (the fifth and fourth centuries BC) when some of the most famous art in the Western world was created. During this period the models were established for ideal images of women that would endure for the next two thousand years, though what we see now are mostly copies of those early works.

When we turn to Greek civilization and its myths, we find the sources for several ways of understanding women, psychoanalytically speaking. Freud, educated in the classics, presented the Oedipal myth of the son killing his father and marrying his mother, as the primary source for children's emergence from childhood and the development of gendered concepts of themselves. More recently Kulish and Holtzman (2008) have suggested that the mother-daughter relationship, as reflected in the myth of Persephone and Demeter, is central to understanding women's views of their bodies and their sexuality. They argue that it is a more apt source than Oedipus for female psychology and women's self understanding of their bodies and their sexuality.

During the classical period in Greece (c.478–338 BCE), the primary role for women was bearing children, and keeping the home and hearth. Greek women, unlike ancient Egyptian women, could not own property (except their clothing and jewelry) and had no legal rights except as wives and daughters. They were sequestered in a separate part of the house, upstairs, away from men, where they could become adept at spinning and weaving. By age fourteen or fifteen, girls were usually married to a man twice their age, who had been chosen by their male relatives. Thus women were effectively passed from their father's protection to their husband's. Young women were expected to be inconspicuous, their heads covered to obscure most of their faces and necks whenever they left the house, and, unless they were attending to certain religious rites, they had to be accompanied by a male relative. Ironically, a number of powerful Greek goddesses offered a kind of refuge for Greek women, both mentally and physically, as many of the rituals at the temples dedicated to Aphrodite, Athena, Demeter and Persephone, and Hera, had to be performed solely by women.

In early Greek art, men were usually depicted nude, while the female body was almost invariably presented clothed. The young male figures (*Kouroi* in Greek) depicted gods, warriors and athletes. The images of females (called *Kore*, or maidens) were usually depicted standing still. For respectable women (wives and daughters of Greek citizens), nudity as well as free movement, was unthinkable. To be sure, most of what is known about the lives of Greek women in classical times refers to the elite class. The social limits imposed on most Greek women did not apply to slaves and foreigners. Nevertheless, women—like men—were depicted as ideal in classical Greek art. The rationale was inspirational, since Greece was a land where the gods and goddesses were available to humans as heroic models one could emulate and from whom one could receive comfort, advice or correction.

The developing Greek tradition prized greater grace and a more life-like representation of the human form than Egyptian art had done. The famous sculptors Phidias, Myron, Polykleitos, and Praxiteles developed canons for the depiction of the human body that involved a system of ideal mathematical proportions established by Pythagoras. The naked body of a male athlete was depicted in a range of what have become famous poses. *The Spear Bearer, and The Discus Thrower* are two supreme examples of the classical ideals of clarity, balance and completeness in connection with the human body. The story is a little different for images of women.

To see how women looked (mostly to male artists) during the last few millennia of Western art, we will focus primarily on five Greek goddesses and their stories—Hera, Athena, Aphrodite (aka Venus), Demeter, and Persephone. In addition, we shall examine one mortal woman, Medusa, who tangled with a powerful Goddess, Athena, and as a result became a legendary frightening female. These goddesses are handy for psychoanalysts, because they exemplify a wide range of human thought, feeling, fantasy and behaviour. Since there are images of them from vastly different regions over an extended period of time, we inevitably find complex and often conflicting stories and attributes attached to the myth or cult. We shall occasionally also skip forward in time to see how the goddesses appeared to later Western artists.

To begin with, Hera, queen of the gods, was the model of matronly virtue for Greek women. Though she is wife and sister to the King of the Gods, she is far beneath him in status, and must obey him unconditionally. Her philandering husband continually formed liaisons with younger and more beautiful goddesses and humans. Not unreasonably, she is jealous, obstinate and quarrelsome. Hera is the only Greek goddess who is really married, hence she is the goddess of marriage, childbirth and wronged wives. The huge early temples (some dating as far back as eighth century BCE) were dedicated to her cult worship; and the remains of some of the most complete Greek temples in Paestum and Sicily suggest that Hera may have been one of the pre-Greek "Great Goddesses."

In antiquity, Hera is always presented as majestic and crowned, usually shown as a large standing figure. However powerful she had been in past centuries, by the time of classical Greece and Rome, Hera was almost always unhappy about her husband's amorous adventures and repeatedly schemed behind his back to find ways to punish him. Such a consistent presentation of *Hera* (Figure 9) as an irritable wife very likely reflected a woman's reality in the classical period. Psychoanalytic commentators like Kulish, Holtzman (2008) and Seelig (2002) might find Hera familiar as the older woman, the mother; whose power in the female pecking order is supreme.

Aphrodite, or Venus, was the goddess of beauty and love, and one of the oldest goddesses in the Greco-Roman pantheon. Originating in the East as a goddess of fertility, she became one of the most widely worshipped deities throughout Greece and Graecia Minor. She could be Aphrodite Ourania, or Heavenly; the goddess of pure and ideal love. As Aphrodite Genetrix, she was the protectress of marriage. As Aphrodite Porne (the courtesan) she was the goddess of lust and the patroness of prostitutes. Aphrodite was known for taking a wicked delight in rousing the passionate desires of the Olympian gods, most of whom (including her putative father Zeus) yielded to her sexual power. Unlike respectable women in Greece, Aphrodite had many lovers, mortal and immortal.

Figure 9. Hera Ludovisi (1st Century CE).

As the myth of Aphrodite goes, men had no responsibility for their own erotic escapades. It was the goddess's fault that they had to ravish beautiful young women and other immortals. In other words, in absorbing the millennia-old tradition of the Great Goddess cults, the

Greeks managed to turn it into a story about the power of the seductive woman, who could either rouse them sexually or make them feel small and helpless.

The iconic image of her marine birth as *Aphrodite Anadyomene* was established by Apelles, the most famous of all the Greek painters. A copy of Apelles' original painting, now lost, was found in a villa at Pompeii (Figure 10). Renaissance artists emulated Apelles' portraits of feminine beauty, supposedly an image of his mistress, Phryne, and it inspired a cycle of images of *Aphrodite Anadyomene* that lasted for the next 2400 years. Botticelli's *Birth of Venus* standing demurely on her large scallop shell and Titian's *Venus Anadyomene* as the long-haired beautiful female torso rising from the sea, looming against the darkening sky, are two famous fifteenth century depictions. Aphrodite was one of Titian's favourite subjects, just as she was for Ingres and nineteenth century artists Manet and Cabanel; both of whom clearly depict Aphrodite as an alluring seductress (Porne).

The other long-lasting model for feminine beauty was a sculpture by Praxiteles (c.400–330 BCE). The work, also now lost, exists in hundreds if not thousands of Hellenistic and Roman copies as well as in later imitations. Praxiteles was already famous for sculpting smooth,

Figure 10. Aphrodite Anadyomene (Birth of Venus) Pompeii—Roman copy of Greek original.

Figure 11. Aphrodite (Capitoline type); Roman copy of 3rd–2nd century BCE; Greek original.

silky skin, a skill he evidently used when he carved the first completely nude Aphrodite of Cnidos (Figure 11). At least three hundred years later, Pliny the Elder observed that the work was "not only the fin- est sculpture by Praxiteles, but the finest in the whole world." The historian went on to explain how the people on the island of Cos, who had commissioned the work, were shocked by the depiction of a nude goddess and requested a different, clothed version. The citizens of the ancient Greek city of Cnidos, now part of modern-day Turkey, eagerly took the first version. The sculpture became one of the great tourist attractions of the ancient world, and many people sailed to Cnidos simply to see it. The goddess was displayed in a temple that had a door at both the back and the front, so she could be seen directly from behind, and all parts admired.

Aphrodite of Cnidos was also reportedly based upon Phryne, who, in addition to being a handmaiden and ministrant of Aphrodite, was a courtesan, or hetaera. Typically hetaerae were beautiful, educated women, usually foreign born or slaves, who could speak knowledgeably about philosophy and were often accomplished musicians or dancers. Like Japanese Geishas, hetaerae provided high-level entertainment as well as sexual services for well-off Greek citizens. Some, like Phryne, were so wealthy and powerful that they became legendary. She was also the mistress of a famous politician who allegedly paid her more than 100 times the price of a normal prostitute for her services. She was known as Praxiteles' favorite model and lover, and she supposedly wrote to him: "Have no fear; for you have wrought a very beautiful work of art .... You have set up a statue of your own mistress in the sacred precinct" (Alciphron, Letters of the Courtesans, 1949, p. 251).

The story of Phryne is too neat for some scholars who question its authenticity. Courtesans were a popular subject for Greek playwrights, especially comedians, and the idea of a stunningly beautiful professional posing for her two famous artist lovers, Apelles and Praxiteles, was an obvious stereotype that may no longer be creditable. What matters for us is that a few select works of art from Greece in the 4th century-BCE became the model for female beauty for over two thousand years.

The Cnidian Aphrodite is usually shown holding one hand over her genital area, and sometimes also covering her breasts with her other hand. For that reason she came to be called Venus *Pudica* (Figure 11). The Latin word *pudendum* means both external genitalia and shame, and there has been much debate as to whether the goddess is embarrassed by her nudity or whether the gesture represents her divine birth from the sea, where her virginity was constantly renewed. As analysts we can understand the complicated and normally conflicted feelings of young girls—naked or not—who very much want their maturing bodies to be admired, even adored, but who may at the same time struggle with their sexual and exhibitionistic wishes. In her intense desirability, Aphrodite represents the otherness of women, as well as "the other woman" whenever there is a triadic relationship.

Some art historians (including me) place Aphrodite—(particularly the genre of Venus Pudica and other Greco-Roman images of nude figures who seem to exhibit any sign of shame) at the beginning of a continuous line of works representing *Adam and Eve's expulsion from the Garden of Eden*. Masaccio's version in the Brancacci Chapel is one of the best known (Figure 12).

The story of Adam and Eve was a fertile source for fantasy about who tempted whom. In a painting by Van der Goes in Vienna we see a male serpent; in Michelangelo's version in the Sistine Chapel, a female serpent. Cranach demurs on the serpent's sex in his many versions of the theme; and Paul Gauguin makes fun of them all by painting a self portrait with a halo holding the sacred symbolist symbol of a serpent as though it were a cigarette. It is worth noting that most of the serpents depicted in these eviction scenes are female. Thus the blame for erotic interest in sexual knowledge is again placed on female shoulders.

Once in Christian hands Eve became the evil counterpart of the virtuous Virgin; the dichotomy of the Madonna—whore. That Eve is offering an apple to her erstwhile partner in crime suggests that the tempting offering harkens back to a much developmentally earlier oral eroticism, as her breasts and the forbidden fruit are not only visually similar but also a symbolic equivalent frequently found in art. Gauguin was notorious for depicting delicious women as delectable objects, and the many painted and sculpted nursing Madonnas recall the blissful moment of union with mothers.

Athena

Almost the antithesis of Aphrodite, the Greek Goddess Athena is invariably represented clothed and powerful. She was the daughter of Zeus, and her birth story is remarkable. Zeus swallowed his first wife, Metis, just as she was about to give birth to a child whom he expected would be a dangerous male rival for his supremacy. As a result of his unseemly hunger for total power, Zeus had a terrible headache which was only

Figure 12. Masaccio: Expulsion of Adam and Eve (ca. 1425 CE).

cured by having his son, Hephaestus, split open his skull with an axe. Out popped a fully armed and fully grown Athena shouting: "Victory." The bright-eyed goddess became Zeus's favorite child—just as she was Freud's favorite Greek goddess.

Athena was the goddess of civilization—specifically the goddess of wisdom. As an armed warrior-goddess, she was also known as Athena Parthenos, and her most famous temple was the Parthenon in Athens, with its huge standing cult statue to her in gold and ivory by Phidias. Co-opted by Greek mythmakers as the woman who knew how to help men, Athena became the powerful mother figure who loomed large over Athens, and who must be seen as non-sexual, tough, wise, and always supportive. Athena is a dutiful daughter, a perfect pre-pubescent tomboy who will not threaten her father, but whose masculine attributes will enhance his glory. When this powerful goddess is seen as having masculine characteristics, she becomes the ultimate phallic woman—adored as well as feared—the opposite of Aphrodite who could only be adored and desired.

Since she fights for and with men, Athena is not particularly dangerous to them—As the asexual protector and advisor to her mortal half-brothers, Hercules and Perseus, she wears her protective aegis, a goatskin wrap fringed with serpents. Much later, Athena put the serpent-haired head of Medusa on her shield as protection. When we address the Medusa problem, I will take up the question of serpents and Athena's more dangerous side.

Demeter and Persephone

Demeter, Goddess of Agriculture and Grain, is the fertile producer and nurturer, whose Latin name, *Deus mater*, means "earth mother." Like Hera, she is usually presented as a somber matronly figure. Though she is often simply the goddess of the harvest, Demeter presided over the sanctity of marriage; the sacred law, and the cycle of life and death. She is most famous for being the mother of Persephone, the maiden who was taken by Hades, her uncle and lord of the underworld.

According to the myth, the girl had been gathering flowers with friends. When she reached out for a narcissus flower, the earth opened up, at which point Hades appeared on his chariot and abducted her into his kingdom. You don't have to be an analyst to get the hint that a young girl's narcissistic self-admiration can get her into big trouble.

This abduction had been pre-approved by Hades' brother, Zeus, who was also her father.

Once taken captive by Hades, Persephone became his wife and Queen of the Underworld, while her distraught mother mourned and searched fruitlessly for her. As controller of the seasons, Demeter refused to let crops grow, thus the first winter came to pass. Under pressure from Zeus, Hades agreed to return Persephone to her mother, but only for part of the year. In the months when Persephone came back to earth, she and her mother were joyfully reunited and the earth flourished; spring reigned and plants came back to life. During her absence, the period when she had to go back to Hades, winter again dominated the earth.

The story of Demeter, who, whilst mourning her lost child, refused to let the world have the nurture that she as goddess of the harvest was supposed to provide, symbolizes the double nature of women as both nurturers and withholders. It also demonstrates the power of the apparently powerless woman in a patriarchal society. She can use her power to deprive, a power quite unlike the aggressive, intrusive force characteristic of the gods or of the masculinized goddesses such as Athena. In the end however, Demeter seems to represent another annoyed, complaining wife, whose main connection is to her child— just like the good Greek woman in classical times, whose life is focused on home and family.

Kulish and Holtzman (2008) maintain that, for women, the Persephone-Demeter bond offers a far more helpful way of understanding triadic relationships than the Oedipal. According to their thinking, the triadic relation involves competition with the same sex-parent, which is a bigger problem for girls than for boys. At the point where competition becomes part of the developmental process, it conflicts with the little girl's need to remain close to a nurturing, supportive mother. To preserve that tie to the mother, sexual and aggressive drives must either remain hidden or be abdicated. Either way, the young girl can easily become passive. Thus girls have psychological reasons for handling aggression and competition differently from boys. By being subtle and indirect, they can maintain relations with both father and mother, something that Persephone accomplishes. Furthermore Kulish and Holtzman (2008) argue that, rather than pre-dominantly feeling shame when she discovers the differences between the genders, a girl can take pride in her body, with its capacity for pleasure and pregnancy, by identifying with her mother.

As analysts, we can see how Persephone's abduction suggests the complex fears and desires of both women and men about the triadic relationship. Was Persephone asking for trouble by wandering off from her mother, or did her uncle make her do it—thus denying her own forbidden wishes? In his depiction of the dramatic moment of the abduction, Bernini shows the unwillingness of the beautiful, usually nude, young woman, to be carried off by a powerful lust-ridden, older, bearded man.

What may be surprising is that in many ancient images of the event's aftermath, Persephone and Hades appear as a companionable couple— King and Queen of the underworld. They are presented seated together as equals, sharing a meal or some joint activity, often seeming to be the same age. Sometimes they are presented working together, with Hades sowing seeds and Persephone tilling the ground. Indeed, in a third-century Tanagra sculpture, where Persephone is shown ostentatiously holding up her pomegranate, a symbol of the sexual experience she enjoyed as a wife, she does not look distressed at all, but rather like a proud married woman. The complaisant normality of these ancient images of Persephone, with or without her husband Hades, has led a number of interpreters to see the myth as an allegory of ancient Greek marriage rituals. In these, the groom's act of taking the bride away from her family is portrayed as a fact of life rather than a criminal matter, and the eating of the pomegranate as a symbol of the sexual experience the bride enjoys with him.

However, in Rossetti's nineteenth century painting, Persephone is depicted as a brooding, troubled young woman who urges the viewer to empathize with her pain and perplexity. Her conflict is evident. Holding a red pomegranate near her lusciously full red lips, this modern young woman appears to know about her sexual desires and her guilty abandonment of her mother. Clearly, whether Persephone is seen as a gratified wife and queen, or traumatized victim, depends on the time and the artist's portayal.

Indeed, in ancient Greece, marriage was a double-edged sword for the maiden, for, along with fecundity, it also had a connotation of death. Just as women were the bearers of children and the harbingers of new growth, they were also the ones who mourned and prepared the dead for burial, reuniting them with mother earth. In that sense Demeter and Persephone were understood as two aspects of the same goddess. Again, we can view this an instance of the way women's bodies have been seen as a living metaphor for the relationship between this world and the afterlife.

Renaissance artists Giovanni Bellini and Michelangelo both suggested the connection between womb and tomb by using symbolic links it was assumed viewers could easily decipher. In Bellini's *Resurrection* in Berlin, the empty sepulcher surmounted by the rising Christ and a dying fig tree above the grave, with its several green leaves of new growth, tell the ancient story of the triumph of life over death. In each of Michelangelo's several Pietas, especially his first at St Peter's Basilica in Rome, the dead Christ in the young virgin's lap was a coded reference for the tie between birth and death.

Medusa

The gods and goddesses of Greece and Rome are as varied as the individuals we treat. In the mythic stories we have just discussed, we have seen a variety of benevolent, essentially nurturing, maternal woman. Now we come to a dangerous one, who strikes her male witnesses with horror: the evil temptress Medusa.

Medusa was originally a beautiful young woman with gorgeous blond hair, celebrated for her charms. One day she was worshiping in Athena's temple where she was a priestess, and Poseidon either raped her or was seduced by her. Outraged at the sacrilege (and also by the competition), Athena changed Medusa's beautiful long blond locks into serpents and made her hideously ugly—and so terrifying that one glance at her would turn a man to stone.

When Perseus, the legendary founder of Mycenae, wanted to rescue his mother, he needed to slay Medusa. With the help of Athena, who provided a mirror-like shield that allowed him to approach Medusa without having to look directly at her horrible head, Perseus killed and decapitated her. Eventually he gave the severed head to Athena, who put it on her shield as a terrifying weapon.

Medusa was emblematic of the dark side of women and the frightening aspect of femininity, and because she could use her immense power to defeat men, she was the prototypical goddess of a matriarchal society. Her snaky hair and reptilian skin symbolize the natural cycle of birth and rebirth. Snakes shedding their skin are parallel to women during their menstrual cycle. But in the ancient world Medusa still retained her beauty as can be seen in the fifth century BC *Rondanini Medusa* (Figure 13).

Figure 13. Medusa Rondanini (ca. 440 BCE).

Seelig has proposed that the story of Medusa and her relationship to Athena reveals other aspects of female psychology and the mother and daughter's competition for the father. Medusa's fate epitomizes the possibility that a sexually maturing daughter must repudiate her forbidden wishes for a sexual relationship with her father, lest her envious mother destroy her by making her ugly and frightening, and even kill her.

As we have seen, a woman who appropriates a masculine symbol can be frightening to men from whom the phallic equipment has been stolen. Thus Athena, the maiden protectress of Athens, was also the bearer of the terrifying shield emblazoned with the deadly head of Medusa.

In his essay on the Medusa head, Freud (1940c (1922)) argues that the frightening sight of the mother's "castrated" genitalia is symbolized by Medusa's terrifying decapitated head. Seelig's (2002) more cogent argument emphasizes the complicated dyadic conflict between the younger and older woman. The eternal maiden Athena, whose choice was to side with powerful men, will not allow another woman to use the power of her own sexual desirability.

Sculptural images of Medusa's head by Renaissance artists Bernini and Cellini hark back to the beauty of the ancient images. Rubens, not surprisingly, created a flamboyant vision of the horrifying female just after her decapitation, and, like Caravaggio's equally gory but even more terrifying painting in the Uffizi, both present the horrible gorgon as a monstrous bloody creature. But to my eye, none of the depictions is as frightening as the late nineteenth century version by Arnold Boecklin, who produced a painting worthy of the overheated symbolist movement of which he was one of the chief pioneers. His painted Medusa (1878) stares out of the canvas with otherworldly eyes that are designed to chill us to our very bones.

Before we arrive at the Renaissance, we shall speed through to the end of the ancient world to see how the images of women fared as the purity of classical Greek culture was mixed with the oriental influences in the huge territory that made up the remains of Alexander's empire, and that eventually became subject to Rome.

Hellenistic period (323 BC-30 BC) through Roman art (250 BC-410 AD)

By the time Alexander (356–323 BCE) had finished conquering the known world, Greek art, language and culture had spread from most parts of the Mediterranean across southwest Asia to the Near and Middle East. By virtue of the vastness of the territory and the variety and diversity of the ethnic groups involved, his successors had to straddle the competing goals of Hellenizing non-Hellenic cultural areas while at the same time maintaining control of the barbarian populations by adopting local customs. As a result Hellenistic civilization represents a fusion of the Ancient Greek world with that of the Near East, Middle East and Southwest Asia.

Rome's conquest of the remains of the Alexander's kingdoms in the third century BCE was relatively rapid. Roman emperors perceived Greek culture as the highest model. Starting in the middle of the second-century BCE, Greek culture was in ascendancy in every aspect of the private culture of elite Roman life. Greek household slaves taught the Roman young (sometimes even the girls). Wealthy Romans decorated their homes and gardens with "Greek masterpieces"—usually copies of past works made-to-order by Greek craftsmen. Greek gods and goddesses were worshipped, but their names were changed into Latin.

As the dominant position of Classical Greek culture gradually gave way, reality seeped into the conventions of artists. The images of women grew more varied during Hellenistic and Roman times, as did their lives. Age, individuality and intense expression found their place, as did portraits of ordinary people, such the image of an *Old Market Woman* (Figure 14).

The greatest difference between the periods that precede and follow the Hellenistic period are images of life lived with pleasure, and the body not only enjoyed but celebrated, as can be seen in the *Bikini Girls* from the 4th century CE Roman villa at Piazza Amerina (Figure 15). During this time an abundance of remarkably modern scenes, including images of perversion can be found. Frank scenes of lovemaking and exotically gendered creatures such as hermaphrodites were all on display. Art became looser; both more realistic and more fantastical; and less conventional than at any time since Akhenaten. Artists had a kind of free reign, and they used it with great imagination and panache.

Goodbye Rome, hello Christianity

By the fourth and fifth centuries AD, however, all that had changed. The Roman Empire had been beset from within by Christianity and disease that decimated the population, and from without by the barbarians. Christianity, whether in the West in Rome and Ravenna, or in the East in Constantinople (Byzantium), gradually imposed new standards on art and artists. Instead of the glorification of the body, the rule became the glorification of the spirit—specifically the Holy Spirit.

When the three principal monotheistic religions took over the ancient world, the tide turned against the celebration of the body. In Islam human figuration was restricted to secular imagery. Judaism, with few exceptions, eliminated the human image altogether. While

Figure 14. Old Market Woman (14–68 CE).

there were plenty of bodies in early Christian art, most belonged to holy figures and saints, whose stories were meant to awe and instruct. Many human figures were presented in an idealized way with sizable haloes and bejeweled belongings, but the sensual life has drained out of them. When nude bodies were depicted they were shown as sensuous but shameful. Recall Masaccio's image of *Adam and Eve expelled from the Garden of Eden.*

Figure 15. Bikini Girls—Piazza Amerina (3rd–4th Century CE).

These hypotheses must be presented with caution, given that the surviving artifacts and documentation may be skewing our understanding of an entire period. High art has represented history for centuries, and only relatively recently has the much more mundane cultural material indicated alternative versions. Ancient laundry lists as well as reports of imperial conquests are now studied.

The Byzantine era was far more complicated than is usually supposed, and the turn of the Holy Roman Empire to Christianity in 329 CE sanitized the story of how women behaved and were experienced. Theodora, wife of the Emperor Justinian, is a superb case in point. Seen in the magnificent Byzantine mosaics at Ravenna, *Theodora* (Figure 16), dating from the sixth century CE, is royal and richly robed. In fact, she began her rise very much like Phryne; as a beautiful foreign prostitute who performed risqué acts in the circus. She was a favourite on the stage where she delighted in displaying her beautiful body nude. Like all actresses of the time she was also a courtesan, and a very successful one. She eventually converted to Christianity, gave up her former lifestyle and moved to Constantinople where she made a living spinning wool.

Figure 16. Empress Theodora (6th century CE).

Theodora was twenty years younger than Justinian when they met and fell in love. He was able to change the laws forbidding aristocrats to form legal alliances with heterae so that he could marry her. They became equal partners in ruling the vast kingdom, and she was proclaimed Empress. In time, her native nobility and sagacity were as celebrated as her beauty and charm. Yet in the official depiction of Theodora, in the church of San Vitale in Ravenna, she and her retinue do not have living breathing bodies, instead, they have magnificently embroidered outfits and are elaborately bejeweled.

Throughout the medieval era and early renaissance, erotic images of female nudity and sex were equated with sin and death. That did not necessarily mean that artists were as rigid as the doctrine. Masterpieces of Romanesque and Gothic art demonstrate the slow but sure turn toward greater naturalism. This development could be seen in the one area where the worship of women was permitted. Indeed one of the triumphs of Christian art was that it launched the Madonna—a woman who could give birth as a virgin—as an object of veneration. Mary, mother of Jesus, became a masterful combination of Aphrodite and Athena. She became a sacred and glorious container, and many beautiful paintings and sculptures of women resulted.

Renaissance and beyond

With the help of antiquity, the Renaissance (1300–1600 AD) once again placed human beings at the centre of the universe and both sacred and secular themes reveal the return to full-bodied presentations. The seemingly magical ability of women to become pregnant and give birth was captured and maintained in the Catholic Church's formulation of a virgin birth, epitomized in some extraordinarily beautiful Renaissance paintings. In Van Eyck's famous *Madonna in a Church* in Berlin, for example, the light streaming through the unbroken stained-glass windows was understood as the penetration of the immaculate virgin by the Holy Spirit.

Variations on the Madonna-and-child theme are sometimes reflected in the piety or personal lives of the artists themselves—a point that is particularly notable when one compares the paintings of holy subjects done with grace and sweetness by the truly pious Dominican Fra Angelico with those of the much more worldly madonnas, angels, and children of Fillippo Lippi. The latter's fame as a painter was equal to his renown as a renegade priest, whose affair with a nun led to marriage, fatherhood and numerous other amorous adventures.

While the predominance of religious images continued throughout the Renaissance, the depiction of the pleasures of the flesh was no longer prohibited. Women as well as men were shown nude in mythological scenes, together with ancient gods and goddesses, frolicking in ways prohibited to good Christians. For example, Rubens was notorious for his evident pleasure in painting fleshy females. Titian frequently moved back and forth between religious themes and secular ones. Scholars still debate whether the alluring nude in his *Venus with an Organist* in Berlin, whose beautiful breasts are being tenderly caressed by cupid, represents the goddess of love or a courtesan being ogled and adored by her musician-courtier. The ancient Greeks and Romans would have no difficulty with such a combined identification.

Another intriguing example of women's bodies displayed nude is *The Fountain of Youth* by Cranach, also in Berlin, which revisits the Egyptian obsession with achieving bodily perfection despite the passage of time. Sagging bodies of elderly women enter the fabulous fountain from the left and when they emerge on the right side of the canvas, they are young and beautiful. Cranach's painting reflects the universal wish to overcome death and aging. Additionally, biblical stories about women bathing allowed artists to depict female nudes in various states of comfort or discomfort with their bodies. Rembrandt's *"Bathsheba with Her Servant"* is a clear instance of sensuous pleasure. The glorious display of female beauty shows a woman comfortable in her own body. While *"Susanna and the Elders"* presents a young woman's concern with the intrusive, voyeuristic actions of the older men, the scene does not seem ominous. Susanna looks surprised and mildly perturbed, but Rembrandt was an artist who clearly liked women, and his depictions of them are always sympathetic.

When we think about the individual lives of the artists, it is instructive to compare Rembrandt's painting of Susanna with that of Artemisia Gentileschi. First of all, we have (for a change) a woman's view of a female experience. In Gentileschi's painting of *Susanna and the Elders* (Figure 17), the perplexity and pain on Susanna's face, along with the helpless awkwardness of her pose, suggests something very different from what is visible in Rembrandt's painting. The two men in Gentileschi's paintings look much more threatening. Can we tell from the painting that Gentileschi herself had been sexually harassed by men in whose profession, painting, she was seen as an interloper? Scholarly opinion is in general agreement that we can, supported by many academics who have unearthed the existence of a number of female artists whose history and works had disappeared; misattributed to men, usually their brothers, fathers or colleagues.

19th–20th century

We shall skip several centuries in Western art to reach the nineteenth century, a time when the rigidity of female positions of wife and mother, and keepers of the household, began to soften. The Victorian role of proper women had been suffocating for many years, as the prohibitions against women's freedom of movement outside the house were almost as restrictive as they had been in classical Greece. Despite some outstanding exceptions (Queen Victoria, Florence Nightingale,

Figure 17. Artemisia Gentileschi: Susanna and The Elders, ca. 1610 CE.

Marie Curie) most nineteenth century women were unable to obtain advanced education, respectable employment or legal rights as wives and mothers. In England and all parts of its large empire, a woman's property, including any money she might earn, belonged to her husband. Only toward the end of the century did the situation begin to change, as the call for universal suffrage activated many frustrated and angry women.

An evolution in art can be seen during the latter half of the nineteenth century. In the 1860s and 70s, in the works of Manet, Renoir and most of the Impressionists, women are almost invariably shown in a charming but restrictive light, in scenes of pleasurable family outings and domestic harmony. Several decades later, those amiable images seemed tame and dated. Social forces and historical events had created a new context for women, who were beginning to break out of their constricted roles.

Freud and the early psychoanalysts provided new conventions for an understanding of women. They were the Dark Continent; they were more complicated than men because they had to switch their loyalties from mother to father; they had weaker superegos and were less likely to be loyal. Worse than any of those negative views, women were being seen by many people as a threat to civilized society.

During the Symbolist and Art Nouveau periods, some influential artists divided women dramatically into dangerous or innocent creatures. A clear example can be seen in the work of Giovanni Segantini, who separated women into good and bad mothers. Abraham (1911, 1937), in one of the earliest applied analytic essays on Segantini, proposed that the artist's early loss of his mother had left him susceptible to idealizing her and demonizing the unsatisfactory mother replacements he had endured. Segantini depicted the bad mothers as cold, uncaring, red-haired sirens whose overtly sensual bare breasts are emphasized by their posture, hanging from barren trees (*Evil Mothers* 1897). These dreadful dames can be contrasted with his images of a good, loving, blonde, nurturing mother, who is also in a tree but who comfortably cradles a smiling young child in *Angel of Life* (1894). But it was not only Segantini who made this kind of distinction. A similar division appears in the work of Edvard Munch, whose seductive women lead men to their downfall and to death—presumably because these excitingly erotic creatures carry the dread syphilitic bacteria that afflicted so many men at the turn of the century.

One of most vivid examples of a successful turn-of-the-century artist who specialized in depicting dangerous women is Franz von Stuck (1863–1928). Von Stuck was a German symbolist painter who taught some of the most important modern artists, including Klee, Kandinsky, and Albers at the Munich Academy. His work; especially his erotic work in classical guise; created a sensation and helped establish the visual icon of the femme fatale. His most popular and influential work, painted in at least three versions, was *Sin*—alternately named *Eve and the Snake, or Sensuality*—for which he won the gold medal at the Chicago World's Fair in 1893 (Figure 18). In each version of the numerous versions he created, an exceptionally sensuous and pale female nude is entwined by a huge dark snake that coils itself between and thorough her legs and around her naked body. Seven years later he won the same coveted award in Paris, and in 1906 this talented son from a family of farmers was knighted for his artistic contributions. Von Stuck was well-versed in classical mythology and recycled, for his contemporary world, the familiar ancient and biblical themes we have seen now many times: *Temptation in the Garden of Eden, Oedipus, Medusa and the Sphinx*, newly popular subjects at the turn of the century. But his paintings reflect the myths from the quintessential macho view of the danger of women appropriating men's prerogatives; mainly aggression and sexuality.

Von Stuck's mediocre painting, *Fighting for a Woman* (1905), captures all the stereotypes common to the concept of the femme fatale. She stands off to the right, arrogant, sure of her erotic power and red-headed, her pale flesh contrasting with the two darker-skinned and equally naked men who are poised for battle. She is depicted as the cause of the trouble, having stirred their bestial side and forced them to fight to the death for her favours. Again, it expresses the conventional nineteenth century-male viewpoint of female sexual power. It is the reverse of the earlier nineteenth century concept of how women were actually supposed to behave; docile, obedient and gracious. To be fair, von Stuck did represent some so-called good, innocent women in his paintings, but these just happened to be portraits of his wife and daughter. In contrast to the femme fatale, the safe women painted at the turn of the century were represented as young, frightened and ashamed, or completely innocent and untouched by men. The paintings of Maurice Denis were typical of such artists, who painted images of the safe women draped in chaste white garments.

Everything changed with the First World War. Men died and women worked. A new era began and new artists like Picasso and Matisse were kings. A trace of the femme fatale could still be found in surrealism where works of Alberto Giacometti, the surrealist sculptor, expressed

Figure 18. Franz von Stuck: Sin (1893).

the same combination of fear and sadistic hostility, which emerged fully after the war.

To end our condensed tour of the past ten millennia we recall the women of Henri Matisse. In Matisse—the French painter and counterpart to Pablo Picasso as a giant of artistic greatness in the 20th century—we have a male artist who adored women and could portray them un-ambivalently over his entire lifetime. Like Alexander the Great, Henri Matisse had a mother who gave him total support, and it shows. It is impossible to find a painting of a woman by Matisse that does not celebrate his love of women and colour. And on that positive note I'll stop.

References

Abraham, K. (1911). Giovanni Segantini a Psychoanalytic Essay, *Psychoanalytic Quarterly, 6:* 453–512.

Benner, A. R. & Fobes, F. H. (1949). Alciphron, Letters of the Courtesans: Phryne to Praxitles. In: *Letters of Alciphron, Aelian and Philostratus* (p. 251). Cambridge, Massachusetts: Loeb Classical Library, 1979.

Baxandall, M. (1972). *Painting and Experience in 15th Century Italy.* Oxford and New York: Oxford University Press.

Chodorow, N. (2010). Beyond the Dyad: Individual Psychology, Social World. *Journal of the American Psychoanalytic Association, 58:* 207–230.

Freud, S. (1940c (1922)). Medusa's head, *S.E., 18:* 273–274.

Johnson, J. H. The Instructions (of a man named) Any. In: Anne K. Capel; Glenn E. Makrone, *Mistress of the House, Mistress of Heaven: Women in Ancient Egypt* (p. 175). New York: Hudson Hills Press, 1996.

Kubie, L. (1974). The Drive to Become both Sexes, *Psychoanalytic Quarterly, 43:* 349–426.

Kulish, N. & Holzman D. (2008). *A Story of her Own: The Female Oedipus Complex Reexamined and Renamed.* New York: Jason Aronson.

Seelig, B. (2002). The Rape of Medusa in the Temple of Athena: Aspects of Triangulation in the Girl. *International Journal of Psychoanalysis, 83:* 895–911.

Note

1. I am grateful for the help received from Nellie Thompson, Carol Neumann de Vegvar, Beth Seelig, Kitty Ross, and Jennifer Stuart.

CHAPTER TWO

How deep is the skin? Surface and depth in Lucian Freud´s female nudes

Rotraut De Clerck

Abstract

The skin has a prominent place in Lucian Freud's work, notably in his representations of female nudes. To Freud, the skin is the principal means for expression of individuality, more important even than the face. With his pronounced presentation of the skin in his *Naked Portraits* he raises issues of individuality and identity in a modern society. This paper will trace the development of the skin, the rendering of surface and depth throughout Freud's work. The translucent skins in his early paintings can be seen as an expression of inner feelings on the surface—*seeing through the skin*. Conversely, the heavy pastoso in hog brush technique in his later years presents a different illusion, shielding the inner world of the individual from the outside—*"as dressed in paint"*. This paper thus links his development as an artist to psychoanalytic concepts, such as Anzieu's Skin-Ego as well as Britton's and Rosenfeld's thin—skinned and thick-skinned presentations, highlighting the importance of the skin in relation to trauma.

Naked Portraits

Lucian Freud's representation of skin is most striking in his representations of female nudes. He is master of giving the skin life and texture. In his naturalistic rendering of the skin Lucian Freud has been compared to Rembrandt and Rubens. However, Lucian Freud´s intentions are not retrograde; copying "Old Masters". To him, the skin is the principal vehicle for the expression of individuality, more important in this way than the face. In his *Naked Portrait*; his candid representations of male and female nudes; he raises issues of identity in modern society, such as the place of mental life, of thinking and phantasies, the place of the body, of pleasure and pain, the place of sex and of sexuality (the two being different) and he raises issues of time and space in relation to the physical existence of death and decay (Fig. 1).

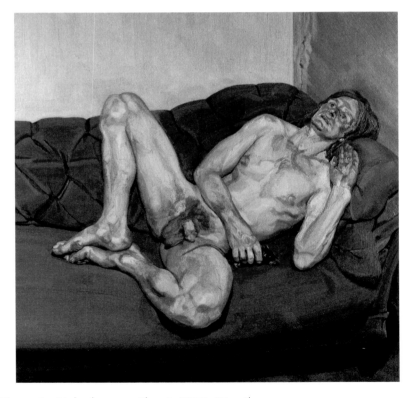

Figure 1. Naked man with rat, 1977–78, oil on canvas.

The skin with its double surface, one inside and one outside, is the membrane on which reflects both internal and external influences. The skin, generally considered the mirror of the soul, can be seen as a reflection of the tensions and demands of society upon the individual.

Lucian Freud's nudes are too overwhelming to be ignored. This is the first explanation for the uproar they have created. Larger than life, they bear down on us, flooding us with their flesh and genitals. This may be considered an indication of the weight and importance that Lucian Freud attaches to the human physical existence (Fig. 2).

Lucian Freud calls things by their proper name: he uses no fig leaf. He paints every part of the body in realistic detail, thereby not excluding the genitals, treating them simply as another part of the body. Nothing is spared from his meticulous investigation; his "penetrating glance", as I have referred to elsewhere (De Clerck, 2005). But Lucian Freud does not only paint bodies. He paints people, personalities portrayed through their bodies. His portraits do not focus on the face as representative of mental life, intelligence, thoughts, and temperament; for

Figure 2. Nude with leg up, Leigh Bovery, 1992, oil on canvas.

Lucian Freud the whole body is the person and the person is the body vice versa. It is in the body that all psychic experience is contained. This notion would be in line with the view of his grandfather, Sigmund Freud in his paper "The ego and the id" (Freud, 1923b), when he stated that "the ego is first and foremost a body—ego" (ibid., p. 31). Psychic life, inseparably bound to physical life, merge together in sexuality. The term sexuality is here being used in the widest sense as Sigmund Freud had conceptualized it, encompassing the totality of the psycho-sexual experience of the individual throughout the span of his development from infancy to old age—and finally death.

I will focus on the painting *Sleeping by the Lion Carpet* (1995) for illustration of Lucian Freud´s views on the inseparability of mind and body. It is a portrait of the model, Sue Tilley, who worked at the Camden Council housing benefit department in London (Fig. 3).

We see a dark-haired woman, naked, in a brown leather armchair. Her immense body is placed in the foreground of the painting, whereas the head is bent backwards. The face is for the most part in the shadow of a bright light coming from the right, and half covered by a hand that supports the head and distorts the face. The whole of the face is only half the size of one of the huge breasts, which sit heavy and full on the arching mound of the fleshy belly. The breasts, together with the upper part of the arms, form the widest part of the figure. The light of the studio lamps falls onto these breasts, the belly and thighs, illuminating them as normally the head and face would be lit. The skin, expanding over almost two thirds of the space of the whole painting, glares at the viewer. This indicates that the skin is accorded the most prominent place in this portrait. It is not smooth, soft skin. It is skin with marks and dents and bumps and bruises. It shows the age of the woman and the imprints a life of sorrow, frustration, greed, and lust have left on it. Unlike most of the other paintings from the *Naked Portrait*s where the genitals are fully exposed, here they are covered by a flap of fatty tissue hanging from the belly of this woman. The knees are big and malformed, the lower parts of the legs are spread apart due to the enormous thighs, and the feet are placed clumsily on the wooden floor.

The hand and arm which hold up the head touch the skin of the right breast all along the inner side, whereas the other arm, pointing downwards, is tightly adjoining the other side of the body with the left hand and coming to rest on the left thigh. This woman is touching herself twice skin to skin: the skin of her right breast rests against her right

Figure 3. Sleeping by the Lion Carpet, 1995–96, oil on canvas.

arm and on the opposite side; the skin of her abdomen and thigh makes contact with her left arm. The thumb of her left hand, resting relaxed on her thigh, almost reaches her genitals, pointing towards them and leading the viewer's gaze towards her "secret". This position suggests the possibility that the hand might wander about, and half dreamingly start some sort of sexual activity on the genitals. This then would be a third instance of her touching herself.

The woman is alone in the room. She seems asleep, unaware of herself. She does not pose in front of the viewer; she is lost in her dreams. We see her as a big, wrongly proportioned, middle-aged woman with hanging flesh; her enormous body perhaps eliciting half repugnance, half pity. But she is definitely a woman who has her own sexuality. She may not stimulate sexual feelings in the viewer, but she has sexuality. From the contact that her arms make with the skin of her breasts and the possible self-stimulation of her genitals by the "wandering hand", this representation of her sexuality is suggested as auto-erotic. Her auto-erotic fantasies would be indicated by the hanging carpet in the background, the "Lion Carpet". Trivial as it might seem, it is probably justified to see this as the representation of the nature of her sexual fantasies. Sexuality is individual and intimate, but its symbolic representation is not original. Lucian Freud resorts to the same metaphors as Sigmund Freud, who discovered these symbols repeating themselves in the dreams and daydreams of his patients, metaphors like "wild animals"; snakes and lions hunting in the savannah.

Sexuality, as Sigmund Freud conceptualized it, has a *general* component common to all humans, which is the energetic source from which all psychic activity emanates, ranging from the lowest to the highest level, and it has a *specific* component, the highly intricate and personally furnished world of each individual's sexual fantasies. In this sense Lucian Freud's painting *Sleeping by the Lion Carpet* is a representation of both the general as well as the specific. The general component, as represented by the hunting lions, makes us aware that sexuality is universal, common to us all, conveying that this woman, no matter what she is like, no matter what she looks like, is a sexual being. This also is true regarding the specific component: no doubt she has a sexuality of her own which she truly experiences, perhaps she is lonely and has to resort to auto-erotism for satisfaction, perhaps she prefers it. She is also not depicted as an idealized icon; she is carefully, almost tenderly, painted with all her personal fat, pointing to her very individual, aggressively unrestrained form of greed. In this respect, one could interpret Lucian

Freud in a certain light: Sexuality and aggression are bound together, its wild territory, with excitements and dangers, untamed and unrestrained, be it in auto-erotism or with a sexual partner.

Nothing has changed since his grandfather's investigations into sexuality in 1900 when he discovered the unconscious representations of sexual wishes in the symbols of the dreams and phantasies of his patients; and of himself. The basic general patterns are fixed and have been so for centuries. What is portrayed in the painting *Sleeping by the Lion Carpet* is not a "sleeping beauty"; it is the normality of the sexual which resists idealization, idealization of beauty, power, status or money. This sexuality occurs in ordinary lives, with ordinary people in ordinary homes—with family members and friends, as described by Sigmund Freud, in his home and in his studio as depicted by Lucian Freud in his paintings. It is this normality of the sexual which breeds incestuous wishes, neuroses. Put in the psychoanalytic terms: it is the representation of the universality of the Oedipus complex, incestuous feelings, forever projected from the early objects on to the present. To come to realize this is at the same time shocking and moving. But it also comes as a relief: is it not liberating to see characters who retain their identities, who do not deny their own history of psycho-sexual development as it has shaped itself from the beginnings throughout childhood experience and who expose themselves in all their nudity, which is representative of the nudity of their desires? To elicit deep sexual wishes, not the worldwide internet but rather narrow, even cramped living conditions, are required. They promote a sensation of closeness, of touch, of skin contact. Unspectacular events, such as a particular way of walking, the sound of a voice or the smell of skin, can stimulate passion.

It is this kind of ideosyncracy of desire that is fairly independent of larger society. It is deeply democratic as it belongs to everyone, offering a degree of freedom to the individual from prescribed roles in society.

The knowledge of the idiosyncrasies of desire—a knowledge that is by no means reserved to psychoanalysis alone—this knowledge is brought back to our attention, represented in the paintings of Lucian Freud. In today's society, sex and smooth skin are ubiquitous—in the images in tabloids and advertising. Lucian Freud makes us aware that sex and pornography can be virtual and globalized, but not sexuality. Real bodies relate a story, real bodies have volume and weight (Butler, 1993). They are three dimensional. They leave an imprint that cannot be erased. This is vividly evident in Sigmund Freud's account of his early case, Dora, who was beset by an elder friend of her parents. Even a long time afterwards, Dora felt the pressure of Herr K.'s body on the skin of her chest.

Lucian Freud has to emphasise the skin to bring out the personal erotic and auto-erotic dimensions of his subjects. He makes the skin the centre of his painting, granting it the largest extension and the most light. Moreover, for his purpose, the skin has to be painted in such a way that it can transmit the warmth and the soft pressure of touch, the longing for stimulation or self-stimulation. To give it this sense of physicality, Lucian Freud has to paint the skin in a realistic manner with heavy layers of paint. This is one of the reasons for the allusion to "Old Masters". An abstract person has no autoerotism.

Against the virtual, globalized bodies, Lucian Freud manifests figures of impressive stature in which the shocking thing is not the subjects' nudity but the nudity of desire. In his *Naked Portraits* Lucian Freud shows people who are self-possessed in that they are endowed with the rich inner world of their own sexual phantasies—whether they be homosexual, heterosexual or bisexual in nature. Such people are independent, they are not sex objects; they "own themselves". To show this in art is far from pornographic. It is to make people self-aware, and embrace their bodies as they are. It is to take a stand against liposuction and tanning studios, botox and surgery, against a sleek façade that pretends to be reality but is empty inside.

When one agrees with Sigmund Freud that it is not the image of what is there that is pornographic, but the perverse fantasy that is attributed to the picture, then it is evident that Lucian Freud's paintings are counter pornographic. What is so startling is the awareness they transmit; not pornography, the constant repetition of "belly, tits, and ass", is really upsetting. The shock that Lucian Freud's *Naked Portraits* produce has to do with the recognition that we are faced with the reality of ourselves, our own sexuality, our own aging bodies, that one day we could or would look the same, or at least to some extent similar. We stare into a mirror, hope that it is a distorting mirror, and feel stripped bare. We cannot distance ourselves easily as with a pin-up or centre-fold. Lucian Freud's paintings do not invite distance, they leave no space for it. They make us feel our own bodies, trapped in a skin that will record the imprints of our life with no way to ever erase it.

Through this experience they bring back the awareness that our own sexuality is not a given but a creation, a "work in progress", to take place in the egoover years of anxiety and confusion, shame and guilt, desire and lust, something intimate and vulnerable, painfully experienced in its failures, enjoyed in its satisfaction. Remaining truthful to the subject, Lucian Freud unmasks the lies of the videos and the internetabout the potential virtuality and globalization of the body, the promise to enjoy forever the "snappy, crunchy sides of life" (AOL website). He makes us aware that sexuality is, stretched out in time, from infancy to old age, linked with suffering and decay.

Sexuality and the skin

The skin, and not the genitals, is, next to the brain (the importance of which for sexuality is just being rediscovered) the largest sexual organ. The skin has an average surface of 18,000 square centimetres, thus exhibiting the greatest surface and the heaviest weight of all body organs. Skin and brain are composed of the same membrane which is a surface membrane. The skin is connected to the nervous system through over 7,135 sensory receptors per square centimetre and over half a million sensitive nerve fibres. It is the sense of touch that first develops in the foetus, when the eyes and ears are still underdeveloped. Thus it is our most archaic sense (Detig-Kohler, 2000).

As Sigmund Freud´s Dora case shows, early psychoanalytic literature was predominantly concerned with the skin at the orifices; the mucous membranes at the erogenous zones, the mouth, the anus, and the genitals; which Freud saw as predestined for the development of symptoms in conjunction with the sexual drives. In the case of Dora, Sigmund Freud had shown the intricate interplay between a physical precondition, (i.e. "Dora´s spoiled lip zone") and phantasy. Dora, the "little thumb-sucker" as he literally put it, develops, on the basis of her oral fixation, an Oedipal phantasy about her parent's intercourse which takes the nature of a fellatio phantasy. In the scene of the kiss from Herr K., and in her first encounter with the erect penis of a grown man, she becomes consciously aware of such phantasies that had until then been repressed. From then on she is so repelled and shocked that according to Freud she falls ill and develops all the symptoms of a conversion neurosis.

Contemporary psychoanalytic literature, in contrast, would be more concerned with aspects of the skin related to object relations and states of the self. It conceives of the skin as a container in the meaning of holding (together), protection and boundaries, aspects that arose from the influence of object relations theory, particularly the Kleinian school.

The idea of the skin as a container for early psychic processes seems to be related to the conceptualization of a skin-ego (Anzieu 1989). According to this the skin has a prominent place in the development of the self. Meta-psychologically it is linked to the concept of the body ego, showing how the concrete concept of skin can be imagined to separate, bind, and layer various parts of the mental apparatus; conscious, preconscious and perception. There is even the notion that mother and baby have a mutual skin, an idea put forward by authors that have studied the skin in early processes like Bick (1986). The concept of envelope or container relates to the different layers of the skin or the body image. In this sense, the skin, in its earliest sense of warmth and touch, represents the relation to the primary object, the mother. The child then progressively differentiates a surface which has an inner and outer face, permitting distinction of self and object. Thus, Anzieu links ego functions that are concerned with the differentiation between different ego states to body sensations and draws a parallel between ego functions and the functions of the skin.

In recent years, medical and feminist sociology claim to perceive a deferral of symptoms from hysteric enactments involving the body as a whole in the patients whom Freud described, towards enactments that use the skin as a stage for the projection of inner conflicts as well as conflicts between the individual and society. Nowadays it seems that motor disturbances of the hysteric kind (paralysis, spasms) have been replaced by disturbances of the skin (Borkenhagen, 2000). The skin then functions not only as the real boundary between inside and outside, but also serves as a highly symbolic surface which undergoes historic and cultural change. Benthien (1998) states that "never before in the western world have such large amounts of money been spent on lifting procedures, liposuction or anti-aging creams as is the case today" (ibid., p. 49) The two sociologists note further that parallel to the increased meaning given to the skin, active injuries to it by burning, cutting and carving have soared as is evident in the fad of tattooing and piercing. Through the attacks on the skin, the individual may express inner states such as self-hate but also hate against the objects or against society as a whole. The skin may itch, the skin may weep, the skin may rage (Pines, 1988).

These findings may well reflect social change regarding the symbolic meaning of the skin for problems of identity in contemporary society.

The boundaries no longer seem secure; society's demands enter through the skin into the body and conversely, inner conflicts manifest themselves on the surface of the skin, and are apparent to the external world.

> The self-injuries seem to have a twofold meaning for the stabiliza-
> tion of the sense of identity: for one, the body is marked by scars,
> leaving traces that give the body, and thereby the fragile ego, a sense
> of unmistakable individuality. Further, through the self-injury (and
> the pain that goes with it) the experience of the boundaries of the
> body is revived and thus the ego boundary reinstated. (Benthien,
> 1998, p. 15)

Furthermore one may say that contemporary diseases of the skin are less distinctly circumscribed than those hysterical symptoms that Sigmund Freud described as being based on a conflict of drives. They may, therefore, mirror the diffusion of identity that would be specific to the conditions of modern life.

What may be true in postmodern society is that problems of identity receive more attention and have increased in importance, compared to an apparent reduction of sexual problems. This shift may well be metaphorically expressed on the skin as the boundary between the interior and the exterior. By putting the emphasis on the skin, Lucian Freud in his *Naked Portraits* would have come to the core of the matter, touching on pressing issues of identity today. From this perspective, reflecting the shift, his work could be seen as a commentary on a society that denies the individual the expression of self, of conflict between the individual and society; an issue that was the hallmark of Sigmund Freud's (1930a) great essay, *Civilization and its Discontents*.

My clinical experience shows me that matters of sexuality and the skin are closely related. I have patients, in fact most of them, who exhibit both; conflicts of the sexual sphere and a disorder of the skin. Today, in clinical psychoanalytic discussions, the symptomatologies are linked to either one or the other of the two schools; Freud´s drive theory or object relations theory. The two are considered to be etiologically different or belonging to different stages of development (earlier or later as regards the development of the child). But I question whether they are really different in the sense of origin or whether they are merely an expression of a shift in modalities, in that we are seeing a change only in the *form* of expression, and not in underlying pathology, following trends and changes of fashion in society.

To give some clinical vignettes:

- I have a patient who suffers from erythrophobia, a fear of blushing, which is very disabling for her as she holds a high position in public life. We have come to see that she blushes because of her hidden incestuous wishes and phantasies towards her father and her hate for her mother, phantasies for which she feels intense shame. She fears being discovered—but at the same time generates a cry for help on the surface of her skin.
- I have a young patient who phantasizes about cutting her skin. She does not do it, out of fear that she would lose me as her analyst because I would have to transfer her to a clinic if she did. Instead, she draws the outline of a larger than life figure on her wardrobe and applies "stitches" to it with the tip of her pen. This patient suffered from a gruesome abortion which she had consciously decided upon, but which brought about severe self-reproach for being a murderer.
- Another patient suffers from an irritating itch in his anus ever since he moved to Germany. We have ascertained that he cannot ward off his unwanted homosexual fantasies when he feels lonely, as he often does. In the analysis he started to remember that as a boy, new to boarding school and feeling lonely, he was seduced and anally penetrated by one of the elder boys.

I could continue this list. Dora, as was described by Freud, felt disgust at the thought of a kiss from Herr K. In Freud´s view this was the expression of conversion of desire into disgust because of opposition from her super-ego towards the incestuous wishes. Freud located the conflict within the individual. But Dora is also a vivid example of the confusion of roles, of problems of sexual identity as a woman in a society at the brink of modernity.

My patients all have a pronounced sexual problem, not only in the form of conflict between an instinctual wish and a restricting super-ego, but also between themselves and society. They are worried about their "sexual performance, feelings of inferiority, and a fear of failure and isolation". This affects their sense of self, their feelings of competence or despair, fear of disintegration or feeling good within their own skin.

Instinctual conflict and object relations must be seen as intertwined. Where the sexual sphere is affected, we also see problems of identity. What may be evident from the clinical examples I have given is that the glossy façade does not present the true picture. Ideas about easy sex mirror a false reality. As analysts we recognize that disturbances of sexuality have not disappeared with liberalization. They reappear as troubles of the skin because they are related to problems of the self and identity in society. Recently I flipped through the catalogue from a photo agency that a patient had brought to me because she (a photographer) has a photo in it. Nothing but beautiful people: smooth skin, smooth faces, regardless of whether they are babies, youngsters or seniors. No chapped skin, no acne, no lines. No pain, no fear, no doubts. Do the people themselves believe these pictures to portray reality? It is difficult to say. This patient who brought me the catalogue has eczema on the inner side of her middle finger. She rubs it constantly during the sessions. But one can hardly see it, and in a photograph it would not appear at all. We came to understand that this patient has a problem with her masturbatory activity for which she uses fetishes (shoes with high heels). She does not know or accept as yet that she feels guilt and shame; and fear of herself and her desires. Consciously she thinks of herself as being very "cool" in matters of sex. She often has one-night stands with black men, feeling very liberal and tolerant, at the same time realizing that she could never think of confessing this to her mother. Her analysis has revealed that when she was a child she took her mother's bathrobe to smell it when she felt abandoned by her. The bathrobe, we understood, took the place of mother's skin. Now, as an adult woman what she simultaneously fears and craves, is feeling touched, and falling in love.

Lucian Freud's skin paintings represent protections against influences from outside that rob people of their individuality, a shield against the impoverishment of the sex images offered as reality in video performances and the internet, promising satisfaction yet leaving people empty and isolated inside. Lucian Freud, in his figurative painting breaking away from contemporary abstractionism but also from traditionalism, takes his own individual path. He is conservative and ultramodern at the same time in that he shows us a timeless perspective on the subject that defies any attempts to divide body and psyche. In doing so, he emphasizes the difference between sexuality, which is bound up with time and space, as opposed to sex as a momentary event, devoid of meaning and development. In this way he articulates an implicit critique of postmodern mass culture which is geared towards commercialization of sex as a commodity, robbing the individual of his memory and personal history. Lucian Freud's skin paintings "smell". To quote his grandfather Sigmund:

(I)t is the *inter urinas et faeces nascimur* of the early fathers, which is
directly attached to sexual life and cannot be disassociated from it
through any possible attempt at idealization. (Freud, 1905, p. 19)

In this sense, Lucian Freud would be closer to the pronounced individuality of turn of the century Viennese painters, contemporaries such as
Gustav Klimt, Oskar Kokoschka and, particularly, Egon Schiele rather
than Rembrandt or Rubens. In spite of, or rather because of, his "penetrating glance", he is a tender, empathic painter, for whom the human
is accessible through self-reflection.

Surface and depth: "Seeing through the skin"—"As dressed in paint"

So far I have focused on demonstrating how Lucian Freud´s paintings
raise questions of identity in modern society; expressed through his
emphasis on the skin as a representation of the border between inside
and outside. Discussing in more detail the painting *Sleeping by the Lion
Carpet* I have put forward the idea that his *Naked Portraits* reveal the
innermost secrets of the individual rendered visible on the skin. This
was also my approach in a previous paper; Lucian Freud, the scientist
and biologist, dissecting his models with his "penetrating gaze," uses
his skill to paint the layers of the skin in order to represent the personal
inner truth of the subject (De Clerck, 2007).

Even if I hold that this continues to have relevance, upon further
reflection I have come to adopt an alternative view which I am going
to elaborate here further. It may well compliment the first. The portrait of Big Sue was executed by Lucian Freud in 1996 at the age of
seventy-two. In looking once again at his early work, the paintings
from the years 1939 up until the 1950s, figurative paintings that
initially had not interested me (I was coming from a post-war appreciation of abstractionism) I began immersing myself in these paintings
more intensely. This time, after taking in the historical-biographical
perspective, tracing the development in his rendering of the skin
over more than six decades, from the beginning of his career as an
artist to his latest manifestations, I began to think in a new way concerning the visibility of inner life on the surface of the skin. The relation of revealing/concealing is puzzling as mentioned, the skin has
a double surface, one inside and one outside. But it can also have a
double function: to bring something from the inside to the surface

and also to conceal something that is inside. I think that Lucian Freud makes use of both these functions of the skin in his work. Is this an apparent paradox?

Regarding his early paintings of the forties and fifties I have come to see that there is more of a quality of permeability of the skin and in that sense more openness in the portrayal of inner feelings than there is in later years. In his early work from his adolescence, the skin appears thin and translucent—the distress, the anxiety and pain of the person felt inside is revealed on the surface. There is a painfully undisguised communication directed to the onlooker, "look here, I'm suffering"; a cry for help.

These early pictures communicate the idea that one could "look through the skin" and what is to be seen is the trauma that the protagonists may have suffered (Fig. 4).

Figure 4. Girl with leaves, 1948, Pastel, 19 x 16,5 in.

These people appear naked in their emotions, yet they are for the most part dressed, their bodies covered with clothes. There is a sense that one can understand their innermost feelings, apart from the wide open eyes, through the fragility of the skin. The use of light paint and a light stroke make the picture look almost like watercolour rather than an oil even when in reality it is not (with the exception of *Girl with leaves*, which is a pastel).

From the late fifties and early sixties onwards, a reverse process takes place in Lucian Freud´s paintings. He begins to change his technique: instead of sable, he now uses hog brushes which allow him to apply thicker layers of paint, and from the 60s onwards he uses heavy Cremnitz white in his skins (Fig. 5). This move, designated by him to invigorate his painting, seems linked to an anecdote from the 1940s, related by William Feaver (2007).

Figure 5. Naked girl, 1966, oil on canvas.

One day, long ago in the 1940s, when he was living on the
Paddington side of the Grand Union Canal in West London, Lucian
Freud found himself examining the late Mr. Page. "The corpse,
dressed in Sunday best, had been embalmed, the face lavishly
flesh-tinted." He is quoted as saying "This very heavy brush work,
lots of impasto: it looked as though it had been laid on with one of
those wooden spoonish things you do butter with. The work that
went into it. Amazing."… Seeing Mr. Page larded in make up was
a novelty; seeing the human face rendered so elaborately unnatural
was a shock. (Feaver, 2007, p. 7)

Twenty years after this episode, from the late sixties onwards, Lucian
Freud begins to concentrate on painting what became his spectacular
Naked Portraits. They are what he now stands for; the audacity, the
mastery in technique, the portraiture. Every part of the body is revealed
to the eye, the genitals are fully exposed, the skin reflecting the age, the
bruises and scars that life has imprinted on the skin and the psyche
alike. Yet paradoxically, rather than being more telling, the heavy paint
also seems to obscure the affects and emotions of the persons, they
become more and more distanced, eyes averted or closed. They do not
make contact with the viewer.

Throughout his years the crust gets thicker and thicker. And from
the late eighties onwards, he starts using crumbs and specks of paint
on the face and the extremities of his models. The nudes are covered in
heavy splash paint. They do not resemble real people any more. By now
it has become evident that this form of painting has nothing to do with
the realism of Rubens or Rembrandt. It is figurative painting as a form
of expressionism, a technique used to highlight Freud's very personal
view of the individual. In these naked portraits, lust is tied up with
anxiety, sexuality with decay, Eros with Thanatos. If there was a parallel with another painter it would be with Bacon. But unlike in Bacon, in
Lucian Freud we see no injured or opened skins. There is no blood, no
raw flesh. The texture of the surface of the skin always remains intact.
The "skin envelope" (Anzieu, 1989), as a representative of the primary
object, the mother, holds him together. The treatment of the skin in their
paintings would mark, more than anything, the difference between
these two great British artist friends who, at one time, shared a studio
in Paddington together.

A further twenty years later, in the 1980s, any individuality becomes more and more blurred. The paint is splashed in thick splashes to make the painting nearly three dimensional. This three dimensional quality heightens the sense of touch, transforming the flat surface almost into a sculpture. The impression that the persons in the paintings now convey is that of roughness, a coarse skin, not pleasurable to the touch; more like the skin of a reptile, a dinosaur or a dragon (Fig. 6).

The use of Cremnitz white becomes excessive which makes the figures look like corpses. The position of the models is unnatural.

Figure 6. Standing by the rags, 1989–90, oil on canvas.

Figure 7. Ria, Naked Portrait 2006–7, oil on canvas.

This is particularly evident in the book *Freud at Work* (Bateman, 2006), a collection of photographs by Bruce Bernard and David Dawson. In some of the photographs one can see the model in flesh and blood on one side and next to it, on the easel the unfinished painting. The skin of the model in the photograph is rosy and smooth, whereas in the painting the skin is coarse and very pale (Bateman, 1995, p. 87).

In these late paintings Lucian Freud provokes and at the same time conceals the image of Death that lies beneath the skin. In this sense they seem to me to be linked to the episode related by Feaver: the day in 1940 when Freud, examining the late Mr. Page, he realized that one could paint over the image of death (Fig. 7).

In his book *Impasse and Interpretation*, Rosenfeld describes two types of modes in dealing with trauma:

> There are many narcissistic patients whose narcissistic structure provides them with such a "thick skin" that they have become insensitive to deeper feelings. ... By contrast to those with a "thick skin", some narcisstistic patients are "thin-skinned". They are hypersensitive and easily hurt in everyday life and analysis. ... In my experience, the "thin-skinned" narcissistic patients were, as children, repeatedly severely traumatized in their feelings of self-regard. They seem to have felt persistently and excessively inferior, ashamed and vulnerable, and rejected by everybody (Rosenfeld, 1987, p. 274).

The development of a protective shield against early vulnerability by moving from a "thin-skinned" syndrome, the translucent skins in his early period, to the "thick-skinned " syndrome of a "crustacious ego" (Anzieu 1989), would not be surprising in Lucian Freud´s life. To account for the time span of more than twenty years between these two orientations, Sigmund Freud's notion of "Nachträglichkeit" offers an explanation: Nachträglichkeit (deferred action), is a psychic mechanism which refers to the fact that an early trauma may remain fairly unnoticed until later it is reactivated by a similar event in the persons life. Only then it may become noticible to the outside world and produce symptoms. In that sense, the translucent skins of the figures in Lucian Freud's early paintings, would represent the reverse side of his later thick skins and vice versa: both would refer to the same enigma that is encapsulated within each person, as in Lucian Freud himself, a narcissistic wound that is constantly revealed and concealed, in his art, but never fully captured.

The dialectics of the process of revealing/concealing is linked to the emanations of the unconscious. As with dreams whose function it is to reveal as much as the ego is prepared to give away and, in a defensive movement, conceal as much as it finds necessary in order to maintain its stability, Lucian Freud's paintings create a mystery that requires interpretation. They do not give away their secret easily. This is because they deal with the duality of Sex and Death, Eros and Thanatos, the two major determinants of the life of the individual and their representations in the deepest layers of the psyche. They exhibit and hide at the same time that what is being made to see and at the same time to be concealed: an early trauma that wants to be recognized and yet is denied making itself known to the world. This would explain the apparent contradiction of surface and depth, the dialectics of transparency and impermeability in Lucian Freud´s *Naked Portraits*.

Postscript

When, for an earlier publication (De Clerck, 2007), I needed permission to reproduce some of Lucian Freud's paintings, I was put through to his solicitor in England. She passed my request on to Lucian Freud himself who let me know that he wanted to know how I saw the link between him and his grandfather. I sent him my paper and consequently he granted me permission. Curious to hear about his thoughts, I asked the solicitor if he had commented some more on the content of my paper. In an email she wrote back:

> I am sorry to disappoint you but Lucian Freud does not wish to make any further comment. He spends his time painting and rarely allows himself to be distracted from his all absorbing interest in his work. (Message sent 18 July 2006)

References

Anzieu, D. (1989). *The Skin Ego*. New Haven: Yale University Press.

Author. *The Naked Truth*. (2005). Exhibition catalogue. Schirn Kunsthalle, Frankfurt am Main.

Bateman, N. (1995). *Freud at Work*. London: Random House.

Bateman, N. (2006). *Freud at work. Lucian Freud in Conversation with Sebastian Smee*. London: Random House.

Benthien, C. (1998). *Im Leibe wohnen. Literarische Imagologie und historische Anthropologie der Haut* (Living in the body: Literary images and a historical anthropology of the skin). Berlin: Berlin Verlag.

Bick, E. (1968.) The experience of the skin in early object relations. *International Journal of Psycho-Analysis 49*: 236–240.

Borkenhagen, A. (2000). "Zum Wandel weiblicher Körperinszenierungen" (On changes in women's perceptions of their bodies). *Psychoanalyse, Texte zur Sozialforschung 2000*: 6.

Britton, R. (2010) Belief and Imagination, The New Library of Psych. ed by Elisabeth Spillius. London, Routledge.

Butler, J. (1993). *Bodies that Matter*. New York, NY: Routledge.

De Clerck, R. (2005). *The Penetrating Glance*. Paper read at the Culture and Unconscious Conference London.

De Clerck, R. (2007). Der zudringliche Blick. Sexualität und Körper. Subjektvorstellungen bei Sigmund Freud und Lucian Freud ("The penetrating gaze." Sexuality and body. Sigmund Freud—Lucian Freud). In: Philipp Soldt (Ed.) *Ästhetische Erfahrungen* (Aesthetic Experience), Psychosozial-Verlag, Giessen, 2007.

Detig—Kohler, C. (2000). *Hautnah: Im psychoanalytischen Dialog mit Hautkranken* (Skintight: A psychoanalytical dialogue with sufferers of dermatological illnesses). Giessen: Psychosozial-Verlag.

Feaver, W. (2007). *Lucian Freud*. New York: Rizzoli.

Freud, S. (1905e). *Fragment of a case of hysteria, S.E 7*.

Freud, S. (1923b). *The ego and the id. S.E 19*.

Freud, S. (1930a). *Civilization and its discontents. S.E 21.*

Freud, S. (1975). *Briefe an Wilhelm Fliess: 1887–1904. Hrsg. Von J M Masson* (Letters to Wilhelm Fliess: 1887–1904). Frankfurt am Main: Fischer Verlag.

Lauter, R. (2000). *Lucian Freud.* Exhibition Catalogue, Museum für Moderne Kunst, Frankfurt/M.

Marcuse, H. (1965). *Triebstruktur und Gesellschaft: ein philosophischer Beitrag zu Sigmund Freud* (Eros and civilization: a philosophical inquiry into Freud). Frankfurt am Main: Suhrkamp.

Naked Portraits. (2000). Exhibition catalogue, Museum für Moderne Kunst, Frankfurt am Main.

Pines, D. (1988). *A Woman's Unconscious use of her Body.* London: Virago.

Rosenfeld, H. (1987). *Impasse and Interpretation. Therapeutic and anti-therapeutic factors in psychoanalysis.* London: Tavistock.

CHAPTER THREE

Alberto Giacometti's Caress/Despite the Hands: Developing and vanished life as a reversible figure—nucleus of an adequate expression of the struggle for the acknowledgment of space and time?

Claudia Frank

Abstract

This Chapter will explore the possible meaning of Alberto Giacometti's 1932 sculpture *Caresse/Malgré les mains*. By taking the reflection of counter-transference manifestations as an approach on which a specific psychoanalytical contribution can be based, I develop my hypothesis that Giacometti—by choosing the form of a reversible figure—expressed an impasse he felt. By using this form he was able to then overcome his mental block. I then outline a few steps which in my view might have been decisive on Giacometti's way to the sculptures from 1947–1952 that made him famous.

"Because I never succeeded, I kept going"

"Ever since 1935 I have never, not for one day, done anything the way I wanted to. I always ended up with something else. Always. I wanted to make heads, ordinary figures. I never succeeded. But as I always failed, I always wanted to keep trying .... I wanted to succeed to make one head the way I saw it, you see. But because I never succeeded, I kept going. You have to have a certain stupidity about you to continue. I really should have given up when I saw that I was unable to do anything. If I had some intelligence I would have given up but as I love this work more than any other …." This is what Alberto Giacometti said in a television interview in the summer of 1964 (quoted in Hohl, 1998, p. 87).

Preparing this Chapter I had the feeling that I had experienced comparable stupidity by accepting the friendly invitation to participate in *The female body—inside and outside*. For weeks I had been working on new versions of this Chapter but sooner or later I always had the impression of having failed to grasp what is "essential". Every time I felt that I had succeeded in getting a better grasp of some essential element; but I still felt that, I had failed to grasp the project as a whole. Everything that had not been touched upon made the project appear lopsided, disproportional and therefore "wrong". Eventually the feeling of never being able to grasp what I was looking for could not be shaken off any more. Still, I kept trying and eventually acknowledged that I cannot present any "final" version, but just the current state of affairs.

I had not expected to have to struggle so hard to find a version that I could more or less stand by—that did not seem too artificial or constructed, but that gives a reasonably lively impression of my view of the discussion. However, if I had taken my first reaction seriously I would have been somewhat prepared. When one of the organisers invited me to participate in the project, as I had worked on Giacometti on various occasions, the idea had been that I might present some of my reflections. At first I felt that I had nothing to contribute. In retrospect, however, I believe my first spontaneous idea to be revealing; I "knew" (although I would at the time have been quite unable to discursively and accurately explain this) that Giacometti's works are not primarily concerned with the representation of the female body. That, in any case, is what I want to suggest and what I have come to be convinced of in the course of my exploration. Intuitively I had very quickly, almost immediately, come to this assessment. But as we also know from initial scenes, initial dreams and further initial phenomena in analyses, these phenomena only disclose their (over determined) meanings in the course of a long process.

This said, I have already indicated that in my reflections on Giacometti's works I follow an approach based on reflecting the reception of art. As a psychoanalyst—and a lay woman in art history—this is the only approach I can imagine allowing for a methodologically founded contribution. I thus see myself as following Freud who, in his famous work *The Moses of Michelangelo* (1914b), expressed the supposed connection between reception and artistic intention as follows:

> In my opinion, what grips us so powerfully can only be the artist's intention, in so far as he has succeeded in expressing it in his work and in getting us to understand it. I realize that this cannot be merely a matter of intellectual comprehension; what he aims at is to awaken in us the same emotional attitude, the same mental constellation as that which in him produced the impetus to create. (ibid., p. 212)

In considering the reflection on countertransference responses as central to the insights that psychoanalysts can contribute to artistic discussion; I assume that we can apply our method as a research tool in non-clinical contexts. It does not, of course, follow the same lines then as it does in the clinical setting (cf. e.g. Frank, 2002) and it requires careful handling and an awareness of the limitations of its validity. Given these provisos the psychoanalytic method can enrich the discussions, just as we as psychoanalysts can learn from artistic creation. In the case of Giacometti, this enrichment might lie in the gauging of a human dilemma, as discussed by Schneider (2006) under the heading of the aporetic situation. Having made these few orienting remarks about the basic procedure of my Chapter, I now want to return to the concrete example. I will sketch my understanding of the reflections on Giacometti's work, with regard to the topic *The female body—inside and outside*.

Swabian Venus versus Femme debut

Previously the thought of focussing my attention on the female body in Giacometti's work had not crossed my mind. The human figure is the central object of Giacometti's principal work, he deals almost exclusively with men and women; however, even though the female body is always clearly discernible it did not, to my eyes, stand out as a separate topic. Perhaps this becomes clearer when we take archaic female statuettes as the epitome of femininity (or for instance pertinent works of Giacometti's contemporary Henry Moore). The contrast between the *Swabian Eve* (on the cover of this book) and Alberto Giacometti's typical female figures could hardly be greater. This *Swabian Eve* (or rather the fragments that, when put together, form this figure) was found at an excavation of the cave of the *Hohle Fels* (hollow rock). It is probably between 35000–40000 years old (cf. the catalogue for the exhibition *Eiszeit—Kunst und Kultur* (*Ice Age—Art and Culture*) in Stuttgart 2009, p. 268ff). Here we have the female statuette, just six cm long, 3.46 cm wide and 3.13 cm thick, made of ivory, without head and neck (but with an eyelet), with voluptuous, widely protruding breasts, short arms (the fingers on the belly underneath the breasts), wide shoulders and hips as well as a distinctly formed vulva. The short, tapering legs are less elaborated. This exterior points to a specific interior. This figure seems immediately compatible—to take only one tradition of psychoanalytic thought—with Melanie Klein's explanations of the infantile (unconscious) phantasies of an inexhaustible breast and a mother's body full of babies and other riches.

In Giacometti's sculpture (Figure 1 *Femme debout/Standing Woman* (1948) from the Staatsgalerie Stuttgart) we have the female figure almost life-sized, very thin, made of bronze, her arms stretched and held close by her side, overly long legs and massive feet on a pedestal. We can discern her breasts, belly and hips schematically, but the agitated surface allows for no detailed ascription. While the outer appearance of the Stone Age figurine pointed to a specific inside, Giacometti's *Standing Woman* appears as a materialisation of the inside in its intensity, dignity and fundamentality—an inside that actually cannot be grasped directly.

This confrontation perhaps lets you understand why I did not concentrate primarily on the female body in Giacometti's work. His statues do not conform to the established consensus of the topic (as far as it is possible to speak of more or less common procedures in view of the many individual approaches artists take in their works on this topic). This observation surprised me as it may have been the starting point for further reflection. I have dealt extensively with typical standing female sculptures. I have also discussed *Mains tenant le vide* and considered in some detail paintings and drawings, for which Giacometti's mother, his wife Annette and others sat him. Had I just been blind when I organised my reflections around my experiences with Giacometti's representation of bodies in the 1947–1952 sculptures that made him famous, yet only ever touched lightly on the aspect of the female body? Possibly. For now I will have to leave this question unanswered.

I realised that with my first reaction to the invitation I had been riveted by Giacometti's principal work. For if one takes Giacometti's early

Figure 1.

sculpture from 1932, that also gives this Chapter its title *Caress/Despite the Hands* (Figure 2), a connection to the topic *The female body—inside and outside* is immediately apparent. Here we have a modern representation of a central aspect of our age old Venus: the pregnant body. Instead of the protruding breast, here there is only the maternal belly. On first impression, this marble sculpture seems to be the idea of a pregnant body turned into matter, abstracted from lived corporality, representing it perfectly. Thus, with this sculpture, the direct link to the book's theme was found. I had previously presented some hypotheses about it, and knew that I had something to say about it and gladly accepted the invitation. I was planning a renewed and more profound reflection on this and other selected sculptures by Giacometti, and took the invitation

Figure 2.

as a chance to gain some understanding of the meaning (or aspects of it) of the female body in his work. *Caress* seemed to me to be the ideal starting point for an investigation of the project topic with regard to Giacometti's oeuvre.

Before inviting you to look at this sculpture, I want to very briefly sketch Giacometti's career. Alberto Giacometti (1901–1966), the son of the renowned Swiss painter Giovanni Giacometti, grew up in natural contact with other artists and the world of painting and drawing. He himself was very gifted in this field but chose a career as a sculptor. His first creative period started in 1925, lasting for about ten years. His dissatisfaction with the chosen artistic style of his early sculpted work (Grisebach, book, p. 117) led to a long period of crisis. During this time he fell back, amongst other things, to drawing and painting, which did, according to Giacometti himself, help him to express the immediate experience of reality. As a sculptor he tried from 1935 (unsuccessfully in his own judgement) to create heads from a model. A little later he was modelling figures that turned out smaller and smaller, until eventually there was hardly anything left (see e.g. the photo Giacometti in his studio 1946–7 by H. Cartier-Bresson, in Ausstellungskatalog der Nationalgalerie Berlin und Staatsgalerie Stuttgart 1988, p. 30). Then, in 1947, after more than ten years, he had found the style that would characterize his mature work.

Caress/Malgré les mains (1932)

Turning now to the marble sculpture *Caress* from 1932, one might say that it initially presents a counterpoint to these introductory remarks about failure. Instead, there is light, comfortable stillness, and tranquillity. It depicts a pregnant body containing the developing child, the sketched outline of hands on both sides. The delicately drawn hands embrace it in a gentle and tender way. The light marble seems to emanate hope and a sense of calm confidence. If we consider that later on Giacometti could wipe out his clay figures, nothing seems to be more unlikely than this portrayal. These fine hands cannot possibly harm the solid stone. There is no danger to the unborn child. Bonnefoy interprets thus: "The smoothness of the marble, its plain, peaceful capacity to absorb the light and let it glide over its surface, indicates a most human, blissful sensuality." Regarding the hands, he speaks of a doubtless "fatherly gesture" (Bonnefoy, 1991, p. 46).

I assume that for most of you Giacometti is the least likely artist to be linked to such tenderness—not through the typically thin and elongated standing women and walking men with their amorphously shaped surfaces that had made him famous; those could not be further removed from any association of pregnancy. Nor through the less well-known surrealistic sculptures, some of which convey a considerable degree of aggression (as well as the pleasure derived from it)—the *Woman with the Throat Cut* (1932) spells it out in its title, whilst *Man and Woman* (1928–1929) immediately conveys it via its visual impact. A picture of Giacometti's hands working on a head, taken fourteen years after "our" sculpture, does, however, seem to me to convey a similar tender and gentle quality (see monograph by Hohl, p. 119). Perhaps a hint at how tenderly he himself identified with (feminine) care could be expressed through his creations.

There is no trace of this type of cruelty in our marble sculpture of roughly fifty cm. Yet, despite the overall positive impression, something gets in the way of unblemished round happiness. Two pinnacle-shaped indentations, declining to the left, leave a disturbing mark. As much as we might welcome this outline of a counterweight to the protruding belly, which creates a connection to the vertebrae of the spine, it still does not quite add up. In the face of all clarity, something disquieting remains. This disturbance suddenly gets a face, as soon as one considers the sculpture from a different perspective; rather than the side view of a standing/sitting person, one can look at a lying one. From this view we can see a lying skull. Bonnefoy writes:

> The unexpected hard, cruel lines, the geometry, which now pierces what a moment ago seemed to be warmest flesh, as if the external room had triumphed over life, that is the profile of a head, thrown back in the face of death, its eyes empty, its mouth wide open (ibid., p. 202).

This association gains credibility through the sculpture *Head of a Man on a Rod* (1947) (Figure 3), created fifteen years later.

If we look at it this way, we can see the hands as covering the eyes of the dead. *Despite the Hands*, the second title of this sculpture, could then be read as death that could not be prevented and held back by these hands, which are powerless in the face of death, and even that something/someone was dying "in these hands". Terrible and irrevocable things are happening despite the helpful, tender and loving hands;

Figure 3.

they are not omnipotent after all. In this sense the first part of the title does indeed refer to the second, and the other way round, *Despite the Hands* refers to the first view of our sculpture. The harsh reality remains "*Despite the Hands*", offering firmness, but also limitations and breaks.

As you will realize, I am fascinated by this sculpture. Looking at it, I always used to feel a bit irritated because it radiates something that I could not immediately associate with my former image of Giacometti's work. Reflecting now in more depth I realised that this piece is a unique representation of something that is at the core of Giacometti's oeuvre: creativity and death. It is a representation that reminds me of the tradition of reversible figures or of reversible perspective. This seemed to me to be important. One sees both things in alternation, in an either/or format. Both ways of looking at it are statically connected to one another. How can we reconcile these two perspectives with our topic, the view of the female body? Put in somewhat exaggerated terms, we might perhaps say that there is, on the one hand, tender, childlike (I believe we can also view the carved hand as a child's hand) curiosity and concern; and, on the other hand, the result of murderous impulse. (Note 1)

I was curious to see how this was being discussed in art historical secondary literature; what importance was attached to this figure that seemed such a significant step in Giacometti's developmental process? I was surprised to find that the figure is neither accorded special significance nor studied in much detail at all, contrary to *Hands Holding the Void* (1932–34), about which numerous analyses exist. This latter piece is doubtless a very expressive sculpture from these years (cf. Frank 2002) but, to my mind, the meaning of "our" sculpture does not fall short in comparison. *Caress* vividly depicts things that are directly incompatible—an aspect that is expressed more in the title of *Mains tenant le vide* or *Invisible Object* than in the form itself. But it is not only that *Caress* has not attracted as much attention as I had expected—the attention it did receive is itself striking.

For one thing, what I have called the second title, *Despite the Hands*, is often omitted (for instance by Bonnefoy). This is all the more surprising since the sculpture was (as far as can be reconstructed) first exhibited by Christian Zervos in 1932 under title *Malgré les mains* (cf. Hohl, 1972, p. 84). In *Cahiers d'art* Man Ray's picture of the plaster mould is reprinted; in the article itself Zervos wrote:

> So the hand that can be seen on the original work in plaster (reprinted at the beginning of this article) is no longer there in the stone version, as its plastic function without message is disturbing, (Vitali, 1998, p. 255).

A marble version with the hands does, however, exist. We can thus establish that the sculpture is obviously able to evoke something disturbing that people for this very reason would like to get rid of. Further observations in this direction can be made. The second reading, focussing on the skull, is often omitted (in Klemm, 2001; Hohl, 1972; Zervos, 1932) or the fright is interpreted away. Wilson for instance writes:

> The artist has conflated a gently swelling head with a pregnant woman's belly. By making them equal he has made a philosopher's stone … . In Caress, the miracle of birth is discovered by the delicately man's or boy's hands as he tenderly touches her stomach. When the work is construed as a head, the hands cover its eyes, forcing it to look inward, where new life is discovered through imagination. (Wilson, book, p. 132)

On the other hand, Inboden's view is, to my mind, too one-sided when she writes:

> *Caress* focuses *exclusively* on not-seeing, the missing face—*death*. In this sculpture the hands cover … the eyes. They touch the head, intending to get hold of it, to make it "visible", and by doing so they rob it of its lively part, its look. Under the touch that wants to grasp something, it petrifies … (Inboden, 1988, p. 90; emphasis added)

Neither do I think that the following, somewhat disparaging, formulation does the work justice, namely that the title forces us to "give an interpretation that is concrete, almost an anecdote" (Hohl, 1971, p. 83). What we actually want to do, according to Hohl, is class it with the family of Hans Arp's "(contemporaneous) inventions of form" (ibid.). Likewise Bonnefoy's biographical interpretations are too one-sided (although they are more cautiously phrased):

> It is not impossible that at the end of this time of mutual love [Bonnefoy is here referring to a love affair Giacometti had at that time], Alberto thought to give the intimacy a character of lasting attachment … . (Bonnefoy, 1991, p. 46).

And further on:

> ... once more the memory of the terrible hours at van M.'s deathbed
> (ibid., p. 102)—referring to the death of van Meurs on the journey
> with A. Giacometti in 1921.

Nevertheless, I, too, had to self-diagnose a tendency towards disambiguation regarding one detail. On second consideration of the sculpture, despite experiencing the hands as "tender and gentle", I also felt bothered by their carved and restricted nature. I remembered that on one occasion Giacometti had tried to sign his autograph on his cousin's arm, by cutting his initials into her skin, using the same penknife with which he was ordinarily carving his sculptures (Lord, book, p. 88). Initially I dismissed this thought; I attributed it to my possibly hypersensitive reactions and played it down. It was not until later on, when I came across Klemm's statement of the engraved hands "*injuring* the abstract perfection of the object" (Klemm, 2001, p. 93; emphasis added), that I reconsidered and thought my initial thoughts might have been significant after all. What is important for our purposes here is that I attempted to view the hands as "only good". In this context I also noticed that in Giacometti's pencil drawing *My studio* from 1932 (for the history of this drawing see Hohl) the hands are omitted—he may have made this drawing of the sculpture at the stage that Zervos wrote about; when it did not yet include the hands. Or perhaps they were hard to draw and would have appeared only as tender.

What is this tendency towards disambiguation? Is it about a tension that is hard to bear, namely that we "hold in our hands" neither creativity nor death? That the sculpture represents both—pregnant belly and skull—without it being clear how these facts of life, might be integrated? In 1947 Giacometti wrote a now famous letter to Matisse, in which he also reflects on this period (1932–34):

> The external reproduction of a figure wasn't the point for me anymore; what counted for me instead was to live and only to realize what really moved me, what I really desired. But all this got detached, became inconsistent, and carried on in glaring contradictions. There was the longing to arrive at a resolution between the simple and quiet, and the sharp and impetuous things. In those years (c. 1932–34) this resulted in things that moved into quite opposite directions—a lying landscape-head, a strangled woman with a cut throat .... (Stoos, Elliott, Doswald, 1996, p. 356)

As we can see, he does not name "our" sculpture but refers rather to another one, *Paysage—tête couchée*, in which we can discern our element in a slightly altered and thus softer form, as part of a composition that he juxtaposes with death. In his description, the contrast between the two sculptures that he puts in opposition to each other becomes clear— peacefully lying landscape-head versus strangled woman. Looking at them, however, the contrast is not so clear. If it really is about "glaring contradictions" with the two marked extremes of light, pregnant body on the one side, and pale skull on the other side, then these contradictions are at their most impressive in *Caress*. It is here that the contradiction of creativity, fertility, and death culminates, because in this sculpture they are presented in one.

Giacometti wanted to create a materialisation of what moved him. And you will remember that Freud assumed that what grips us so powerfully can only be the artist's intention, in so far as he has succeeded in expressing it in his work and in getting us to understand it. With regard to the reception of his work Giacometti succeeded; interpretations move in "opposite directions". Nevertheless, the meaning of the form chosen is still not sufficiently resolved. What is the reversible figure about? I could not find much about the function of reversible figures in the course of art history; as far as I can see one aspect is thwarting a (supposedly) awe-inspiring representation. I am indebted to Carina Weiß for pointing out to me, amongst other things, the satirical medals that were used as means of propaganda; for instance in religious controversies images (depicting both the pope and the devil or the cardinal and the fool). Reversible figures function as a means that aim at effect and can be revealing and funny, but do not necessarily contribute to a profound understanding of the situation in question.

We do find, however, that Bion has resorted to visual phenomena in order to illustrate a particular problem that can occur in psychoanalyses. I believe that his reflections can help us in reverse as well, which is why I want to quickly summarise them. Bion used the example of "Rubin's vase". One sees either two faces or a vase. He uses the reversible figure in order to illustrate how we can imagine an initially invisible stand-still in an analysis. Bion assumes that patient and analyst see the same lines, as it were; however, inwardly each sees something different in them. In such cases the analysis may outwardly seem to progress fruit-fully; the patient associates, the analyst interprets. But after a while it may become obvious that the analytic process has not been progressing.

Bion described how this can be due to the patient (seemingly) accept-ing the analyst's interpretation, "but the premises have been rejected and others silently substituted" (Bion, 1963, p. 54). The interpretation thus has no effect. As long as the reversible perspective remains unrec-ognised, this leads to an impasse in the analytic process. The dynamic connections cease to exist and are replaced by static splitting. Realising such an impasse during an analysis will be accompanied by an intense despair that misconceptions have been governing the situation. That might open at least a chance for change.

It appears that it was with the reversible figure that Giacometti found a form to express the impasse he felt himself to be in. He felt he did not progress with regard to his wish to produce works that corresponded to his perception of reality (cf. his remarks in the letter to Matisse, quoted in Stoos, Elliott, Doswald, 1996, p. 356). There is also a third reading that I thought of while looking at *Caress*, namely that of a mutilated hand. A somehow deformed and damaged hand—a (cut?) thumb, index and middle finger merging with the rest of the fingers. This hand might stand for his "knowledge", and the expression of it, that his "creat-ing hand" was not yet producing that which would conform to what he was searching and imagining, an art seeking truth/reality. I thus believe that in *Caress* Giacometti might have got to the heart of his aim. He was working on perverse solutions, in which incompatible facts are not realized as such, with emotional consequences. These "solutions" are characterized by the fact that they subvert the acknowledgment of the irreversibility of time and space that connect but also separate. The artistic connections (seemingly) spare one the painful task of working through. When Marcel Jean reports Giacometti's statement by the end of 1934, that "everything he had made up until now was nothing but masturbation"(quoted from Hohl, 1998, p. 82), this might indicate his feeling that he had not really confronted his experiences, and that his artwork might have been impressive but was lacking the depth of really moving the viewer.

At the same time, however, *Caress* also stands for the hope that something in him would mature, that his creating hand would con-form to the carved one that feels something growing underneath. In this function, it might have been inspired by a representation of Venus by Laussel; Giacometti copied this Venus by sketching it on the page opposite the reproduction in a book (Figure 4, in the exhibition catalogue of the Museo d'arte Mendriso, 2000, p. 72) and probably also again on a

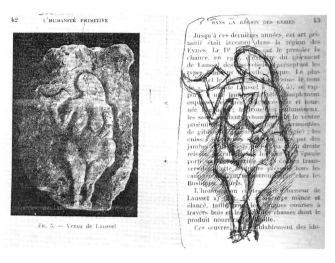

Figure 4.

separate sheet of paper. The book came out in 1924, though it is unclear when Giacometti purchased it. His copy is not dated but probably belongs to the early ones (cf. Carluccio, p. 23). On the photograph of the Venus, the fingers can be discerned more clearly (see e.g. catalogue of the Ice Age exhibition 2009, p. 276).

Where has this investigation taken us? With regards to the topic of the female body, we might say that for Giacometti the female body functioned as the epitome of fertility and creativity. The focus on the pregnant body as an image for this bears witness to an intuitive knowledge that time and space are necessary for creativity to evolve. It is likely, however, that this phase was also dominated by a rather abstract idea of what creating means; the idea of a perfect creation, fed only by life drives. The reverse side was thus death and mutilation, the split off manifestations of the death drive. In the carved and yet tender hand, however, there might already be an appearance of the further direction, namely that what is needed is to find a form capable of integrating these opposing forces. I think that *Caress* is both climax and turning point at the same time. Henceforth Giacometti struggled for true creativity; symbolization that bears the traces of working through, for the evolution of a thinking space with the necessary distance for movement; and thus for the dimension of time.

"Impossible to capture a figure in its entirety"

How did Giacometti's development continue? How did he eventually find a way out of this impasse? What part was played by the female body? I wanted to look at the originals again. Filled with enthusiasm and curiosity I went to several exhibitions (apart from the room dedicated to Giacometti at the Staatsgalerie Stuttgart, the sculpture exhibition *From Rodin to Giacometti* in Karlsruhe and *Woman with a Chariot* in Duisburg were of great interest). I wanted to look at the objects intensively—quite literally and with a third eye; to paraphrase Theodor Reik's word about the analyst's third ear for listening to inner experience. It was then that I entered into the unexpected crisis that I mentioned before.

Trying to summarise how I felt during those weeks, I would say that I made many new small discoveries and also experienced some old aspects in a new way. Initially this experience was very enriching. I saw before me various details from Giacometti's different representations of women. Then, however, I got stuck with an abundance of images in my head. No figure emerged; no golden thread was in sight. Time passed. I felt stupid. (End note 2). Eventually I came across another phrase of Giacometti's in his letter to Matisse:

> Impossible to capture a figure in its entirety (we were sitting too close to the model and in starting from a detail, a heel or a nose, all hope was lost of ever reaching the whole). (Vitali, 1998, p. 158)

Again, the dilemma existed in glaring contradiction; either a complete opening (every detail, every work would have to be captured in its entirety, which tends to become pointless as it threatens to override form) or limitation to a certain design element (which in turn threatens to amount to a closing off with regard to any individuality). At this time I also remembered difficult experiences from when I had first worked on Giacometti; difficulties that I had not properly understood at the time and that, as became clear to me now, had a similar pattern as did my present dilemma. It was more than ten years ago that I first presented my hypothesis that Giacometti's sculptures affirm and illustrate Segal's reflections on great artworks in a particular way; namely that they present the greatest possible acknowledgement of the death drive that is curbed for the needs of the life drives. I proposed that the specific aspect of these sculptures lies in the mediation of the experience that an impermeable core (within a permeable object) is indispensible as a condition for aliveness (cf. Frank 2002). There were many who found their own experiences well expressed in my theses but I also encountered some criticism, the vehemence of which surprised me.

Such criticism was directed on one side against my method, the reflection of countertransference responses, which, according to such critics, is not permissible outside the analytic situation. On the other hand, it was directed against the content of my hypothesis, which was taken as a plea for the necessity of a "merely" impermeable object. The common denominator, as I see it now after so many years, was that I was disclosing essentials of the analytic situation. That on the one hand I betray clinical psychoanalysis when I understand applied psychoanalysis as a science, in which our method can be used. And that on the other hand I betrayed the core of psychoanalysis in assuming an impermeable core; as if giving up an indispensable part of our work, namely being open towards all the different projective identifications in order to be able to achieve meaningful understanding. It seemed as though I was propagating either an opening that levelled all differences and thus opened the way for wild, arbitrary and random analyses, or that I was proposing a complete shutting off and declaring masochistic involvement with it to be the cure. In terms of content, both attitudes seem absurd to me. I think what was involved here were enormous emotions that, lacking a containing thought, dressed themselves up as pseudo-plausible. But what kind of thought would present an adequate container? What is it that actually has to be understood? Does it have to do with the intuition that reversible perspective needs to be given up if mental maturation aimed for?

In conclusion, claims to totality of one sort or the other thus presented a considerable obstacle. From this stemmed the necessity to search consciously for adequate limitation and sensible reduction. In terms of our discussion here this also means that I will only be able to sketch one line (from a complex nexus and also without being able to prove it in detail). I will now trace the line that eventually stood out to my eyes.

... what was lacking was my feeling for the whole; a structure, a certain sharpness that I saw before me, something skeleton-like in the room. Giacometti, (Stoos, Elliott, Doswald, 1996, p. 356).

Giacometti tried time and again to move on by studying heads. I think he knew that he had to find a mental solution. He knew for a long time that in order to attain this limitation, a reduction was necessary. At the beginning of the 1920s he had occupied himself for some months with skulls. The sculpture *Gazing Head* from 1927–28 represents his first important step in this direction. It expresses about the importance of seeing but, at the heart of it, not about the sort of seeing that we can achieve with our concrete eyes. Following our sculpture (*Caress*), Giacometti positioned life and death side by side; for example in *Head-Skull* (1934). An edge running through the middle divides the face into two areas. Klemm puts it this way:

His right, dead side appears far more vigorous and lively than the smooth and abstract left one. (Klemm, year, p. 111)

A formal connection can also be found in the face of *Hands Holding the Void*, where the right eye holds the wheel of life, but the left is broken into three pieces. These sculptures present an attempt to depict opposites in one, so that both sides are visible simultaneously. In this, however, the living and fertile half has lost force; it has become abstract and sleek. This can also be observed in a further form of reduction that Giacometti tried out on another figure; *Walking Woman* (1932/36), a sculpture where the stretching of the legs with the simultaneous flattening of the body will have been another unsatisfying attempt. A few years later, he tried out the extreme reduction of size—and his play with fire (by letting the figures end in nothingness).

On the one hand, it is central that Giacometti was able to represent the impasse in one work, namely in *Caress*; but on the other, I suspect that what was needed in the following years was again a separate representation of the object and its shadow, in order to distil the reality that he saw but for a long time was unable to grasp. In 1942–43 Giacometti made *Woman with a Chariot* from plaster and painted her shadow on the (wooden) wall of his studio in Maloja (Figure 5). If we look at this plaster figure it becomes clear that it was again something that is alive that has gained the upper hand; a woman who has adorned herself. Perhaps

Figure 5.

he was driven to complete his perception of reality. What he had tried to capture until then in a skull or a dead half-face, he now tried to represent in the form of a "shadow" on the wall. Not a real shadow but a constructed one that he could take apart and thus grasp. Concretely speaking, this shadow consists of the draft drawn in pencil, elaborated with colour but also plaster (see the catalogue of the Duisburg exhibition, edited by Wiesinger and Lenz for details). This is arguably when the seed for the "something skeleton-like in the room" (Giacometti in his letter to Matisse, quoted from Stoos, Elliott, Doswald, 1996, p. 356) was planted, that can be discerned on a sheet depicting *Woman with a Chariot* from the beginning of the 1950s (see e.g. Wiesinger & Lenz, 2010, p. 25).

Why were two related pieces necessary? Reflecting on my own condition while I was thinking about what is known about Giacometti's life during these years of crisis, I could not help but think of Freud's famous characterisation of the central mechanism of melancholia:

> The ego mourns because it has lost its object through devaluation, but it projects this object onto itself and then finds itself devalued. The shadow of the object falls on the ego and obscures it (Freud, p. 107, Letter from Sigmund Freud to Sándor Ferenczi, February 7, 1915.).

In being able to represent both object and shadow separately, a step towards the overcoming of this obstacle was accomplished (End note 3). I believe that he was able to define the moment of absolute separation, which is not destructible (but can only be denied or similar), from variable contingent experiences.

That 1947 became the year of breakthrough might also have had something to do with a commission. Giacometti was asked to do a portrait of a resistance fighter, Henri Rol-Tanguy, who obviously impressed him (Wilson Alberto Giacometti. Myth, Magic, and the Man, p. 196ff). Was a resistance fighter awakened in him too? Did it help him to be able and willing to trust that there was a resisting core in him as well as others? Was that the point when he was able to conclusively combine the contradictory perceptions of an inner force that was stable, not dead but impalpable; a mental skeleton; and experiences that were constantly changing and alive?

In his mature work, which is characterized amongst other things by the fact that the individual details (nose, heel, etc.) are indistinguishable, Giacometti gave up his claim to totality. It was only by doing so that his proper striving could become fertile, that it could convey something of his perception of reality. His perceptions did not allow themselves to be pinned down in precise external details and did not allow themselves be reduced to limited experiences of birth and death; even though these latter phenomena are indispensible precisely as limitations. The concise overall form with its amorphous surface then shaped his most important sculptures in a unique way that was symbiotically rooted in tradition.

With regard to the topic of the female body, my investigations revealed that even though it was in his preoccupation with (amongst other things) female figures that Giacometti was eventually able to form to his satisfaction that which he intended, the exploration of the female body as such was not his primary concern.

Concluding remarks

I have described how difficult and full of crises my undertaking has been. Here and there, time was an essential factor. It was only then that meaningful approaches became possible; with all their uncertainty, emptiness and ignorance. And space, in which dimensions became essential. As soon as thinking in absolutes crept in, I had once more reached an impasse.

Let us now turn back one last time to the Stone Age figures. The *Swabian Eve* as well as Laussel's *Venus* are characterized by distorted proportions. These distortions in width and depth of the torsos appear as fully sensual, plump fertility. This seems fairly uncontested; if anything it is the function of these female statuettes that is the object of controversy. The hand on the body of Laussel's *Venus* might have inspired Giacometti's *Caress*. It refers to an inside that stood for Giacometti's own maturing creations. In 1932 he felt driven into opposite directions; a sensation he conveyed in a unique way through *Caress/Despite the Hands*. What would become characteristic of his principal work were the distortions of length; as for instance in *Femme debout* (1948); and the many other standing women and walking men. These sculptures undoubtedly speak to many people, without one being able to define what specifically appeals to them.

There are diverse interpretations of the standing women and walking men, for which he became famous. What is often said is that the figures represent haggard bodies that bear witness to the victims of the Holocaust. This implies that our sculpture can be read as the expression of an external gaze on a female body. This reading suggests that the piece might represent an envious attack that was made; internally or externally; on the body. Also emphasized is the immobility and enforced passivity. In support of this one suspects inner reasons that make it appear safer (for a man) not to imagine a woman as alive and fertile, but as immobile. Both approaches assume, for different reasons, that the figure represents the counter-figure to the Stone Age Venus, and that female fertility is the bone of contention. Further associations emerge from "goddesses" to "prostitutes"; just to hint at the width of the spectrum of interpretation. What cannot be overlooked is the fact that what the female figures confront us with are projections, and without projections, understanding is impossible. Profound understanding, however, requires revoking projections time and again, reflecting on what evoked them and they might be understood.

I suggest that we should seriously consider the emergence of opposing associations, and we should link this to the irregular surface structure. These associations are to be understood as the humps that are supposed to be determined, while the essence of representation evades such determinations. They are part of constantly changing outward experiences. I examined the stages that Giacometti had to pass through in order to convey a life-like experience of the constantly changing and at the same time fundamental presence of a counterpart. This can never be definitely achieved as it is ultimately a near—impossible undertaking, but "because I never succeeded, I kept going". (Giacometti quoted in Hohl, 1998, p. 87)

References

Archäologischen Landesmuseum Baden-Württemberg und der Abteilung Ältere Urgeschichte und Quartärökologie der Eberhard Karls Universität Tübingen (Ed.): Begleitband zur Großen Landesausstellung Eiszeit—Kunst und Kultur im Kunstgebäude Stuttgart September 2009—January 2010. Hg. v. Bern: Thorbeke.
Bezzola, T. (2001). Phänomen und Phantasie. In: C. Klemm et al (Eds.), *Alberto Giacometti* (pp. 30–39). Kunsthaus Zürich und Nicolaische Verlagbuchhandlung. Berlin.
Bion, W. (1963). *Elements of Psychoanalysis*. London: Heinemann.
Bonnefoy, Y. (1991). *Alberto Giacometti. Eine Biographie seines Werkes*. Bern: Benteliverlag.

Carluccio, L. (1965). Bemerkungen zu den Kopien. In: *Alberto Giacometti. Begegnungen mit der Vergangenheit* (pp. 15–35). Zürich: Verlag Ernst Scheidegger.

Frank, C. (2002). Mains tenant le vide—Maintenant le vide: Überlegungen zu Giacomettis Skulpturen (von ca. 1947 bis ca. 1952) und zum analytischen Prozeß. *Jahrbuch der Psychoanalyse, 44*: 63–104.

Frank, C. (2009). „Es ist ein Suchen ohne Ende." Überlegungen einer Psychoanalytikerin zu Alberto Giacometti Lithographie *Beunruhigender Gegenstand II* von 1963/64. Zeitschrift *für psychoanalytische Theorie und Praxis, 24*: 135–150.

Freud, S. (1914b). The Moses of Michelangelo. *S.E., 13*: 209–238.

Freud, S. (1996 (7.2.1915)). Entwurf von Trauer und Melancholie. In: E. Falzeder und E. Brabant (Eds.): *Sigmund Freud/Sandor Ferenczi, Briefwechsel* Bd. II, 1, 1914–1916 (pp. 106–108). Wien, Köln, Weimar: Böhlau.

Giacometti, A. (1948). Brief an Pierre Matisse. In: *Alberto Giacometti.* Ausstellungskatalog der Nationalgalerie Berlin und Staatsgalerie Stuttgart (pp. 336–344). München: Prestel Verlag, 1988 and In: C. Vitali (Ed.) *Entweder Objekte oder Poesie sonst nichts. Alberto Giacometti Werke und Schriften* (pp. 152–162). Zürich: Scheidegger und Spieß, 1988.

Giacometti, A. (1950). Brief an Pierre Matisse. In: C. Vitali (Ed.) *Entweder Objekte oder Poesie sonst nichts. Alberto Giacometti Werke und Schriften* (pp. 163–169). Zürich: Scheidegger und Spieß, 1998.

Grisebach, L. (1988). Die Malerei. In: Nationalgalerie Berlin und Staatsgalerie Stuttgart, *Alberto Giacometti.* Ausstellungskatalog der Nationalgalerie Berlin und Staatsgalerie Stuttgart (pp. 115–127). München: Prestel Verlag, 1988.

Hohl, R. (1971). *Alberto Giacometti*. Stuttgart: Gerd Hatje.

Hohl, R. (1981). Giacomettis Atelier im Jahr 1932. In: Hohl,R., *Alberto Giacometti. Zeichnungen und Druckgraphik.* Stuttgart: Verlag Gerd Hatje, 1981.

Hohl, R. (1998). *Giacometti. Eine Bildbiographie.* Stuttgart: Verlag Gerd Hatje.

Inboden, G. (1988). Das Gesicht des Raumes. Beobachtungen zum reifen Werk Alberto Giacomettis. In: Nationalgalerie Berlin und Staatsgalerie Stuttgart (pp. 87–97). München: Prestel Verlag, 1988.

Klemm, G. (2001). *Alberto Giacometti.* Kunsthaus Zürich und Nicolaische Verlagbuchhandlung Berlin.

Museo d'arte Mendriso (2000). *Alberto Giacometti. Dialoghi con l'arte.* Mendriso: Tiratura.

Lord, J. (1995). *Alberto Giacometti. Ein Portrait.* Weinheim: Athenäum-Verlag.

Schmied, W. (1997). Schatten aus einer anderen Welt. Alberto Giacometti und sein Bild der Realität. In: *Alberto Giacometti*. Ausstellungskatalog der Kunsthalle der Hypo-Kulturstiftung München (pp. 39–53). München: Hirmer Verlag, 1997.

Schneider, G. (2006). Ein "'unmöglicher' Beruf" (Freud)—zur aporetischen Grundlegung der psychoanalytischen Behandlungstechnik und ihrer Entwicklung. *Psyche—Z Psychoanal, 60*: 900–931.

Segal, H. (1952). A Psycho-Analytical Approach to Aesthetics. *Int. J. Psycho-Anal., 33*: 196–207.

Stoos, T., Elliott, P. & Doswald, C. (Eds.) (1996). *Alberto Giacometti 1901–1966*. Stuttgart: Verlag Gerd Hatje.

Vitali, C. (Ed.) (1998). *Entweder Objekte oder Poesie sonst nichts. Alberto Giacometti Werke und Schriften*. Zürich: Scheidegger und Spieß.

Weiß, H. (2003). Zeiterfahrung und depressive Position. *Psyche—Z Psychoanal, 57*: 857–873.

Weiß, H. (2005). Wenn das Geschehene erst dann geschieht, wenn wir es denken können—Überlegungen zur Konstruktion des inneren Raums und zur zeitlichen Rekonstruktion. *Psyche—Z Psychoanal, 59* (Beiheft): 65–77.

Wiesinger, V. & Lenz, G. (Eds.) (2010). *Die Frau auf dem Wagen. Triumph und Tod*. München: Hirmer Verlag.

Wilson, L. (2003). *Alberto Giacometti. Myth, Magic, and the Man*. New Haven, London: Yale University Press.

Zervos, C. (1932). Einige Anmerkungen zu Giacoemttis Skulpturen. In: C. Vitali (Ed.), *Entweder Objekte oder Poesie sonst nichts. Alberto Giacometti Werke und Schriften* (pp. 253–255). Zürich: Scheidegger und Spieß, 1998.

Notes

1. Laurie Wilson has postulated a trauma that Giacometti supposedly suffered. She bases it on the observation that numerous deaths and births took place during the same period of time; before Giacometti's birth (stillbirth of Amiet's son) and later deaths (amongst others the grandmother's death and the birth of the sister Ottilia in 1904). Reading this I found it to be a speculative construction that is not sufficiently grounded in direct material from Giacometti; to my mind we are lacking hints that it mirrors his (conscious and unconscious) experience. Nonetheless, Wilson's point would be compatible with the reversible aspect of my interpretation. Overall, perhaps we can do without this sort of biographical construction. We cannot know in detail Giacometti's personal background (as he is not lying on our couch), in

order to understand the universal aspect that concerns us as recipients due to our own singular biographical backgrounds.

2. Giacometti's varied expressions about his failure were often not taken seriously but instead understood as a *façon de parler*, a coquettish whim, and in turn interpreted as successes (Bezzola, Phänomen und Phantasie, p. 31ff). On the other hand, they were sometimes taken too literally, as for instance by Schmied (1997) who writes: "Giacometti was not interested in quick results; ultimately he was not interested in results at all. For him it was about being constantly on the move towards some tremendously far and high aim, the attainability of which was never called into question" (Schmied, Schatten aus einer anderen Welt. Alberto Giacometti und sein Bild der Realität., p. 49). These perceptions all capture one aspect but then threaten to make it absolute, creating academic tension. Suddenly, discussing this failing seemed to me to be itself in danger of sounding coquettish. Or perhaps this idea was due to the fear of never reaching a presentable (interim) result? It might turn into an end in itself and thus subvert not only the joys of discovery but more importantly the inevitably painful aspects of such an undertaking. How far is this, too, another reflection of Giacometti's creative processes?

3. It is probable that following the death of his father, Giacometti identified in this way with the dead father or the father killed in phantasy (Wilson, 2003). However, I am not primarily concerned with detailed biographical background that we only have limited access to. In every development we are also concerned with melancholic mechanisms, which is why the creative ways of dealing with them that an artist might find can become relevant for the viewer. And, of course, Giacometti himself studied other artist's compositions. In our context it might not be accidental that Giacometti was inspired for *Kubus* (1933–34) in which he saw a head, by Dürer's famous engraving *Melencolia* (cf. Bonnefoy, p. 213f).

Figures

1. Femme debout/Standing woman (1948).
2. Caress/Despite the Hands (1932).
3. Head of a man on the Rod (1947).
4. Copy of the Venus of Laussel.
5. Woman with a charcot (1942–43).

PART II

PREGNANCY AND MOTHERHOOD

CHAPTER FOUR

The female cauldron: reproductive body schemata fore-grounded by infertility

Joan Raphael-Leff

Abstract

We have all emerged from within it. For both sexes the female reproductive body is therefore a receptacle of unconscious fantasy and creative primary identifications as well as a "cauldron" of magical powers and malevolent projections. For today's women with access to efficient contraception and safe abortion, "generative identity" incorporates a sense of power; holding unconscious representations in check by matter-of-fact control over the life-forming female body and its preventive or death-dealing forces. However, when they contemplate creating a baby of their own, fantasies of that archaic cauldron intrude, taking on a personal material form and centripetal anxieties concerning the female body interior. That is to say the maternal intrauterine space, and its awesome "feminine mysteries" of conception, implantation, formation and sustenance; and destruction.

This chapter focuses on representations of the numinous "cauldron" fore-grounded with the desire for offspring. Infertility constitutes a severe blow, especially in a culture that cultivates an illusion of reproductive control. Diagnosis disrupts lifelong axioms of Russian-doll type lineage, with dire social consequences in some societies. Fertility treatment further unleashes unconscious oedipal anxieties as tacit belief in personal generative power, and body-management is dismantled to be relocated in potent fertility experts and their bizarre technology. Verbatim clinical material demonstrates shifting imagery with the crisis in self-perception, as failure to conceive naturally undermines long established facts of life, transferring the primal scene from bedroom to laboratory.

Body schema

> I have given suck, and know/How tender 'tis to love the babe that milks me: /I would, while it was smiling in my face, /Have pluck'd my nipple from his boneless gums, /And dash'd the brains out, had I so sworn as you/Have done to this. (Shakespeare, Macbeth, Act 1, scene 7, 54–9)

Mothers have absolute life and death powers. Neonaticide of an unwanted baby or infanticide in a fit of violent rage, dire necessity, or delusional belief are accompanied by states of denial, dissociation or ego disorganisation (Marks, 2008). I suggest, these acts, whether "merciful" or persecutory killings, relate to a powerful upsurge of the repressed "cauldron".

Each "babe" imbibes not only milk but maternal emotions. With great prescience, Winnicott described the mother's face as the baby's mirror (1967). Discovery of mirror neurons, and micro-analytic techniques in studies of pre-linguistic infants, demonstrate the dialogical process through which the baby's self is constituted, and that adverse neonatal experiencescan even alter brain development (re psychoanalytic research see Beebe, et al., 2003). I propose that our sense of embodiment and psychic mapping of the body's interior, as well as its skin-bound exterior, also transpire interactively.

From the start, our first home, the female reproductive body, is a receptacle for reciprocal mother-baby projections and projective identifications, also reflected in cultural practice. The permeable boundary between the infant's inside and out, comes into being between the mother's breasts. Her unconscious imagery of the still-bubbling "cauldron" primes the baby's intrapsychic affects and own sub-symbolic bodily schema.

As already noted by both Freud and Ferenczi, the exquisitely sensitive raw material of the baby's sensory apparatus is activated, "seduced" and formulated by maternal passions and projections, as well as through pro-prioceptive feelings originating within the sensorium. Bodily care, implicitly invested with the caregiver's ascriptions, enigmatic erotic messages and fantasy, is unconsciously absorbed by the infant, to be incorporated in his/her psychosocial body image, and gendered embodiment. But in the case of the biological mother, her own body is highly charged and sensitised by pregnancy and the experience of childbirth. Not only does she deal with the neonate's primal substances, but fertile, lactating, bleeding and aromatic the maternal body is empowered with primitive female mysteries which imprint themselves on the child. A bodily language of smell, sound and soothing, fire and passion, hunger-slaking milk; slumber inducing and arousing caresses. The mother's embrace and handling of her daughter's body, will differ from unconscious evocations regarding her bodily experience of a male child. The girl baby born with a womb and full component of ova out of a same-sex body, will imbibe the mother's fantasies about the procreative interior and its social interface.

Similarly, primary relationships are co-constructed through interweaving. Back and forth, conscious and non-conscious bi-directional influences co-create the particular relational ambiance of each specific dyad. The mother's attitude towards her baby's body, bodily substances and gendering, expresses issues of her own sensuality, sexuality, corporeality, contagious arousal, emotional receptivity or defensiveness. Representations of the maternal partake of her inevitable ambivalence and myriad failures, counterbalanced by her positive input, and the degree of her attunement to the full range of the child's affects (Raphael-Leff, 2007, 2010b, c, d).

Fundamentally, we are cultured beings. From conception or even before, our bodies and minds are psychosocially primed. Although the domain of psychoanalysis explores the timeless unconscious of an individual psyche-soma, our subjective grasp of female bodies "inside and out" is contextual; our own representations of maternal alchemy glimpsed through the specific prism of our milieu. What is permitted, encouraged or forbidden also reflect the general societal climate and its imposed social constraints. Thus, I argue that as psychoanalysts we cannot afford to overlook psychosocial expectations and manifestations, which in our own era strain to adapt to extraordinary changes.

In this Chapter I will propose that the contemporary western notion of the female body as an ever-curable self-possession contrasts markedly with conceptualizations at another time and elsewhere today: of female bodies as the functional and disposable property of men. Furthermore, that in both cases, unconscious fears and fantasies about the maternal body and its awesome reproductive "cauldron" evolve defensively, influencing the way female bodies are perceived, controlled and (mal)treated. In societies in-transition such as our own, these have been affected by two major forces:

> I suggest that conscious representations of subjective body ownership crystallized in the late 1960s when availability of the contraceptive Pill coincided with the Women's Movement's objection to objectification of the female body. Repudiating domestic violence and non-consensual sex, and demanding access to birth control and reproductive choices for all women, the feminist body politic also designated the personal as political. This was intended to enable ideas of female bodily liberation to infiltrate every household, highlighting each woman's personal right to claim authority over, and pleasure in, her own body. Needless to say, intimate partner control is still with us. But nevertheless, many mothers bequeathed this sense of self-regulating female entitlement and agency to their daughters, and now grand—and even great-granddaughters.

Furthermore, although formation of the female procreative body schema continues to evolve much as before, its psychosocial meanings are now permeated by technological innovations of life and death control. These include efficient contraception (including hormonal pills, devices, implants, injections, barriers and spermicides, IUDs, and tubal ligation/clamping); safe abortion; reversible sterilization; the "morning-after pill"; pre-implantation selection; IVF; donated gametes; multiple conception and selective feticide, and most recently ovarian transplants, and the potential for young women to freeze their own eggs for later use. Incorporated into the implicit body schema these technological levers offer women new choices as to whether, when, how and with whom to have a baby.

Linked to this I wish to make two central points. First, that such innovations both defensively negate and yet actualize darker destructive dimensions of the maternal imago, in an undisguised daily reality. (For instance, using ultrasound imaging, sex-selective termination of female fetuses is widely practiced in China, India, Pakistan and the Caucasus). Second, that medical bio-technology reinforces an illusion of reproductive control. Absorbed into self-representations of the female body schema, this is drastically undermined by involuntary infertility.

Conscious and non-conscious choices

Contemporary women live in a different reality to that of our own mothers and grand-mothers. Efficient female-based contraception starkly exposes a paradox: for the species reproduction is a necessity; for a woman it is an option. Maternity is no longer the unquestioned female destiny.

Worldwide, women are having fewer children than their mothers, especially in lower income societies where reduction of child mortality decreases the necessity of having many children to ensure survival of a few. Contraception allows sex without fear of conception. Where available, safe abortion allows conception without a baby. Reproductive Technology now even produces conceptions without sex! These extraordinary changes have extraordinary consequences: perhaps most strikingly, for the first time in world history—the death rate exceeds the birth rate (Note 1).

In the West, with educational parity and greater opportunities for personal fulfillment, an estimated twelve to twenty per cent of European women choose to not reproduce at all. Thirty-nine per cent (!) of educated German women voluntarily remain "child-free". As their biological clock approaches menopause, some women who have postponed childbearing decide to have a baby. Spurning casual sex, many single women opt for artificial insemination by donor sperm. Those who fail to conceive within a relationship turn to the reproductive "industry" which has arisen to counteract waning fertility. However, media hype about the omnipotence of medical technology promotes unrealistic hopes: despite an increasingly bizarre treatment helter-skelter, a live and healthy "take-home" baby is delivered to only a very small proportion of those wishing to start a family.

In societies in-transition, family formation varies with today's changing norms:

- Single mothers by choice
- Primary care fathers
- Non-cohabiting and/or "live-in" parental couples
- Same-sex parents (gamete/embryo donors)

- Multi-parent (three generational, polygamous)
- Grandparental or child-headed families (AIDS decimated parental generation)
- Composite ("blended") step-families or of different fathers
- Unrelated small groups/communes/gangs
- Adolescent parent/s, etc

Regardless of its composition, in addition to offering nurture, protection and support, society designates the family to teach meaning and social values to enable the child to form a construction of the world according to that belief system. By definition a family remains a group of people linked by a common ethos and—a founding myth. Ideally, it also helps the child to process and resolve fundamental problems. The toddler's gradual discovery that s/he did not always exist, nor was self-created, impels complex questions: "Who am I and where do I come from? How are babies made? What are my origins? Whose tummy did I come out of?" As well as "Who looked after me?", "How?" and "Who would I be if I weren't me?…"

Generative identity

Psychoanalytic research has long noted the emotional upheaval during early toddlerhood, instigated by awareness of sexual difference. I emphasize that a young child's conscious re-appraisal of her/his budding genitality is very much dependent on the particular psychosocial restrictions, and socially defined anatomical markers of sex and bodily configurations in their own family and social milieu (see Note 2).

In line with contemporary thinking, elsewhere I reframed the three traditional constituents of gender as embodiment (a psychic construct of the "core gender" of male or female sexed identity), reconfiguration (psychic imagery of psychosocially determined "gender role" and feminine/masculine self-evaluation and performance) and *erotic desire* (negotiations of "sexual orientation") rooted in parental "enigmatic" sexual messages and Oedipal solutions to the incest taboo, leading to hetero/homo configurations and partner choice. In addition, to accommodate the current diversity of family formations and new responses to reproductive choices now expanded by medical bio-technology, I have introduced a fourth gender component; that of generative identity (awareness of oneself as a potential (pro)-creator) (Raphael-Leff, 2007,

2008). These four constituents are useful in charting various, not always compatible, psychic configurations, social manifestations, and dynamic processes of unconscious desire, fantasy, conflict and generative agency within a single subject.

The growing toddler is challenged by the "oldest and most burning question that confronts immature humanity" (Freud, 1908, p.135)—the origins of human life. The question "where do babies come from?" demonstrates a child's perplexity about the puzzle of the creation of one by two. With the discovery of sexual dimorphism, as the young child learns to reconcile realistic limitations, several factors converge, leading to loss of the previous sense of inclusive bisexuality. Thus, in toddlerhood (and again at puberty), we each faced (and rebelled against) fundamental restrictions that punctured our sense of omnipotence and invincibility—the basic generative facts of life:

Gender ("I am either female or male, not the other sex, neither or both")
Genesis ("I am not self-made. Two others made me")
Generation (Adults make babies; children cannot)
Generativity (Females gestate, give birth & may lactate; males impregnate).

These generative facts are further linked to what I termed "genitive" issues consisting of arbitrariness; the chance meeting of genitors, and gametes; irreversibility of life's trajectory—the impossibility, once born, of ever returning to the womb. In addition, the idea of finitude—separateness, and the universal inevitability of ultimate death. These issues are addressed again in depth during adolescence.

Acceptance of these facts of life in toddlerhood gives rise to a new psychic construction of him/herself as a potential (pro)-creator. Symbolic representation of the generative body "inside and out" now changes to incorporate the little girl or boy child's own reproductive organs as potentially procreative. Compensation for current generative limitations is promise of a baby in the future baby and exogamy— becoming a mother or father oneself, with an as yet unknown mate (Note 3). Today, potential creativity (rather than pro-creativity) is highlighted. The contemporary psychosocial concept of generative agency encompasses many rewarding endeavors for westerners. In non-traditional societies, having babies is no longer seen as the female *raison d'être*. Like their male counterparts, their productivity can be expressed alongside, or even replace reproductive aims (Raphael-Leff, 2010a).

Contemporary sex, origins and generativity

However, in recent years, these seemingly eternal and absolute universal limitations and facts of life have become malleable. Until recently, we acceded to the functional specificity, fixity and finality of the male or female body, and of procreative difference. However, today, generative facts have altered dramatically: embedded in gender self-designation is the social reality that sex itself now can be changed. Similarly, that conception can occur without sexual intercourse. Two-sex reproduction can be manipulated; postmenopausal pregnancy is a reality, and conversely, with earlier puberty, even children as young as ten may conceive. With pre-implantation selection, genitive arbitrariness no longer holds; HRT, transplants and cosmetic surgery seemingly halt the effects of time; and even death is stalled by life-support machines.

As generative issues come to the fore, the parental couple is regarded afresh by the toddler. Not only as sexual partners who exclude the Oedipal child from their erotic exchange, but as genitors; people with life-stories that began long before conception of their child. In these days of non-traditional family formation, the child's disillusionment of self-made autogenesis does not necessarily earmark two, or even different-sexed, parents. For children born of reproductive technologies, primal fantasies about ancestral origins proliferate and may multiply exponentially into ovarian, incubatory and social maternal components, with known or untold origins.

Technology invades the "cauldron's" numinous mix. Self-image may need to incorporate science fiction realities: "It is a bit weird to think I was once a ball of cells sitting in a freezer" says Emily Boothroyd, first IVF baby born from a frozen embryo (www.cambridge-news.co.uk, August, 2008). The need for assistance in reproduction, punctures the view of parental omnipotence, as does their inability to prevent perinatal loss or complications in siblings. And like adoption, a child conceived of donor gametes may split the fertile and non-fertile parental imagos (Raphael-Leff, 1991, 2002). A child one born of donated sperm may harbour fantasies of

Immaculate Conception (Ehrensaft, 2000) or triumphant superhero competition with the infertile father.

Trying to conceive

Contraception renders conception a conscious act. Whereas in the past marriage carried an explicit biblical injunction to "be fruitful and multiply", today's couples have other reasons for being together. Lovers do not necessarily cohabit, and temporary "hooking up" with anonymous partners may take place for purposes of sex or reproduction. The decision to make love with the explicit aim of making a baby lifts the old taboo on procreative sex, arousing excitement yet trepidation, unconsciously fraught with tensions about rotating the original Oedipal triangle. The excluded witness to the parental primal-scene now couples within it. Indeed, this heady feeling, and fear of activating the awesome cauldron's witchcraft so alarms some people that they procure assisted reproduction to shift the reproductive primal scene from marital bed to a Petri dish, seeking the protection of potent fertility experts and their permission to create a baby.

Our parents are the first intimately known adults, inextricably linking adulthood and parenthood. For some people, a sense of full maturity can only be achieved by parenting, and conversely, a childless state may be associated with childishness. The conscious engagement with a desire to conceive evokes archaic fantasies and influential residues of one's own parents' feelings about gender, sexuality and generativity, imbibed since babyhood. If, when dwelling on our innate bisexuality Freud saw "every sexual act as an event between four individuals", I suggest that in reproductive sex at least four more join in—unconscious representations of the respective female and male progenitors of each partner. *Recreational sex may be liberated but pro-creational sex retains the imprint of the original copulation* (Raphael-Leff, 2003).

So whilst using contraception denotes body ownership, mindfully suspending it requires daring. There are thrilling months of suspense as a procreating couple awaits the magical moment of conception: "I feel incredibly alive" says Rachel (see below). "I'm not used to being on this level—a mixture of joy and excitement filtering into everything, and generating so much energy it's quite over-whelming!"

But finding the temerity to shift a generation may seem the ultimate act of self-assertion, defiance or theft. Subject to the ambience of her internal mother (and associations to the numinous "cauldron"), for a woman the deliberate pursuit of childbearing may feel like symbolic matricide. Indeed, it was such trepidation that prompted Rachel to refer herself to me for twice weekly psychoanalytical therapy, seeking to explore her complicated relationship with her own mother when contemplating becoming a mother herself.

Writing this Chapter is informed by my clinical work as a Psychoanalyst in London, in a practice devoted to various aspects of the life course of reproduction, seeing around two hundred individuals, couples and families over the past forty years. These included twenty-eight infertile women seen individually one to five times a week, and thirteen sub-fertile couples seen weekly or fortnightly for some years each, pre-conceptually, during fertility treatment, and in some cases, over the course of more than one pregnancy. Some suffered from unexplained infertility while others had a firm diagnosis. My work is also informed by my training as a Social Psychologist, by my research and academic career as Professor of Psychoanalysis, and a wide range of consultancy work with primary health carers on six continents.

Motivation for conception

Double, double toil and trouble; / Fire burn, and cauldron bubble.
(Shakespeare, Macbeth, Act 4, scene 1, 11–12).

Apart from the biological clock, there are many impulsions to set the cauldron bubbling, some more conscious than others. To name but a few:

- conception as proof of fecundity
- a desire to be pregnant; and/or to be a mother
- wish for *a* baby; or for one's *own* genetic baby to perpetuate oneself or the genealogical family
- loneliness—to have "someone to love/to love me"
- seeking a purpose; responding to social/family/peer pressures
- wishing to be "feminine"/"fully adult"/to emulate mother
- unprotected sex—ignorance, denial or dicing with consequences
- desire to keep or "fire" up a failing relationship
- a wish to "double", to flesh out a fantasy baby or glimpse the partner as a child

- to recapture/repair lost aspects of one's baby-self and to renegotiate incomplete developmental tasks
- to create a "perfect" loving family and/or rewrite history
- to cheat Death (the threat of terminal illnesses, and increasingly, HIV+)

While awaiting conception, the fine-grained focus on the body's interior displaces primacy of its periphery. The circumstances of conception and each woman's personal psycho-history conjure up specific imagery of gestation:

> "I'm not pregnant. Again" says Rachel sadly, after trying for some months. "I don't know if I'm making too much of it. People imply I should accept that it will take time, but I want to know the very second I become pregnant so I can begin to nurture the baby straight away. I feel so ready—inside me there's a nest just waiting to be filled" she gently cups her hands to show me: "I carefully plan where we are on ovulation days and make sure we eat well and listen to nice music. I'm so much more aware of subtle changes in my body; when my breasts get tender I find myself wanting to talk to the cells that may have begun dividing inside me. I think of it with such delight and want to make it welcome from the very start. I was an unexpected "mistake" for my parents ... Would I know if I was pregnant right now? Could I detect subtle changes in my body just 48 hours after conception of a baby smaller than a full stop? I will say "hello" to the dot just in case it's there."

The vacant inner "nest" and yearning to welcome the fledgling are common themes. However reactions can vary tremendously, depending on the emotional ambiance of a woman's internal world, her unconscious body schema, representations of the female cauldron and her personal sense of generative agency. Compare Rachel's response to that of another patient, of equivalent age, ethnic group, education and career status:

> As soon as I feel there is life inside—I snuff it out. Seems like a frightening alien being in there—weird, fishlike stages. I don't know why I use my power to kill embryos when I want a baby so. Perhaps I envy them their comfort or am afraid of them attacking me inside. When I got a positive result on the pregnancy test I thumped myself

on the belly. Couldn't overcome my urge ... just confirms that I'm not good enough to have a baby. My womb feels rotten, full of rubbish and yucky things inside which can't let a baby grow.

Similarly, both these two western career women's introspective communications differ from nubile child brides or established wives elsewhere, whose thwarted attempts to conceive, or successful abortive measures, may lead to divorce, replacement, banishment or worse. In traditional societies, motherhood is often the only way for a woman to enhance her position within her husband's family and community. Infertility not only deprives her of her central role and infringes upon her status and human right to health provisions, but can result in "a violation of the most basic moral protections that are intrinsic to humanity itself" (Daar & Merali, 2004, p. 17).

Ironically, expenditure on reproductive technology in the West far exceeds the budget for antenatal provision in low income countries where ninety per cent of the world's babies are born. And where much infertility is secondary (due to poor health and nutrition, sparse maternity services and high levels of infections) and hence, curable. Yet despite childlessness being highly stigmatized in the third world, ART (Assisted Reproductive Technology) is still largely unavailable. Thus the experience of the female body and its reproductive processes are physically affected not only by internal reality and unconscious body schema but by external resources, social beliefs and cultural practices.

The Female imago

"... how can he be clean that is born of a woman?" (Job 25: 4, King James Bible)

Throughout life the female body schema and the experience of feminine selfhood are constituted within the social unconscious. These constraining socio-cultural factors metaphorically reflect the unconscious collective of a specific social system (see Hopper, 2003). Local myths and beliefs condense communal experience, reinforcing dominant social values. Folklore that justifies the subordination of women focuses on curbing dangerous aspects of that female "cauldron"—and its terrifying modes of seduction, engulfment, paralysis or murderous intent.

In many cultural representations, split figures contrast idealised and denigrated aspects, virginal Madonnas and unclean sexual whores.

One recurrent theme around the maternal imago in legends is that of the mysteriousness of female transformational processes, a cauldron of seething reproductive substances including menstrual blood, amniotic fluid, placental nutrients and toxic fluids.

Time reversals in Celtic fable has dead warriors put into a cauldron and returned to life, to go back into battle to be killed again. Myths expressing a deep-seated fascination with stealing female secrets, hint at primal anxiety and envy of women's procreative and birth-giving ability. In addition to the originary mother's awesome power of gestation and our universal exile from her body in birth, we cannot neglect postnatal aspects of maternal power, associated not with childbearing but childrearing. Typically, primary helplessness and annihilation anxieties compel us to negate the archaic carer's subjectivity, treating her as an "object"—a cauldron of good resources and bad magic. In fact, Winnicott notes that we are all "[I]n infinite debt to a woman". And that "if there is no true recognition of the mother's part, then there must remain a vague fear of dependence … a fear of woman in general or … less easily recognized forms, always including the fear of domination" (Winnicott, 1964, pp. 9–10).

This truism has implications for therapeutic interpretations which conflate the unconscious imago with objective experience. Pathologizing the never good-enough, over-controlling, over-involved or abandoning mother as cause of our patient's sufferings renders the fantasy real—negating maternal subjectivity by accepting as real the poisonous, intoxicating and toxic mother-monster. Such scapegoating affects reality testing. Ettinger says it turns an "important, painful and vital conscious and unconscious real-phantasmatic experience" into a symbolic "truth-cause" with no compassion for the actual maternal figure, which in turn, makes "the intimate mother to whom we are trans-connected (whether we like it or not) into the craziest of all figures" (Ettinger, 2010, p. 4, citing Marguerite Duras "Our mothers always remain the strangest, craziest people we've ever met").

As an aside, although the primordial witch and her cauldron are now decidedly female, it will be interesting to see the effect of primary care (unemployed) fathers on the next generation's unconscious imagos. Similarly, we can consider the effects on female self-representations.

Women's internalization of a mythical perception of dangerous female impulses and shameful lasciviousness has led even relatively "liberated" westerners to voluntarily starve, reshape and mutilate their own bodies. Hiding unconscious associations with the ferocious "cauldron" may also underpin strict inner controls, to curb expression of their sexuality and appetites. Aggression, envy, and even ambitions are often inhibited (see Harris, 1997) and in our own societies women are still underrepresented in positions of power.

In many other places women are excluded from public life altogether, lacking political, economic and civil rights. Their bodies are not their own to feed or starve, but carry the imprint of their men-folk, whose control is implemented with devastating effects. Female circumcision, infibulations with partial or total removal of the external labia, clitoridectomies and vaginal incisions or scarification are executed to ensure chastity and to reduce female sexual pleasure and desire. Intended as a "portcullis" safeguarding a girl's body as virgin territory for her future husband, ironically, these procedures also become portals of entry for genital infections which damage their fallopian tubes. Genital mutilation thus contributes to sexual problems, birth complications and infertility, as do unsafe abortions, precocious pregnancies, and unhygienic labour and delivery conditions (see Osato & Giwa-Osagie, 2004) (Note 4).

Sex-specificity

My cross-cultural consultancy and clinical experience have confirmed a central fact. Once sex is geared to producing a baby even egalitarian partners diverge dramatically with sex-related reproductive preoccupations: male concerns with erection and potency contrast with anxieties about the female interior. The male must be virile to impregnate; his offspring is sired by ejaculation. The female partner is geared to do what only members of her sex can do. Conception, implantation, pregnancy occur in her. She will be the one to contain the baby; her placenta will nourish it; her womb will carry or miscarry their joint baby.

Whatever her relation to her birth-mother, as a primordial process, childbearing reactivates a woman's primary identifications with the woman who carried her for better or worse. Representations of the life-giving womb/death dealing "cauldron" invade her mind triggering feelings of anxiety or triumph, and idealized or persecutory fantasies about prenatal life. The awesome female cauldron comes ever closer, intruding inwards with unsolicited imagery of maternal reproductive process and the shared bodily space between foetus and mother. Essentially alone with her fantasies while tethered to a partial-stranger feeding off her internal resources, each pregnant woman is locked into an inexorable course which, one way or another will end in their disjunction.

During pregnancy two people reside in one body. But it no longer need be *her* body.

Surrogates have existed since biblical times. But now they can carry the official mother's egg as well as her partner's sperm. She need not be infertile to procure pregnancy by proxy. India now offers an international trade in rented wombs for career women who have no time to be pregnant, or those who wish to avoid stretch-marks and the agony of birth. Donor eggs can be procured over the internet, and sperm chosen through catalogues. Technology offers greater control over the unknown. Birth may be painless, even sensation-free with epidural relief. Labour may be medically induced; delivery, instrumentally assisted (increasing to twelve and thirteen per cent in the UK over the past years), and elective caesarean sections can be scheduled to avoid uncertainty (e.g. twenty five per cent of births in the UK, and forty-six per cent in China). According to the WHO, these now reach "epidemic" levels worldwide, commanding a disproportionate share of global economic resources. Even premature birth now can be procured to avoid unsightly weight gain (a common occurrence among educated women in Brazil).

Over the past years, further bio-technological development such as cloning has developed hugely, and artificial wombs have successfully gestated lambs. It is only be a matter of time before one hosts a human baby. But in the meantime, childbearing still remains sex-specific. The female is both bearer and mediator. As gate keeper, she may decide with whom to share her news; a man may not even know about his impending fatherhood. In lesbian couples the issue is which of the partners will conceive, and how. Usually one is designated the bearer but in some cases when they have swapped eggs, both may conceive each other's baby.

Expectant partners

The impact of pregnancy on the human body is not to be underestimated. Pregnant women experience a host of symptoms, including nausea, tiredness, muscle laxity, swollen feet, bodily transformation, with tripled estrogen and progesterone surges. Yet interestingly, expectant partners also undergo changes. Studies show that they put on weight, and visit their family doctors more frequently, complaining of pregnancy-like symptoms of queasiness, backache and sleep disturbances. Couvade has been known for centuries but recent research finds that amazingly, co-habiting expectant partners, like pregnant mothers, have stage-specific changes in hormone levels. In men, stimulated by the pregnant woman's pheromones the "stress-hormone" cortisol spikes four to six weeks after being told of the pregnancy, seemingly providing a "wake-up call", followed by higher concentrations of prolactin just before the birth and a testosterone drop by a third during the three weeks immediately after the birth (Note 5).

Reproductive sex imagery

When conception fails to occur, couples engage in an increasingly desperate quest to procure the generative combination of egg and sperm. Some western men may concur in seeking "perfect" conditions to attract the elusive baby, but their frustration increases with the pressure to desist from spontaneous sex, and only make love on ovulation dates. Each month her bleeding deflates hopeful elation, taking a heavy emotional toll. One English husband commented: "we live under the tyranny of her cycle".

Becoming sexually polarized, some partners unconsciously begin to live out their respective representations. Imagery of an inactive ovum passively waiting to be pierced by the fittest sperm may be replicated in the sexual fantasy of their bodies coming together, as she patiently awaits his penetration. Sensing her husband's sexual reluctance, she may feel as helplessly dependent on him to impregnate her as she believes her ripe egg is upon his "sluggish" sperm. Unconsciously equating his wife with her egg, a male partner fears her female engulfment of his masculinity: "… when she snaps at me, I'm afraid she'll bite my head off!" Fantasies of the dark cauldron of her sexual body, her penis-grabbing *vagina dentata*, and the dangerous depths of her noncompliant womb often induce temporary impotence. Infrequent or ineffective sex contributes to non-conception. Alarmed by the intensity of his partner's sexual demands, a man may feel sapped by his pro-creative endeavours. In some cultures semen is regarded as a non-regenerative precious commodity. Hindus, for instance, believe a hundred drops of blood go into making a single drop of semen. Common aspects of contemporary western life style, such as intra-uterine (IUD) contraceptive devices, multiple sexual partners lead to silent pelvic inflammations and sexually transmitted diseases (STD). These contribute to subfertility, as starvation diets or anorexia in women and heavy use of certain medications, alcohol, tobacco or drugs; career stress and excessive exercising in men; exposure to lead, pesticides, plastics and environmental oestrogen, or even tight underwear (Note 6).

Similarly, in other cultures there are fertility issues. In sub-Saharan Africa (where up to a third of couples are infertile) despite the aim of maximizing the number of offspring, polygamous marriage both reduces frequency of sex and the likelihood of intercourse at fertile times, and the rotation of mating visits among wives also introduces cross-infection. Finally, in many low-income societies, male command over finances also filters female access to medical services.

Although seemingly universal, procreation is clearly affected by deeply ingrained cultural dictates. The reproductive body schema is psycho-socially contoured, and unconsciously primed, bound by local social constraints which, however, can, and do, change over time. For instance, social stigma. Until recently unwed mothers and their illegitimate children were ostracized in western societies, with a high incidence of neonaticide and adoption. Today in the United Kingdom over forty-five per cent of births are to unmarried mothers (up from twelve per cent in 1980) and in Scandinavia the figure is higher (Note 7). Similarly, habituation to novelty. Birth of the first "test-tube" baby was only forty years ago, yet to date over a million babies worldwide have been born following IVF & ICSI treatments. Moreover, even fertile women seek ART. In this era of sexually transmitted diseases, many single women opt for sperm screening and medical insemination, rather than relying on sex to conceive. Virgin conceptions and non-vaginal births are increasingly common. Earlier puberty (dropping from 16.6 years in 1860, to 14.6 in 1920, 13.1 in 1950, 12.5 in 1980 to 11.7 years in 2010), and mass-media sexualization of pre-teens, have lowered the western threshold for maternity considerably, with a high prevalence of very young mothers in the USA and UK. On the other end of the spectrum, egg-donation spawns an ever rising maximum age of childbearing, rapidly ratcheting social norms upwards, currently set at age seventy (Note 8).

Sadly, despite contraceptive ease and reproductive technologies, we are still a far cry from the mantra "every child is a wanted child". Given maternal powers of termination or contraceptive and iatrogenic non-reproduction, the "enigmatic" message to offspring of older mothers and infertile parents is that generativity is neither inevitable nor straightforward. Neither is mothering. Educational parity has led to postponed motherhood, with career women in particular, finding a high discordance between their personal expectations which have changed dramatically over the past forty years, and the infant's needs, which have changed very little over the millennia.

Body "ownership"

"I so envy women who just get pregnant and don't have to agonise or root for the baby" says Rachel sadly, nine months into her mission to conceive "After each cycle I search—I *will* there to be a sign, a symptom. I count up the months when the baby would be due. I fix on special dates on the calendar and when my period comes, at first I tell myself 'it's only a little bleed' .... I feel such a failure. I've always felt in control of my body. Now it lets me down ...."

As noted, embodiment is a lifelong ongoing interactive psychic process, encompassing a person's core sense of corporeality, sexuality and unconscious body schema. This is inter-woven with an interpersonally-influenced changing sense of femininity/masculinity and erotic desire (Raphael-Leff, 2010c). Our illusion of body malleability is all-pervasive in western women who diet, jog, train, take HRT, undergo Botox, cosmetic surgery, breast implantations. Postponed childbearing is merely another facet of the attempt to suspend Time. Convinced that conception will occur as soon as they stop contraception, many women are shocked by the delay.

However, far from our commanding "owner-occupancy", our body is assailed by undermining forces from within and without. Domestic violence, childhood sexual abuse, rape and pornographic images of women provide further evidence of the fragility of our female bodily ownership. And psychic fluctuations, repudiations, and discontinuities both express and subvert the wish for bodily control, manifesting in addictions, eating disorders, self-harm cutting and burning. As psychoanalysts we recognize that the many unconscious uses of the body demonstrate internal schemata symptomatically, in conversion hysteria, accident proneness and psycho-somatic illnesses.

On a social level, institutionalized control over female generative "cauldrons" is evident in China's one-child policy or governmental pro-natalism (see Note 9 regarding Ceausescu's Romania). Horrific examples of colonization of the female childbearing body are also found in deliberate impregnation geared towards destroying nationalism (e.g. the systematic war rape of 20,000 Bosnian Muslim women organized by Radovan Karadžić). Marginalised and impoverished, such women, their trauma and resultant children are justified as mere collateral damage of (male) war. On the other hand, allegedly, women may take their ancient powers into their own murderous hands. In November 2008 it was reported that women in Agibu and Amosa villages of Gimi region in the Eastern Highlands province of Papua New Guinea agreed to smother all newborn male babies to combat their men-folk's incessant tribal warring (http://www.thenational.com.pg/281108/nation5.php).

Elsewhere, vengeful attitudes towards the female "cauldron" manifest in sexual exploitation and impregnation (even of children by their care-givers). Sanctioned violence, genital mutilation, child marriage, mail-order brides and female trafficking for prostitution are rife across Europe and Asia. Women who stray or try to reclaim their own bodies are subjected in many places to "corrective rape" (for lesbians), and stoning or "honour" killings in cases of adultery (Note 10).

Much of this oppression cannot be challenged, or even contemplated by women, who are stigmatized and shunned even by their families as "unclean", and/or have internalized these prohibitions and shame to the point of justifying their punishment. "Yes, my husband must beat me if I burn the food—I have to atone for my disgrace" Ethiopian Merheret tells me matter-of-factly through an interpreter.

Fertility and infertility

Human speech is like a cracked cauldron on which we bang out tunes that make bears dance, when what we want is to move the stars to pity (Gustave Flaubert, *Madame Bovary*, 1856; London: Penguin, 1992).

Magic enters where words and deeds fail to "move the stars to pity". Approaches to sterility vary within the myriad cultures of the world. Traditional therapies for barrenness include wearing amulets and talismans; binding fertility dolls to the woman's back; drinking herbal potions; saying magical incantations; belly massage with creams and concoctions; application of herbs to the vagina to aid the outflow of impurities; manual trans-abdominal massage of the uterine fundus or trans-vaginal repositioning of the uterus for presumed retroversion, to name but a few. In addition to these, in some places sacrifices of poultry, goats or rams are made to ancestral spirits. Biblical Hannah beseeched God in the Temple courtyard. Roman Catholics pray to the Madonna or to St. Anthony. In some societies gifts are rendered to pacify annoyed gods/goddesses, or to invite their favour so that pregnancy may occur. Ritual practices often involve diverse items ranging from threads, raw eggs, seed pods, hair, garlic, to milk and urine.

Followers of various religions, including Christianity, often fast, applying anointed oil to their bodies or drink holy water to hasten conception. Infertile women in Japan hang prayers on temple-trees. Jewish women insert requests into the crevices of the Wailing Wall. Chinese herbalists recognize foods with different energetic, moistening and nourishing qualities. These are now becoming popular in the West, where glossy magazines and weekend "Fertility Shows" advocate holistic, complementary and alternative systems for enhancing fertility. These complement reproductive surgery: Ovarian Reserve tests; international egg donation or surrogacy; scrotum sonography; new IVF techniques such as IMSI (a variation of ICSI using a more high-powered microscope or OOSIGHT, ™) to improve the quality of sperm or egg selection to avoid producing chromosomally abnormal embryos. Other more natural remedies, such as "Mind and Body stress-reducing groups" take place at major clinics; fertility-boosting nutrition or herbal "hormone rebalancing" said to prevent miscarriages; or conception earmarked through Biorhythmic Lunar Cycles, corresponding a woman's most fertile time to the phase of the moon at her birth.

These find willing candidates. As Rachel says almost a year into trying to conceive:

> "I am prepared to try any magic! I feel so raw. Like an egg without a shell. I used to like my periods—a sign of my body working. Now they're a sign it's not. John and I used to be so close when we made

love. Now it feels mechanical; a means to an end. I've been cry-ing for a week—feeling trapped, yearning for a baby. I sit chairing important meetings but it feels as if I have a thin veneer of grown-upness over a chasm of craving to be looked after. I just couldn't bear yet another month of high hopes and disappointment. I pray and plead to some invisible God—'release me from this intermi-nable phase so I can go on to the next' but feel I'm caught up in a process that's indifferent to my fate ...."

Investigations

Infertility is on the rise in the West. Due to environmental and social factors, it strikes indiscriminately. Nonetheless, even in cases of clear cut physiological obstacles to fertility, internal conflicts and fantasies are exacerbated by the protracted disillusionment of failing to conceive, which alters one's body and self-image, putting one in touch with the unconscious numinous cauldron. The sense of undermined hegemony permeates life on every level, affecting life style, relationships, sexual-ity, work, and even spirituality.

Fertility investigations change the nature of intercourse itself. A third party, the medical expert (or team), now invades the couple's intimate lovemaking. Their generative incapacity infantilizes the couple. Like pre-fecund children they are scrutinized and instructed by experts—potent adults who *can* create life. Invasive procedures reveal hidden bodily inadequacies. Sperm counts and evaluation, temperature charts and a cocktail of tablets and injections intrude into the private space between partners as others try to "fix" their non-productive bodies. Post-coital reports must be made to fertile authority figures wanting to know when, how often, and how they make love; conducting tests and coming up with verdicts. Not surprisingly, sexual disturbances are common at this phase.

Prejudice, guilt and superstition

As menstrual cycles continue un-fructified, the search for meaning generates self-doubt:

"Wherever I look there are pregnant women" says Rachel "It must be me. Am I being singled out and punished. Forbidden to have a baby? Or is it that I'm not good enough to grow one?"

Rachel expresses three common notions: prohibition, punishment, and inadequacy. The unconscious repository of social recrimination, unacceptable wishes or desires, traumatic memories, and painful emotions erupt with the female body's failure to oblige. Feelings over non-conception are filtered through unconscious guilt. Seeking an explanation a self-critical woman ascribes her infertility to her own transgressive thoughts, deeds or omissions. Socially, too, she shoulders the "moral" responsibility for non-conception. Despite the equal incidence of male infertility women are more likely to be held responsible. In fact, until some ten years ago western clinics commenced with female fertility investigations despite their invasive nature. Only after completion of the woman's workup was a simple semen test carried out. Yet it is crucial to note that problems due to deficiencies in the volume, count, motility and/or formation of sperm account for almost half the infertility in couples worldwide. Recent studies find that sperm concentration has decreased by a third since the 1990s and continues to fall.

In many Latin American and African societies where machismo prevails, male infertility remains a taboo subject. Psychological conflation of virility and potency renders it an affront to masculine self-esteem to be considered infertile. Male shame at failing to impregnate combines with internalized female guilt and the complex contradictory imagery of the creative/destructive maternal cauldron, contributing to excessive self-blame in women who fail to conceive, or to carry a baby to term. Studies illustrate these gendered meanings of the diagnosis of infertility, calling up different psychological defenses in men and women. As noted, experiencing a loss of power and masculinity, on the whole men tend to be more secretive, declining to reveal their part in infertility. Whilst women tend to share their predicament with confidantes, often assuming full liability for childlessness to cover up for their partner's incapacity (see Note 11).

Social construction of illness and adversity

Rachel believes she is being punished. As noted, this is a common causal theme, often blamed on previous sexual activity, retaliatory maternal malevolence, or sisterly competitiveness. In the past, psychoanalytic writing often attributed infertility to the woman's own repudiation of femininity and inability to identify with her fertile mother. It was assumed that inability to conceive was the *result* of pathological envy having destroyed the fantasy of the internal mother's pro-creative capacities (Langer, 1958; Pines, 1990). However, I suggest these issues often arise in the context of failure. Like all traumatic events, prolonged infertility evokes a resurgence of intrapsychic doubts, anxieties and anguish retriggering unresolved past conflicts and unconscious archaic fantasies. Despite the intricate connection between psyche and soma, we must be cautious in ascribing psychogenic causality. Many neurotics conceive effortlessly, and conversely, infertility can strike indiscriminately. Today, with more sophisticated and refined diagnostic techniques, unexplained infertility (previously ascribed to psychological causes) has fallen from sixty per cent of cases to under twenty per cent. Nonetheless, psychotherapeutic intervention can ease the intensity of suffering and by modifying harsh representations, release their terrorizing grip.

When the diagnosis remains vague even after assessment of ovulation and fallopian tubes in the woman and semen analysis in the man, people seek reasons. Attributions differ geographically, blaming sexual misdemeanours, bad thoughts, nightmares, stress, and the malice of evil spirits or the evil eye of jealous women for barrenness or miscarriage.

Cognizant of the thorny issues of essentialism and syncretic universalism, I would nonetheless suggest that whilst local narratives and imagery vary cross-culturally, a prolonged waiting period of anticipated childbearing commonly activates similar responses. These include unconscious imagery of the reproductive body schema and its dual creative/destructive capacities; concerns over the viability of the foetus, its inter-uterine retention, and sustenance. Anxieties about the enigmatic interior of the female body relate to "feminine mysteries" of formation and magical transformation, of speck to baby, of bodily fluids into milk (Raphael-Leff, 1991). Roles usually allocated to women—of cooking (traditionally in a hung or three legged cauldron pot), potting, weaving, vegetable cultivation, flour-grinding and baking—often presumed "instinctively" female, are merely associative cultural by-products of the primordial transformational processes of childbearing. Failure to bring a pregnancy to fruition therefore has widespread ramifications.

Diagnosis of Infertility

Infertility is defined as failure to conceive after a year of normal intercourse without contraception (Note 12). Today, the diagnosis usually follows investigations, once the increasingly despairing couple decides to seek help. In some cases it may be the outcome of a medical emergency, such as an ectopic pregnancy (when the embryo implants outside the uterus) or multiple miscarriages.

Deteriorating sperm, delayed childbearing, environmental pathogens and sexual infections have increased fertility problems in the West. It is now estimated that at least one in five couples in Britain has difficulty conceiving. Sexual problems may result, caused or exacerbated by the prolonged investigation, medical management and increasingly bizarre treatments for infertility.

Most of us take for granted that like our parents, our bodies have the natural capacity to make babies. When that axiom, tacitly held from infancy, is suddenly called into question, the aspect of gender I termed *generative identity* is threatened. The infertile person now sees themselves as the end, rather than middle, of a genealogical chain. I argue that the manner and intensity with which each person reacts to the diagnosis of infertility is determined by the specific historical resolution of their own generative agency, and the degree to which they have invested it in reproductive (as opposed to productive/creative) generativity (Raphael-Leff, 2002, 2010b).

The excruciatingly slow-motion process of fertility investigations and subsequent treatment, and each patient's constant need to re-question their desire for a baby before committing themselves to another emotionally, physically and financially costly treatment round, show up pre-conscious generative representations. Being party to such forced introspection enables us to draw distinctions between hitherto conflated aspects of gender, generativity, sexuality, fertility, genitive anxieties and reproductive urges and desire.

"One body, one flesh"?

To some Western couples, the diagnosis of incurable infertility constitutes a blow to their most cherished hopes and belief in control. It threatens the epistemological centre of their world, not uncommonly resulting in suicidal ideation. Where only one partner is afflicted, culpability towards the fertile mate may feel so great that s/he suggests divorce to enable the other to find a new spouse. Some childless couples find ways of drawing closer in their sorrow, finding ways to render the unbearable bearable. In other couples guilt, self-recriminations or accusations proliferate. Infertility may be blamed on sexual transgressions, on previous abortions or postponed childbearing. Given the intense suffering and primordial nature of the issues involved, when the partner's desire for a child differs the relationship often deteriorates. An anguished sense of asymmetrical need or let down by the other's failure results in acrimony, and they may split up unless couple or individual therapy intervenes. Even in a loving marriage, such as Rachel's, loneliness can prevail:

> I feel isolated and lonely and left out, as if I am in a box of my own horrible feelings … awful, miserable, unhappy, envious, angry feelings that have been flooring me. I have lost my femininity. There is no forgetfulness. This pain and loss are constant. I am so full of my rage. Hurt by other people's rude health and gross insensitivity. Even my mother wounds me with casual remarks. No one, not even my partner has any conception of my grief. My empty pocket is invisible. We might as well be on different planets.

Tensions rise within the relationship as despair and derision fester below the surface or erupt in desperate attempts to regain equilibrium. Faced with genetic extinction an infertile person or couple may isolate themselves from others, avoiding pregnant friends, people with children and even their own parents, in a world now divided starkly into haves and have-nots. Assailed by primitive forces of shame, deprivation and envy, they often feel singled out, excluded, stigmatized or even ostracized in being unable to fulfill the most fundamental requisite of the human race. The stark options now seem treatment or childlessness. In the West, adoption is increasingly difficult as efficient contraception and de-stigmatized single motherhood has lessened the number of unwanted infants, and adoption agencies operate an age cut-off point for would-be-parents. (Transcultural adoptions involve complex issues beyond the scope of this Chapter.)

In time, some couples gradually come to accept a life without a baby or accustom themselves to the idea of fostering, or find other creative solutions. Others, determined to have a child of their own, embark on further rounds of investigations and expensive fertility treatments, albeit with low success rates. These include intensive medically assisted regimes, biochemical and invasive physical interventions and surgical procedures. [The economically skewed use of fertility services has demographic implications discussed elsewhere (Raphael-Leff, 2010b). Sometimes, it becomes apparent that the desperate wish to conceive represents not a wish for a baby but the desire to be pregnant or the need for reassuring proof of fertility, possibly followed by an abortion.

The emotionally and financially draining consequences of treatment failure come on top of the generative confusion of prolonged inability to conceive naturally. While struggling to produce a baby, the promise of ever-improving techniques may conspire to separate a couple even further. Unless they blindly follow the roller-coaster regime of incessant treatments, many couples have to grapple monthly with fundamental questions as they debate, and do not always agree, whether or not to continue to pursue their dream. Some discover that their need to parent utilizes capacities which could be diverted into social activities. Others, whose generative identity is inextricably fixed in reproduction, cannot relinquish the hope of ultimately producing offspring, their own, or a "second best" genetically unrelated baby.

The technological primal scene

Throughout fertility treatment, archaic emotional conflicts and unconscious numinous schema of the body interior are counterbalanced by idealized fantasies about the omnipotent medical specialists who, like the fecund Oedipal parents, can produce babies. Transference to these parental figures is accompanied by the couple's resentment about infantalization and profound dependence on the control and interference of these authoritative strangers. Ironically, when it does take place, fertilization occurs in the lab in the absence of the procreative couple. As one would-be father put it:

> It seems so obscene that our beloved baby will probably originate in a petri dish from a combination of my wanking off in the clinic toilet and her egg "harvested" up by a pipette.

The technological primal scene shatters age old generative facts of life. Asexual conception occurs. Self-insemination introduces the possibility of a woman on her own achieving fertilization without a potent male in her external (or internal) life. Some women have a baby by proxy, through surrogacy or a relative's generous incubation. Generations may be breached when grandmothers gestate their own grandchildren. Female partners may choose reciprocal conception by egg swapping. Nucleus removal and cloning may bring procreativity out of the exclusive possession of heterosexuality, or indeed, of two-someness. Gametes can even be borrowed from the dead: "necro-impregnation" utilizes eggs from adult cadavers, or cultivates them from dead girls or aborted foetuses, and posthumous insemination. Egg transfer means a woman may be pregnant with a genetically unrelated foetus.

Reproductive technology moves us into situations without precedence and new domains of emotional arousal, ethics, law and kinship. With embryo freezing twins can be born years apart. Early scanning exposes many a twin who fails to develop and vanishes when absorbed after fourteen weeks gestation. Women give birth to litters as the rates of multi-foetal pregnancies increases dramatically with Assisted Reproductive Technology, introducing cruel dilemmas about foetal reduction, and decisions about which and how many embryos to kill off. Gamete donation introduces new types of parent/child/sibling connections, including known or unknown surrogates and donors. US internet websites reveal that up to fifty half-siblings across many families may be sired by a single donor. In heterosexual couples, the unknown donor is a further mythical stranger to the infertile couple, and their offspring—evoking idealized or paranoid ideas about genetic sources. Egg or sperm donor or surrogate may be disavowed or alternatively, elaborate fantasies may be constructed around their omnipotent qualities. Furthermore, a toddler's preoccupation with his/her own genetic history inevitably incorporates fantasies about the original union; as one has to come from somewhere. However, a pan-European study found that only 8.6 per cent of donor children were told of their origins (Golombok, et al., 2002). In the face of non-traditional configurations of family formation, child psychoanalysts are beginning to chart how (formed by assisted and asexual reproduction) generative puzzlement and anxieties predominate, especially when unconsciously fathomed family secrets raise alternative fantasies regarding parental sexuality, reproductive union and gametes (Ehrensaft, 2000; Corbett, 2001).

In sum, within the last few decades eternal and seemingly immutable generative facts of life have changed dramatically. Blurring the boundaries between fact and fiction, science gallops ahead, changing the story of origins faster than our unconscious can keep up.

With treatment, sexuality and procreation become further separated and the sexual act is drained of its excitement, as hope and responsibility for fertilization are relocated to another place (Raphael-Leff, 2003). Stripped of its potential procreative function, intercourse can feel futile and empty of desire, as horrendous aspects of the "cauldron" infiltrate the generative body schema, altering it beyond recognition:

> "Our whole sex life has shut down" wails Rachel almost three years into fertility treatment. "When he wants to make love I feel murderously angry. What for? It can't lead anywhere. We can't make a baby ourselves. I can't bear him to touch me—it's just a reminder that we're useless. As each period approaches I plummet down again. Such a long expensive haul getting nowhere. We've blown another chance.
>
> I dreamed that squatters occupied our house. I woke my partner by screaming 'No!' I know I'm furious with him for putting me through the humiliation of IVF because of his low-motility sperm. But we're *both* such utter failures. I suppose I'm worse than him. My womb's not good enough. I imagine it destroys the fertilised embryos as soon as the doctors put them back into me. Life is so pointless. I hate myself. I hear this voice inside berating me with such loathing—'you're stupid; incompetent; barren!' It builds up inside me like electric power waiting for discharge and I turn on my partner screaming: 'why can't you even do what any animal can!' We can't take control of our lives—we lie there in bed, just he and I together—awake, not touching each other, trapped, separate, wretched, sick with frustration. And sex, the very thing that once brought us comfort is the very last thing we can contemplate."

Clearly, the emotional impact of infertility permeates every aspect of life; intrapsychic, interpersonal, psychosexual and occupational.

Given the ongoing traumatic nature of self-reappraisal, and the lifelong consequences for all involved in assisted reproduction, psychotherapy or counselling are not luxuries but a vital necessity during the five phases of psychological impact:

- trying to conceive
- investigations
- diagnosis
- treatment interventions
- parenting, or timely exit from unsuccessful treatment protocols offering a safe haven of exploration in the presence of a sympathetic, validating, witness (Raphael-Leff, 2005).

Conclusions

> I/Am the arrow, /The dew that flies/Suicidal, at one with the drive/Into the red/Eye, the cauldron of morning. (Sylvia Plath, Ariel 1.26–31, *The Collected Poems*, 1981).

I have argued that the vicissitudes of childbearing constitute profoundly disturbing confrontations with raw pain and archaic desire. Primitive fantasies, unconscious fantasies are reactivated of destructive as well as creative primal powers.

Contraception and abortion aid some women's choice not to bear children at all. In others, infertility diverts their wish to reproduce. Many do become mothers, but have fewer babies than their own mothers. And some cannot survive motherhood, especially under conditions of extreme poverty, adversity and/or personal loss. In these cases, suicide, infanticide and matricide are often emotionally intermingled.

Mothers who suffer intolerable depression or persecutory anxieties may kill their babies., and/or themselves. Weeks after writing that poem, at the witching hour of 4.30 a.m., Sylvia Plath set out milk for her sleeping children's breakfast. She sealed the room between them, put her head deep into the oven's red-eyed "cauldron", and gassed herself.

In this Chapter I made several points:

- Scientific innovations facilitate expression of the darker, destructive dimensions of the maternal imago, reinforcing generative agency with an illusion of reproductive control.

- If in the unconscious mind the archaic mother's power is absolute, inability to conceive or repeated miscarriage exposes powerlessness, and the interwoven life-giving/death-dealing forces inherent in maternity.
- Reproductive failure constitutes an existential crisis, undermining control over the procreative body, taken for granted since infancy and imbuing the female body schema with malevolent destructive powers.
- Bizarre treatments resuscitate archaic disorientation, and taboos, puzzlement about the origin of babies and wild theories of how they are made or destroyed.
- Whilst ART offers hope where barrenness has resided, success rates are low, and the process is fraught with conflict, heartache and painful disillusionment.
- Conversely, as technology subverts the basic facts of life, aided and abetted by potent fertility experts, reality restrictions are flaunted and generative day-dreams actualised.
- Rational cognition, geared to ordinary processes of "copulation, birth and death" lags sorely behind the reality of these unnerving procedures.

These science fiction technological interventions take place not in outer space but in the innermost interior of a woman's body, reviving unconscious imagery of the female cauldron with its attendant fantasies, anxieties and projections.

Psychoanalytic therapy provides necessary time-out from the whirligig to rest, to examine non-conscious motivations, and to articulate and repair the emotional erosion of prolonged failure to conceive, on self-esteem, body schema, generative identity and intimate relations.

References

Beebe, B., Knoblauch, S., Rustin, J. & Sorter, D. (2003). Introduction: A Systems View. *Psychoanalytic Dialogues* 13: 743–775.

Bernstein, D. (1990). Female genital anxieties, conflicts and typical mastery modes. *International Journal of Psychoanalysis*, 71: 151–165.

Corbett, K. (2001). Nontraditional Family Romance. *Psychoanalytic Quarterly*, 70: 599–624.

Daar, A. S. & Merali, Z. (2002). Infertility and social suffering: the case of ART in developing countries. In: *Current Practices and Controversies in Assisted Reproduction* World Health Organization Report on "medical, ethical and social aspects of assisted reproduction".

Ehrensaft, D. (2000). Alternatives to the stork: fatherhood fantasies in donor insemination families. *Studies in Gender and Sexuality, 1*: 371–397.

Ettinger, B. (2010). (M)Other Re-spect: Maternal Subjectivity, the Ready-made mother-monster and the Ethics of Respecting, www.mamsie.bbk.ac.uk/Ettinger.html.

Freud, S. (1905). The Sexual Researches of Childhood: Three Essays on the Theory of Sexuality. *S.E.7*: 194–97.

Freud, S. (1908). On the Sexual Theories of Children. *S.E.9*: 205–26.

Freud, S. (1918). From the History of an Infantile Neurosis, *S.E 17*: 1–124

Golombok, S., Brewaeys, A., Giavazzi, M. T., Guerra, D., MacCallum, F. & Rust, J. (2002). The European study of assisted reproduction families: the transition to adolescence. *Human Reproduction, 17*: 830–40.

Harris, A. (1997). Aggression, envy, and ambition: circulating tensions in women's psychic life. *Gender and Psychoanalysis, 2*: 291–325.

Hopper, E. (2003). *The Social Unconscious: Selected Papers*. London: Jessica Kingsley Pub.

Langer, M. (1958). Sterility and Envy. *International Journal of Psychoanalysis, 39*: 139–143.

Marks, M. (2008). Infanticide. *Psychiatry 8*:10–12.

Mayer, E. L. (1985). "Everybody Must be Just Like Me": Observations on Female Castration Anxiety. *International Journal of Psychoanalysis, 66*: 331–347.

Osato, F. & Giwa-Osagie. (2002). Social and ethical aspects of assisted conception in anglo-phone sub-Saharan Africa. *Current Practices and Controversies in Assisted Reproduction,* World Health Organization Report on "Medical, ethical and social aspects of assisted reproduction". (Eds) E.Vayena, PJ. Rowe & P. D.Griffin. Geneva: WHO

Peterson, B.D., Newton, C.R., Rosen & Skaggs, G.E. (2006). Gender differences in how men and women who are referred for IVF cope with infertility stress. *Human Reproduction, 21*: 2443–2449.

Pines, D. (1990). Emotional Aspects of Infertility and its Remedies. *International Journal of Psycho-analysis, 71*: 561–568.

Raphael-Leff, J. (1991). *Psychological Processes of Childbearing.* 4th edition, London: Anna Freud Centre, 2005.

Raphael-Leff, J. (2002). Eggs between women—the emotional aspects of gamete donation in reproductive technology. In: A.M. Alizade (Ed), *The Embodied Female*, (pp. 53–64). London: Karnac, 2002.

Raphael-Leff, J. (2003). Eros & ART. In: J Haynes & J Miller (Eds), *Inconceivable Conceptions: therapy, fertility and the new reproductive technologies* (pp.33–46). London: Routledge, 2003.

Raphael-Leff, J. (2005). Psychotherapy in the Reproductive Years. In: G. Gabbard, & J. Holmes (Eds), *The Concise Oxford Textbook of Psychotherapy* (pp. 367–380) Oxford: Oxford University Press, 2005.

Raphael-Leff, J. (2007). Femininity and its unconscious "shadows": gender and generative identity in the age of biotechnology. *British Journal of Psychotherapy, 23/4*: 497–515.

Raphael-Leff, J & Perelberg, R.J (Eds.) (2008). *Female Experience: Four Generations of British Women Psychoanalysts on Work with Women,* London: Anna Freud Centre.

Raphael-Leff, J. (2009) Fertility, Gender & Generativity—Romania as a special case. Romanian J. Psychiatry, *9 (4)*:143–150.

Raphael-Leff, J. (2010a). "The dreamer by daylight"—imaginative play, creativity and generative identity, *Psychoanalytic Study of the Child 64*: 14–5.

Raphael-Leff, J. (2010b). The Gift of Gametes: Unconscious Motivation and Problematics of Transcendency, *Feminist Review*, 94: 117–137.

Raphael-Leff, J. (2010c). Contemporary views on Femininity, Gender and Generative Identity, chapter in *Freud's "Femininity. New Introductory Lessons on Psycho-analysis"—divergences and convergences with Freud's works* according to contemporary psychoanalysis. (Eds.) L. Glosser Fiorini & G. Abelin-Sas. lPA publications, London: Karnac.

Raphael-Leff, J. (2010d). Healthy Maternal Ambivalence. *Studies in the Maternal, 2, (1)*: p. www.mamsie.bbk.ac.uk/raphael-leff.html.

Winnicott, D.W. (1964). *The Child, the Family and the Outside World.* Harmondsworth: Penguin.

Winnicott, D. W. (1967). Mirror role of (M) Other and Family in Child Development. In: Name of editors, *Playing and Reality*. (pp. 130–138). London: Penguin, 1971.

Notes

1. Today, sub-replacement fertility rates have contributed to population decline, from North Asia through to Eastern Europe (including Russia, Kazakhstan, Ukraine, Belarus, Moldova, Estonia, Latvia, Lithuania, Bulgaria, Georgia, Armenia, Bosnia, Croatia, Slovenia and Hungary). The human replacement figure is 2.3 children, but today in places as diverse as Hong Kong, Latvia, Korea, Armenia, Spain, Italy, Bulgaria, Russia and Greece childbearing women are having only a single child. In the UK, with a fertility rate of 1.5 it is estimated that unless immigration intervenes, the population will halve in forty four years, with drastic consequences. Anxiety about the decline in Japan's birth rate is so severe they have invented a word for it; *shoshika,* meaning a society without children.

2. According to classical psychoanalysis, discovery of the girl's lack of a penis may result in intense anxiety in a boy, who fears for his own. Castration anxiety revives previous traumatic experiences of "lack"

THE FEMALE CAULDRON   125

characterized by an element of loss; birth, separation, weaning, defecation. Thus Freud (1905, 1908, 1918) noted a chain of symbolic equivalences penis = faeces = child, with the latter treated as a compensation for the "castrated" girl . Clearly, in a patriarchal society, a girl's "penis envy" also signifies yearning for the cultural privilege of males. As suggested earlier, the value assigned to male or female genitalia is implicitly filtered through parental ascriptions, influenced by socio-political forces. Recent post-feminist theories propose that a girl may also celebrate what she *does* have, including cathexis of her own sexed body; labia, vulva, clitoris, vaginal opening and inner reproductive organs. Depending on her particular interpersonal experience, on her parents' desire, and her own unconscious sense of guilt, a girl may experience a sense of grievance about her lack. She may attempt to compensate, to deny—or to seek a way to remedy it. Some authors have de-centralised the "phallic stage" [now termed "early genital"], casting attention to differences between "open" and "closed" bodies, and resultant specifically female anxieties of "access, penetration and diffusivity" (Bernstein, 1990) which differ from the "castrative" fantasy of the imagined lost penis (Mayer, 1985). However, although some theoreticians persist in designating sexed-subjectivity to a biogenetically predetermined bodily sense potentiated by somatic sensations, recent evidence corroborates early findings that genital and other sensations become mental constructs before becoming "incorporated" as a sexed representation, hence self-evaluation of sexuality is dependent neither on genitalia nor chromosomal sex, but on psychic representation which is much affected by the interpersonal dimension of embodiment.

3. This is aided by a prohibition on a child of either sex being exclusively who the mother desires. Conversely, when parental possessiveness infiltrates the child, it triggers anxieties that prohibit realization, or even expression of desire to be other than who the parent desires.

4. Female genital mutilation is still practiced in twenty-five countries in central Africa. Although the practice was outlawed in Britain in 1985, some 63,000 women in the UK have suffered genital mutilation and 20,000 girls are still at risk of genital mutilation. Elsewhere in Europe, Australia, Canada and the USA immigrant populations from Africa, Yemen, south western Asia and South America continue to practice it. An estimated 70 million young girls and women have been subjected to it worldwide with dire effects, including birth complications. The World Health Organization [WHO] estimates that about half of births worldwide occur without access to trained personnel or traditional birth attendants. Nine neonates and parturients die every minute in sub-Saharan Africa, where most maternal and infant deaths occur.

In malnourished, disease stunted, circumcised women, fistulae are commonplace following obstructive births, especially among very young brides. Suppurating urine and feces, they are rejected by their husbands, and relegated to cow sheds or returned in shame to the parental home.

5. The exact effect of these hormones on men is still unclear, but in women pro-lactin stimulates milk-production, and mothers with raised cortisol levels are found to be more sympathetic to their baby's cries, and "bond" better. Male hormonal shifts (sparked by exposure to the pregnant woman's sweat glands) may similarly prepare the man for parenthood, reducing his sex-drive and aggression, promoting dependable behavior.

6. The fear of being infected by "feminine weakness" is a variation on this theme, one Freud (1918b, p. 198) described as a generalized sexual dread of women. More specifically, studies report that following the discovery of male infertility, up to two thirds of western men experience transient impotence lasting one to three months. In addition, STDs are very common and important preventable causes of infertility. An estimated 2.8 million cases of chlamydia and 718,000 cases of gonorrhea occur annually in the United States. Untreated these lead to pelvic inflammatory disease (PID), and "silent" infection in the upper genital tract which may cause permanent damage to the fallopian tubes, uterus, and surrounding tissues. In men they may impair spermatozoa (motility, DNA condensation).

In AIDS-ridden Africa, STDs also increase the chances of transmission of the human immunodeficiency virus (HIV), associated with infectious semen. Perinatal counselling projects reveal the effects on mental health in sero-discordant couples, or stigmatised women whose HIV+ status is discovered through screening in pregnancy. Facing this double crisis is a significant public health issue, especially in low and middle income countries (LMICs) where mental health services in community and primary health care facilities are limited. The risk of mother to baby transmission through birth and breastfeeding is now greatly reduced by retro-virals. Nonetheless, reviews of ante—and postnatal psychological wellbeing in Southern Africa, find exceedingly high rates of major depressive episodes and maternal anxiety due to unintended pregnancy, domestic violence, poverty, lack of social support, stressful life events and previous perinatal loss, especially in densely populated informal settlements.

7. These figures reflect not only reduced stigma but complex demographic vectors, and statistics should be read with a critical eye. Of the thirty four EU countries surveyed, among the highest unwed birth rates

are the Scandinavian nations (sixty-four per cent in Iceland, fifty-five per cent in Sweden and Norway and forty-six per cent in Denmark), France and some Eastern European ones but these figures do not reflect cohabitation rates, which are very low in Bulgaria, Estonia, Slovenia, etc. Likewise, in countries with low divorce rates like Spain, Portugal, Italy and Greece, single motherhood is much less prevalent (around six per cent), but increasingly, women there choose to remain both unmarried and childless, so the general fertility rate is very low indeed (see Eurostat yearbook 2010).

8. In 1980, over forty was considered too old to have children. By 1990 it was over fifty; in 2000 over sixty and in 2010, a seventy year old woman in India obliged her husband's desire for a son, giving birth to twin boys (Raphael-Leff, 2010b).

9. Romania's Total Fertility Rate has fallen from a high of 2.96 in the 1970s to 1.3 in 2000. This drop must be seen against the historical background of the Ceauşescu regime which in 1966 introduced draconian policies to increase the very low birth rate to at least four children per woman. Contraception, abortion and divorce were banned and national demands overrode personal choices. Submission to these imperialistic decrees was exacted through strict control, including taxation (ten to twenty per cent of the incomes of men and women who remained childless after age twenty-five). Romanian women were subjected to mandatory monthly gynaecological examinations. During this period of enforced reproduction, many women were damaged or died by clandestine abortions, leading to the highest maternal mortality rate in Europe. Notoriously, the rise in childbearing was accompanied by unrelenting poverty, resulting in many families having to entrust their children to overcrowded orphanages or one of Romania's six hundred under-stimulating or even abusive institutions (Raphael-Leff, 2009).

10. What the men of the family, clan or tribe seek is control of reproductive power. There may be financial gain. Girls as young as thirteen (mainly from Asia and Eastern Europe) are designated as mail-order brides. Their bodies are not their own. Children from Togo, Mali, Burkina Faso and Ghana are trafficked to Nigeria, Ivory Coast, Cameroon and Gabon; and in most cases these girls are powerless, isolated and at great risk of violence. Honour killings may involve burying the victim alive or stabbing her following a family meeting, stoning, or burning to death. Practiced as a warning strategy to avoid girls becoming pregnant outside marriage, in countries like Bangladesh, Central African Republic, Chad, Guinea, Mali, and Niger more than sixty per cent of girls are married off soon after or before even puberty. In Turkey, honour killings account for half of all the country's murders. Victims have been

killed for refusing to enter a marriage, for committing adultery or being in a relationship that displeased their relatives. In many instances, the crimes are committed by family members against a female relative. In Europe, more cases have reached the courts in recent years, but many remain unresolved or undetected. In some parts of the world, women who have been raped have also been murdered for the dishonour of being a victim and the disgrace it brings to their family. In South Asian and Middle Eastern families, but also in South America honour killing is believed to have originated from tribal customs and motto: "a life without honour is not worth living" where allegations against a woman can be enough to defile the reputation of a whole clan. Legislative provisions allowing for partial or complete defence in that context are still found in the penal codes of Argentina, Brazil, Ecuador, Egypt, Guatemala, Iran, Israel, Jordan, Peru, Syria, Venezuela and the Palestinian National Authority. Corrective rape is a criminal practice in some South African townships, whereby men assault, rape and victimise lesbian women, purportedly as a means of forcing them to change their sexual orientation.

11. Such reactions to infertility are consistent with findings from meta-analyses of coping strategies in general. Finding show that women are more likely than men to ruminate about problems, to seek emotional support, communicate effectively, and use "positive self-talk". Reviews of gender difference in response to infertility (e.g. Peterson et al., 2006) confirm that women are more likely to express problems of self-image and self-esteem and to report distress, looking outside the relationship for support and information. Compared to men, women use proportionately greater amounts of confrontational coping strategies: accepting responsibility and seeking social support. Men use greater amounts of distancing, self-control and problem-solving, tending to focus on work and other time-consuming activities. Both sexes describe diminishing sexual satisfaction. [Yet, it must be remembered that despite these patterns of sex differences, individuals vary within each gender and in different contexts].

12. Medical distinctions are drawn between sterility resulting from irreversible damage or defect, secondary infertility due to correctable causes and sub-fertility attributed to a single cause or several factors in one or both partners, or their particular combination (such as cervical mucous incompatibility); producing problems at any stage before or after the successful meeting of sperm and ovum. Clearly these definitions become invested with personal fantasy

The Medea Fantasy: An evitable burden during prenatal diagnostics? Psychoanalysis, gender and medicine in dialogue

Marianne Leuzinger-Bohleber

Abstract

Analyzing pregnant women has always been a unique opportunity to clinically investigate *"The female body—inside and outside"*. Pregnancy and giving birth to a baby is not only connected with obvious changes to the female body observable from the outside, but also with the stimu-lation of intensive unconscious (inside) fantasies which have a specific gender quality. The "Medea fantasy" presented here is one example of such an unconscious fantasy concerning the female body and mind. The "Medea fantasy" is reactivated when a woman/couple has to decide on life or death of their unborn child after a positive finding in prenatal diagnostics PND. We investigated nearly 2000 women/couples in an interdisciplinary, European-wide study: *Ethical Dilemma due to prena-tal and genetic diagnostics (EDIG)*. As will be illustrated, psychoanalysts have specific professional knowledge and skills to cope with these reac-tivations of archaic unconscious body fantasies. Two case examples will show that this expert knowledge can help women/couples in crises interventions to recognize the archaic state of the mind in such a situa-tion, and to return to a more mature way of psychic functioning. As the EDIG study showed, this is very important for the short and long term consequences of such traumatic experiences. Protective and risk factors coping with possible traumatic experiences after a positive finding in PND will be discussed.

Introduction

"Medea Fantasy"—an ubiquitous unconscious fantasy system? (Note 1)

The "Medea fantasy", which I would like to discuss in this Chapter, is one example for a gender specific unconscious fantasy concerning the female body and mind. This central unconscious fantasy is inevitably reactivated when a woman/couple has to decide on life or death of their unborn child after a positive finding in PND. We had the chance to investigate nearly 2000 women/couples in an interdisciplinary, European—wide study: *Ethical Dilemma due to prenatal and genetic diagnostics, EDIG.* As I would like to show: Psychoanalysts, due to their professional skills to cope with threatening unconscious phantasies, could thus help women/couples in crises interventions to recognize the archaic state of the mind in such a situation of decision-making and to return to a more mature way of psychic functioning which is, as our study showed, very important for the short—and long term consequences of such traumatic experiences.

I would like to illustrate this thesis just with two examples:

a) A summary of an interview from our EDIG study which proved to be helpful for the interviewed woman and
b) A summary of 5 crisis intervention sessions with a woman who reacted with panic and severe psychosomatic symptoms after becoming pregnant by artificial insemination. She had the obsessional impulse to terminate her pregnancy immediately.

How can we characterize the "Medea-Fantasy"?

In the psychoanalyses with nine psychogenic sterile female analysands, and in four psychoanalytical long term psychotherapies with female patients, we discovered first this fantasy which unconsciously seemed to determine the experience of their female body, their femininity and potential motherhood (Leuzinger-Bohleber, 2001).

In the centre of the "Medea-fantasy"(Note 2) was the conviction that female sexuality is connected with the experience of existential dependency on the love partner and the danger of being left and narcissistically hurt by him (as was Medea, a princess from the Black Sea, by Jason, a Greek hero, whom she had helped to bring the Golden Fleece back to Greek, but was deceived by him afterwards. In order to hurt him existentially, she killed her two sons). These women unconsciously feared their own sexual passion might revive uncontrollable destructive impulses in a close, intimate relationship, which could be directed against the autonomous self, the love partner and above all against the offspring of the relationship with him. Thus, their psychogenic frigidity and sterility unconsciously protected these women against these fantasized dangers.

Unfortunately I cannot summarize the interesting psychoanalytical literature concerning the concept of the unconscious fantasy. Susan Isaac (1945), Glover (1947), Arlow & Brenner (1964), Arlow (1969a, 1969b), Sandler (1986), Beland (1989), Inderbitzin & Levy (1990), Sandler & Sandler (1994), Britton (1995), Shane & Shane (1996), Roth (2001) and Perron (2001) have published central papers on this important topic. In summary, these unconscious fantasies may, as Freud presumed, have been early-infantile daydream fantasies of the women, in which earliest bodily and object relational experiences and primal fantasies (as e.g. the primal scene, birth and death etc) had been included. To mention just one example: one surprising common biographical fact of my psychogenic sterile women patients had been that all their mothers had suffered from severe postpartum depressions and had been treated by antidepressant medications for months. These early traumatic object relations and connected fantasies had been part of the early embodied memories of these women.

As Sandler and Sandler (1994) postulated, these fantasies probably have been banished into the unconscious during the Oedipal phase in the fourth or fifth year of life. They may have been rewritten 'nachträglich' again and again, e.g. by masturbation fantasies in adolescence as well as fantasies of motherhood and femininity in late adolescence. Seen from a perspective of the structural model in psychoanalysis, the "Medea fantasy" can be considered as a psychic compromise allowing a certain unconscious satisfaction, as well as a satisfaction of archaic shame and guilt feelings. Besides, as terrible as the unconscious self image of a witch and a child murderer may be, these severely traumatized women preferred to be the actress of their fate (a "Medea" or a psychogenic sterile woman) instead of the passive victim of their love object (Leuzinger-Bohleber, 1998.)

The "Medea-fantasy" in EDIG

Short summary of EDIG

"These things that, by his science and technology, man has brought about on this earth, on which he first appeared as a feeble animal organism ... do not only sound like a fairy tale, they are an actual fulfillment of every—or of almost every—fairy-tale wish. ... Future ages will bring with them new and probably unimaginably great advances in this field of civilization and will increase man's likeness to God still more. But in the interests of our investigations, we will not forget that present-day man does not feel happy in his Godlike character." (Freud, 1939, p. 91f)

When Sigmund Freud published his reflections on modern civilization he could not anticipate the enormous developments in modern technology 20th and 21st century. Do these developments increasingly confront us with new facets of a Faustian seduction? Are we "playing God" as many contemporary critical authors of modernity are claiming?

Technology has always been part of culture and thus of human nature. Without it we would not be able to take control of our lives in a contemporary sense. However techniques, once developed, force us to make responsible decisions about the consequences of their use. We also have to find forms of coping with the ambivalences and dilemmas which are connected to most modern technologies.

In EDIG we have thoroughly studied this topic in a field which is particularly sensitive; prenatal and genetic diagnostics. This short summary is based on the introduction of the book, *The Janus Face of Prenatal Diagnostics. A European Study Bridging Ethics, Psychoanalysis and Medicine*, (Leuzinger-Bohleber, Engels & Tsiantis, 2008). I thank my colleagues for allowing me to quote our joint introduction here again.

Achievements in genetic research produce ethical and moral dilemmas which need to be the subject of reflection and debate in modern societies. Moral dilemmas are seen as situations in which a person has a strong moral obligation to choose each of two alternatives for action, but cannot fulfill both. Denial of ambivalences that moral dilemmas arouse constitutes a threat to societies as well as to individual persons. The EU wide study *"Ethical Dilemmas Due to Prenatal and Genetic Diagnostics" (016716-EDIG),* which was performed from 2005–2008, tried to investigate these dilemmas in a field which seems particularly challenging: prenatal diagnostics (PND). The existence of PND confronts women and their partners with a variety of moral dilemmas: Should they make use of this technique at the risk of hurting the foetus or by being possibly confronted with a question of termination? Once they have undergone PND, abnormalities confront women and their partners with moral dilemmas regarding the decision on the life or death of the unborn child, and their responsibility to it. An important aspect is the conflict of individual beliefs and obligations and those of specific social cultures. These dilemmas have not received full attention in our society and often remain latent, creating a source of distress for women (and partners) and placing stress on relationships. Some couples show better coping capabilities, particularly if support by competent professionals is available. However, more research is needed to identify those with vulnerability to psychopathology as a consequence of abortion after PND results, or to giving birth to severely handicapped children. Pathology sometimes does not appear until years after the decision. Our study was a step in this direction.

The study described existing care systems across participating centres in Germany, Greece, Israel, Italy, Sweden, and the United Kingdom. Data was collected in two sub-studies. All results were integrated into a discourse on ethical dilemmas. Study (A) recruited two groups of couples (positive or negative PND, total n = 1687). Experiences with PND and connected dilemmas have been explored (through questionnaires and interviews). Results have been discussed in interdisciplinary research groups. Study (B) interviewed psychoanalysts and their long-term patients who showed severe psychopathologies as reactions to the dilemmas mentioned previously. Results of the study help to discuss possible protective and risk factors for women and their partners undergoing PND. The perspectives have been discussed with participating couples, experts, the general public, and politicians, in order to develop culturally fair clinical practice within the EU.

The EDIG study offered a unique chance for a multidisciplinary dialogue between ethicists, psychoanalysts, medical doctors, philosophers and cultural anthropologists. Another innovative aspect was the possibility that relatively detailed interviews with women/couples after PND as well as the empirical findings based on large scale questionnaire data could be used by different authors looking at them from different disciplinary and cultural perspectives.

Clinical example

In our book we have summarized seven out of forty-five interviews with women/ couples after PND in detail. The second source, completing the information from the questionnaires, has been interviews with sixteen psychoanalytic colleagues on their insights gained in long term psychoanalyses with women experiencing difficulties with pregnancy. We tried to illustrate the broad spectrum of possible reactions to PND in our book; for one of the women coming from a genetically burdened family PND meant the chance to dare to become pregnant at all. For others, such as Mrs. D., whose interviews will be summarized shortly, the late interruption of pregnancy was a traumatic experience.

Interview 4: A severe crisis in the love relationship after pregnancy interruption

The following interview may illustrate the reactivation of the "Medea-Fantasy" and archaic kinds of guilt feelings after pregnancy interruption (trisomy 21, the most frequent reason for terminating pregnancy in our sample).

Interview with Mrs. D.

I was asked to interview this woman by her partner who told me on the phone of his girlfriend's bad state, and her urgent need to talk to someone. In person, Mrs. D. makes the impression of a person with a capacity of bravely confronting and coping with even the most terrible strokes of fate. Her figure is rather sturdy, and she proves a very sporty person. She is only twenty-eight years old. I am impressed by her deep blue eyes and remarkably long eye lashes, which—apparently to her own surprise—often fill with tears during the interview (she apologizes and wipes the tears away like a courageous little girl).

Five weeks previously Mrs. D.'s pregnancy was interrupted. She is already back at work and "thinks that she is getting over the situation quite well". She is now suffering from being hardly able to endure proximity to her partner. If he had not moved into her house, she would desire "a break in their relationship for a while." Additionally she currently cannot bear bodily contact. This is putting extreme pressure on their relationship. It was an unplanned pregnancy; they had known each other for only a short time. She had been very happy with him, especially in contrast to the relationships she had before. Concerning her present situation in her profession and her age the pregnancy nevertheless seemed to be welcome for her. During a routine examination an abnormality was detected. An amniocentesis was indicated, and the diagnosis was trisomy 21. This was a shock for both. Neither had expected complications. Their family histories are genetically inconspicuous and both are still young. They immediately decided on a termination, which was endorsed by both doctors and their families. "The childbirth was indeed painful, but I am tough, and childbirth itself is not the problem, but the effect the situation is having on my relationship." I explained that many people within traumatic experiences regress to a less mature way of psychic functioning, which corresponds to a relatively easy shift of blame. It could very well be the case that she unconsciously shifts the blame for the suffered traumatic experience on to her partner. This acute process of mourning can often last about one year; which is why I understand her uneasiness about decision-making in her present state. She is reassured to hear that this is a well-known reaction after a traumatic loss, and that it is not her demise into a "crazy mental state."

Her family prioritizes emotional repression and endurance. Her father, for example, diagnosed with cancer, still appears at his shop every day in spite of undergoing chemotherapy. At times he permits her to go home if not feeling well, but she is aware of his disapproving glance (she assists in the family shop). Her family has limited empathy for the impact of the aftermath for her. She chastises herself inwardly, determined not to feel so much self-pity. Then she tries to act as if nothing had happened, tries to take her mind off things, go to parties, and participate in sport competitions.

Only when I explicitly explain that a late abortion is a huge burden for most women, is she able to tentatively report her experience in more detail. She did not feel well informed about the effects of the tablets from which she suffered regurgitation and diarrhoea. Furthermore she did not know that pains could trigger childbirth contractions and generally did not know what labour pains would feel like. She had been to the toilet alone and suddenly held the child in her hand, covered with blood. She put it onto the sink. Then the expulsion of the afterbirth started: (Cooper, 1986)

> Everything was covered with blood—I cleaned everything and left the dead child there …. It was terrible—I felt like a child murderer … (Initially she had not wanted to look at it—and then she was confronted with it alone and totally unexpectedly).

Only when I pointed out how horrifying this experience must have been for her, does she feel free enough to release her tears unashamedly. She agreed with my impression that she unconsciously felt let down by her partner. In any case, she cannot imagine voluntarily going through such an ordeal once more. The thought of a further childbirth is a nightmare to her. "What I think is that your body now might be trying to defend itself; it is taking a rest in order to give time to your mind to come to terms with this experience." I encouraged her to take her time for the process of mourning and offer to arrange more appointments with either myself or one of my colleagues, in case she so wished. She thanked me for the interview. It was of great help for her, for a better understanding of her reactions and for considering them as part of a "normal process of mourning."

Some psychoanalytical considerations

For most of the women/couples, a positive finding of PND, coupled with the need to decide on the life or death of one's unborn child, have a traumatic quality. According to Bohleber (2010) experiencing a trauma can be characterized as having to cope with a situation which has the quality of a *"too much"* (in respect of the so called economical as well as the object relational model of contemporary psychoanalysis). Cooper defined a psychic trauma as an event, in which the capability of the ego, to guarantee a minimal feeling of safety and integrity, is suddenly overwhelmed, evoking anxieties and a state of mind of extreme helplessness. (Cooper, 1986.) Such a traumatic event leads to long lasting changes of the psychic organization (see also Fischer & Riedesser, 1998). From an object relational perspective the basic trust in a helpful, "containing" and empathetic inner object is destroyed because this "good inner object" was not capable of protecting the self in the traumatic situation.

In all the interviews the overwhelming, traumatic quality of PND was obvious. But why do our empirical findings, which have been summarized by Tamara Fischmann and others in our book (Fischmann et al., 2008, p. 89 ff.), replicate the findings of other studies that for around eighty per cent of the women/couples, the trauma seems to have the quality of an extreme short crisis which can be overcome within a relatively short period of time? And what about the other twenty per cent?

Most of the psychoanalysts, who have been interviewed, agree on the following psychoanalytic considerations:

A woman (or couple) going through a traumatic situation (as being confronted with an unexpected, shocking diagnosis (such as the child not having a face) or having to give birth to a dead child), has to mobilize extreme coping mechanisms and defense strategies. The complexity of the situation has (for psychic reasons) to be reduced radically in order to be able to decide and to act in the presence. One of the best known coping mechanisms for trauma is dissociation. The self dissociates from its emotions, fantasies, and thoughts in an extreme way. It flees into a different state of mind which (on the surface) has nothing to do with the overwhelming emotions and fantasies evoked in the traumatic situation. Initially, the individual can function surprisingly well, and can return to everyday functionality shortly after the traumatic event. But at the same time the individual has lost the inner connection to their sense of self, their emotions and thoughts; and perhaps to the object (e.g. the partner) and to reality. This state of dissociation often is not recognized by the individual (as e.g. by Mrs. D) and not connected to the traumatic situation. As we know from long term psychoanalysis such dissociative states may sometimes endure for years and—unconsciously—determine the psychic reality of the individuals. The severely traumatized persons have never found their way back to normal life again. They do not feel connected to other people anymore and have lost the basic feeling of being the active centre; the motor of their own lives (see also Leuzinger-Bohleber, Roth and Buchheim, 2007). As we know from the empirical parts of our study, around eighty per cent of people going through PND seem to overcome the psychic states of dissociation and integrate the trauma into their identities, often by the help of empathetic others in their private lives or in therapy. But again, what about the others?

There are further considerations to note; based on the classical structural model of psychoanalysis and some newer theoretical approaches in psychoanalysis (see Leuzinger-Bohleber, et al., 2008, p. 199ff). According to clinical observations, the trauma of suddenly being confronted with life and death of one´s own child often leads to an extreme regression into an archaic state of psychic functioning. As Freud has already described, the confrontation with one´s own death or the death of a close and beloved person (particularly one´s own child) absorbs all the psychic energy at once. The death anxiety is the most extreme form of anxiety which mobilizes primitive coping and defense strategies. (Freud, 1926) It evokes primitive mechanisms like denial splitting, projections and projective identifications and so on (see Moser, 2005). This archaic state of psychic functioning is dominated by the so called paranoid-schizoid position, an extreme psychic split. Connected with this state of mind is the reactivation of an archaic world of unconscious fantasies of murderers and innocent victims, witches and saints, devils and angels and so on. The Medea fantasy, described above, seems to be just *one* example of such a ubiquitous female (body) fantasy. The women are unconsciously convinced they will murder their own children, fearing revenge and thus suffering from unbearable guilt. Often, (archaic) oral fantasies are evoked, such as the fantasy of an oral conception of the baby; of having poisoned the foetus e.g. by smoking, drinking alcohol or having taken dangerous medicaments. We also have mentioned that the fact that the foetus had to be eliminated in order not to threaten the life of the mother may evoke anal fantasies. In other interviews and therapies we could observe that Oedipal fantasies had been reactivated by PND. Several psychoanalysts reported that the disability of the foetus was unconsciously experienced as a punishment for ubiquitous infantile wishes (secretly kept in the unconscious of each adult woman) to get a child from one´s Oedipal father. Thus the foetus was experienced as the product of an incestuous relationship. The deformation of the foetus and the interruption of pregnancy were both seen as revenge or a punishment for such forbidden wishes.

The regression to this archaic level of psychic functioning with a primitive, pre-ambivalent logic of right and wrong, as well as the reactivation of the just mentioned archaic unconscious fantasies, may be some of the psychic sources for the unbearable guilt. Unconsciously many of the patients, who had interrupted their pregnancy, were convinced they had murdered, and were always expecting revenge and punishment.

From a psychoanalytic point of view a confrontation with such an archaic world of a murderous self and other (often the partner or the medical doctor on which the own murderous impulses are projected) can hardly be prevented when the patient suffers a late interruption of pregnancy. This outside reality is confounded with the archaic inner reality. Therefore it proves to be very important for the women in psychotherapeutic sessions to get in touch with this state of mind and the archaic (of course unrealistic) quality of the fantasies and the specific psychic functioning. This is a presupposition that they are capable to "rediscover" and experience the complexity and the ambivalences which are always connected to PND in a more realistic way. Clinically this proves to be a presupposition to overcome the trauma and to regain psychic health.

Psychoanalysts know that in extreme (traumatic) situations, where an individual is confronted with life and death, the individual's own inner resources mostly prove insufficient. Therefore all the women/couples undergoing late interruptions of pregnancy due to PND need a counterpart to the archaic inner world in the outside reality, in a loving partnership, family and friends, but also in the professional medical or psychotherapeutic care during PND, in order to finally overcome the regression and to regain a more mature level of psychic functioning after a relatively short crisis. If such a support is not given the crisis might end in a dramatic process in which the individual needs professional help in order to overcome it.

Crisis Intervention: Liaison service with a department for PND in Frankfurt

I would like to illustrate this thesis with a second short case example. It is taken from our experience in a liaison service in connection with one of the largest departments for PND in Frankfurt (Prof. Dr. med. Merz) . It was built after a 2008 congress in which we introduced the findings of EDIG to our medical colleagues. We are offering crisis interventions to women/couples during or after PND.

Mrs. P. was sent to me by a gynecologist because, after a successful fertilization, to his surprise she did not show any happiness, pride or joy, but instead panic, severe eating and sleeping disturbances, and other psychosomatic symptoms. She asked for a crisis intervention (five sessions in total). Mrs. P. is in a miserable state when I first see her. A beautiful woman but very thin; I immediately had the association with anorexia nervosa. Mrs. P. informed me that she is not able to eat anything and vomits all the time; she has to take infusions and stay in bed. She complains that ever since she has got the information that she is pregnant she can hardly sleep and has terrible nightmares about carrying a "monster inside of me ... This monster is destroying everything—my body, my job (she is a very successful lawyer), my marriage, my love for my dogs ..." Her gynecologist had told her that she, a thirty-nine year old woman, already shows signs of the menopause. Suddenly she absolutely wanted to have a baby and decided to undergo artificial insemination, but as soon as the pregnancy was diagnosed, she was full of panic.

Spontaneously she tells me that she is an only child and has a very bad relationship with her mother, who seemed to misuse her as a self-object from early childhood onwards. She wants to have a grandchild. Mrs. P. remembers being a very lonely child under high pressure to be an excellent, outstanding student, violin player etc. Her mother seemed incapable of empathizing in a "good enough way" with her needs as a child. To give just one example, each year she forced her little daughter during her pre-school years to bring her most beloved toy to an orphanage before Christmas; so she should learn to share her wealth and privileges with poor children. Mrs. P. reported in an impressive way how difficult it had been to separate from this mother and to build up her own sense of identity and autonomy. She lives far away from her parents but has to talk on the telephone with her mother every day. "My mother is so happy about my pregnancy ... she is not interested how *I* feel at all—my womb does seem to belong to her again: it is her pregnancy not mine". We discussed her fears of losing her autonomy and identity as well as her ambivalent feelings towards her mother and her own feelings about "becoming a mother".

"The growing baby seems to threaten your autonomy, your basic feeling of being a separate human being—a pregnancy is, of course, indeed a process of no return ..."

"I only feel the impulse to get rid of all this and find back to my former equilibrium .... But during the nights I panic because I feel like a murderer of my own child ... there is no solution. Sometimes I even think of suicide .... In any case, I would like to terminate the pregnancy as soon as possible—to finish this terrible physical state."

I offer crisis interventions every day to Mrs. P. "We know from our study that it is helpful to have the courage to look at all the ambivalent feelings before definitively deciding for or against interruption of pregnancy", I tell her. She agrees to wait some more days.

In the second session Mrs. P. reports the following dream:

> I am at the airport—pregnant, feeling horrible—and all alone ... All planes have gone—I have no place to be—feel panic and want to throw myself out of the window.. " "Suicide would be a possibility to kill the monster and myself at the same time..", she associates. I ask her to further associate. She reports her feelings of being left alone by her husband. He has two children from a former marriage, is much older than she is, and did not want to have any more children. But because she absolutely wanted to become pregnant— he finally agreed. "I felt so terribly dependent on him—you cannot become pregnant alone ...."

At the moment he seems to be very tolerant; he leaves the question of termination to Mrs. P. However, his tolerance provokes a different response in Mrs. P; she feels left alone which strengthens her aggressive feelings towards him, and the "monster" being the product of intercourse with him.

Mrs. P. cancelled the next session because she had to be hospitalized, as she was bleeding. In the third session Mrs. P. reported that she felt intensive ambivalent feelings in the clinic. On the one hand she hoped to have a spontaneous abortion. On the other hand she felt something like sadness.

> "I am starting to have something like admiration for the strong little monster within me—he seems to fight for his own life ..." She reports another dream: "I was in the hospital, pregnant and miserable, lying in a bed. I was paralyzed. A black nurse came: she was only dressed with a napkin around her hip. She had huge, huge breasts. She bowed over me. I hardly could breathe because of her huge breasts ... She had a long injection and wanted to kill me—I woke up in panic."

Her associations lead her first to the African look of her own hair. She often was told that her hair made her beautiful. Then she associates to her mother:

> "She was quite fat after the pregnancy with me. She has huge breasts—I hate this and never would like to look similar to her. Pregnancy seems to mean that you are losing your beauty and become an ugly woman like your mother. I am convinced that my husband than will leave me: he hates fat women. I am so angry that he made me pregnant—and will leave me afterwards alone in this vulnerable state, ugly and with a baby whom I can not love …"
>
> "Is it possible that you are struggling with all these intensive negative feelings towards the "monster" as a product of your sexuality with your husband, yourself and your growing body— and perhaps also towards your mother who did not transmit a more beautiful picture of motherhood and femininity to you? Could these aggressive fantasies be one reason why you (the "African look woman") kill yourself and your little monster?" I comment.

This session seemed to have an influence on Mrs. P. She feels better physically, can eat again and starts to get more regularly. In the next two sessions it is possible to talk about all the details of the "Medea-fantasy"; her unbearable feelings of dependency and loss of autonomy, her conviction that her husband will deceive her with another, more beautiful, young woman, her murderous fantasies towards herself, her partner and the "little monster."

It is impressive that recognizing and partially working through the "Medea-fantasy" has an effect on the psychosomatic and psychic state of Mrs. P. She develops the first positive fantasies of the "vital monster" and her becoming a mother. She then decides to continue her pregnancy.

After four weeks Mrs. P. calls me; she had a spontaneous abortion. She feels sad but also relieved: "I did not actively kill my baby son …he obviously had some genetic deformation and was not able to live ….The doctor told me that I could try again to become pregnant after six months—I will have to think about it seriously after all what we have seen in our sessions …"

Crises interventions: a professional offer by psychoanalysts to women/couples after PND?

As I see it, the psychoanalyst in a crisis intervention proves to be a "good real object" who helps; by his or her professional understanding of the world of unconscious fantasies; the patient to find her way back to reality, out of the nightmare of inner persecutions, archaic guilt feelings, shame and despair. Only after such a therapeutic working through is the process of mourning and psychic healing possible.

For overcoming the acute crisis, not only the support in the outside reality, but also a stable inner object world of the individual itself might be a protective factor. This could the eighty per cent of the women to regain their psychic equilibrium, or what Kleinian analysts call the "depressive position", a capability to cope with mature ambivalences and complexities again. If "good inner objects" can be mobilized in the acute crisis and can be supported by the experience with "good objects" in the outside reality, feelings of loss, guilt and shame can be experienced in a more mature way and lose their persecutory quality.

The twenty per cent of the women after PND who became severely depressed, years after the interruption of pregnancy, often do not have such protective factors (good inner objects, good ego resources, stable good relationships in the outside reality, supportive medical, professional and cultural environment etc.). They often had not had stable early relationships and so were not able to develop a secure attachment pattern, the capability to symbolize and mentalize. They also often have gone through severe trauma in early childhood and/or adolescence. Particularly traumatic experiences with former losses (of a child or a close relative) often prove to be risk factors. Therefore we tried to offer some diagnostic considerations in order to discriminate between risk and protective factors during and after PND.

These factors, seen from a psychoanalytic standpoint, are thus due to the idiosyncratic and biographical characteristics of one's own inner psychic world, which are not easily diagnosed because they are not directly observable. Nevertheless experienced clinicians learn how to perceive (and afterwards to test) some indicators for important features in the psychic reality. These indicators for protective and risk factors for women/couples undergoing PND can be transmitted to non-psychoanalytic persons, such as medical doctors and their staff. In the following table we try to summarize some of these indicators.

Inner world	Indicators	Indicators during PND	Inner world	Indicators	Indicators during PND
Good inner objects	Stable relationships with partner, friends, family	Trusting, open contact with medical doctors, staff etc.	Fragile, instable inner objects	Rarely good relationships with partner, friends, family, socially isolated	Strange relationship with doctors and medical staff (no basic trust, difficult communication)
No severe traumatic experiences in childhood and adolescence	Integrated personality (good integration of emotions, fantasies, thoughts, no dissociative state, can communicate one's anxieties, concerns, meets people trustfully	Can communicate with medical doctors and staff in an uncomplicated way, talks about feelings, anxieties etc, shows curiosity, openness for information etc.	Traumatic experiences in childhood and adolescence	Traumatic experiences influence communicative style, no basic trust towards partner, friends, professionals etc.	Not integrated emotions, signs of dissociations, mistrustful attitude towards staff and medical doctors
No former loss of child or close person		Loss is not spontaneous topic in contact with medical doctor or staff	Former loss of child or close person		Person may seem depressive, anxious, talks about former losses

Secure attachment	Individual has access to broad range of feelings, ambivalences etc.	Individual can show broad range of feelings (e.g., anxieties, despair etc.) when the doctor confronts with the problematic findings	Insecure attachment	Individual has either to deny negative emotions (dismissive attachment pattern) or is overfloated by them (preoccupied attachment pattern)	Individual either does not show any emotions while confronted with the problematic findings or is overwhelmed by panic and despair in an extreme way
Depressive position	Individual can perceive and express ambivalent feelings and thoughts	Individual can perceive and express ambivalent feelings and thoughts in talking to medical doctors or staff	Paranoid schizoid position	Individual splits in extreme ways between "good" and "bad", "right" and "wrong" aspects of PND, decisions etc.	Individual splits in extreme ways between "good" and "bad", "right" and "wrong" aspects of PND, decisions etc. while talking to doctors or medical staff
Mature coping with guilt feelings	The self can stand to become guilty without a basic feeling of being destroyed in his or her self concept and esteem	Individual can talk about guilt, shame etc. in a "mature", adequate way	Archaic guilt feelings	The guilt feelings have an archaic, unbearable quality and therefore have to be split of, projected, denied etc.	Individual does not seem to have guilt feelings, others are blamed for the situation, one's decision etc. individuals often show strange psychosomatic reactions instead of direct emotions

(Continued)

Table (Continued).

Protective factors			Risk factors		
Inner world	Indicators	Indicators during PND	Inner world	Indicators	Indicators during PND
Mature quality of aggression	Individual can perceive and accept own aggressive impulses because they are not mainly associated with destruction	Individual can show or talk about aggressive, non destructive impulses	Archaic quality of aggression	Individual denies, splits off, projects own aggressive impulses, fears revenge, destructiveness of others etc.	Individual can not show directly aggressive impulses or is overfloated in an uncontrolled way by them, often individual feels to be the passive victim—others are the persecutors
Stable narcissistic self regulation	Individual has stable narcissistic self-regulation in private relationships, job etc., good developed autonomy, stable narcissistic self regulation is used and a label and an explanation—so not clear to non analysts	Individual shows a socially adequate behaviour towards doctors/medical staff (can accept medical authority without too much submission), seems to be able to use information in an autonomous way	Fragile narcissistic self regulation	Individual needs strong narcissistic support by other persons, is narcissistically vulnerable	Individual seems to be in a constant vulnerable stage, often feels insulted (also by medical doctors, staff), does not show much autonomous thinking, actions etc.

Dominance of mature defence mechanisms	Individual can use sublimations, rationalizations, intellectualizations	In contact with medical staff person is able to show intellectual interest without losing emotional contact	*Dominance of primitive (archaic) defence mechanisms*	*Psychic life seems to be dominated by denial, splitting, projections, reversal in the opposite mode etc.*	*In contact with medical doctors the individual seems to deny important information, splits between "good and bad", tries to project negative feelings onto others*
Mature coping strategies	Individual has a range of mature coping strategies dealing with difficult situations (in professional and private situations)	Individual can take up advice, suggestions by the medical staff and completes them with own suggestions, ideas etc.	*Lack of, or primitive coping strategies*	*Individual can hardly solve difficult situations alone, is extremely dependent on the advice of others*	*Individual shows extreme helplessness and "infantile" ideas on how to cope with the difficult situation of PND, can hardly ask relevant questions etc.*
Sensitive for cultural and ethical factors of PND	Individual is capable to reflect on cultural and ethical issues of PND	Individual takes up cultural and ethical questions in the consultation with medical doctor and staff	*Not sensitive to cultural and ethical factors of PND*	*Individual seems to live in his or her own personal world in an extreme way*	*Individual mentions strange connections between PND and own situation, is not capable to reflect on cultural and ethical issues*

Suggestions for training of medical staff

Perceiving and reflecting on indicators for protective and risk factors of women undergoing PND could be aims of future professionals involved in the process. Of course all the above indicators are not objective findings and therefore would have to be carefully reflected in the exchange with a specific women/couple. Nevertheless, in the best case the knowledge might help professionals to be good real "objects" to women/couples in the traumatic situation after positive findings in PND; helping them to deal with the above mentioned regressive processes and thus increasing the probability of regaining a mature psychic level of functioning.

More research is needed to further test these indicators for protective and risk factors for informing couples in more detail about possible risks of PND and even offering them some help in order to prevent the long lasting consequences of (unexpected) traumatic experiences.

Containing function of culture and society for women/couples undertaking PND

As briefly mentioned in the introduction, the traumatic quality of the decision concerning the life and death of one´s own child often overtaxes women and couples after PND. Helpful "good objects" in the professional world can be a beneficial influence on the woman/ couple. Many of the interviewed women/couples also mentioned the importance of public discourses on PND, handicapped children and, more generally, the responsibility for the next generation. As we had discussed in our book, society and culture seem to have a "containing function" (Bion) for couples in the traumatic situation described and should express empathy and understanding for the extremely difficult situation modern prenatal and genetic diagnostics may lead individuals into. These individuals are members of our society who have the right to be supported, and not devalued or even condemned for their decisions (see Leuzinger-Bohleber, Engels and Tsiantis, 2008). We also should not forget that economical interests might play an increasing role in creating a direct or indirect pressure on a couple who decide to give birth to a handicapped child. As we have discussed in our book, the decisions evoked by PND for or against giving birth to a severely handicapped child touch dimensions which go beyond the responsibility of the individual couples and become social concerns in their own right.

References

Arlow, J.A. (1969a). Unconscious fantasy and disturbances of conscious experience. *Psychoanalytic Quarterly, 38*: 1–27.

Arlow, J.A. (1969b). Fantasy, memory, and reality testing. *Psychoanalytic Quarterly, 38*: 28–51.

Arlow, J.A. & Brenner, C. (1964). *Psychoanalytic Concepts and the Structural Theory*. New York: International Universities Press.

Beland, H. (1989). Die unbewusste Phantasie. Kontroversen um ein Konzept. *Forum der Psychoanalyse*, 5: 85–98.

Bohleber, W. (2000). Die Entwicklung der Traumatheorie in der Psychoanalyse. *Psyche—Z Psychoanal*, 54: 797–839.

Bohleber, W. (2010). *Destructiveness, Intersubjectivity, and Trauma: The Identity Crises of Modern*. London: Karnac.

Britton, R. (1995). Psychic reality and unconscious belief. *International Journal of Psycho-Analysis*, 76: 19–23.

Cooper, A. (1986). Toward a limited definition of psychic trauma. In: Rothstein, A. (ed.), *The reconstruction of trauma*. (pp. 41–56). Madison: International Universities Press.

Fischer, G. & Riedesser, P. (1998). *Lehrbuch der Psychotraumatologie*. München: Reinhardt.

Fischmann, T., Pfenning, N., Laezer, K.L., Rüger, B., Tzivoni, Y:, Vassilopoulou, V., Ladopulou, K., Bianchi, B., Fiandaca, D., Sarchi, F. (2008). Empirical data evaluation on EDIG (Ethical Dilemmas due to Prenatal and Genetic Diagnostics). In: Leuzinger-Bohleber, M., Engels, E.M. & Tsiantis, J. (Eds.), *The Janus Face of prenatal diagnostics: A European study bridging ethics, psychoanalysis, and medicine*. (pp. 89–135) *London*: Karnac.

Freud, S. (1908a). Hysterical phantasies and their relation to bisexuality. *S.E., 9*: 159–166.

Freud, S. (1926). Reflections on war and death. *S.E., 14*: 275–300.

Freud, S. (1930a). Civilization and its discontents. *S.E., 21*: 64–145.

Glover, E. (1947). Basic mental concepts: Their clinical and theoretical value. *Psychoanalytic Quarterly, 16*: 482–506.

Inderbitzin, L.B. & Levy, S.T. (1990). Unconscious fantasy: A reconsideration of the concept. *Journal of the American Psychoanalytic Association, 38*: 113–130.

Isaacs, S. (1945). The nature and function of phantasy. In: Riviere, J. (ed.), *Developments in psychoanalysis* (pp. 67–121). London: Hogarth Press.

Leuzinger-Bohleber, M. (1998). "… J'adore ce qui me brûle …" (Max Frisch). Die "Medea-Phantasie"—eine unbewußte Determinante archaischer Weiblichkeitskonflikte bei einigen psychogen sterilen Frauen. In: Kämmerer, A., Schuchard, M. & Speck, A. (Eds.). *Medeas Wandlungen. Studien zu einem Mythos in Kunst und Wissenschaft* (pp. 199–231). Heidelberg: Mattes Verlag.

Leuzinger-Bohleber, M. (2001). The 'Medea fantasy': An unconscious determinant of psychogenic sterility. *International Journal of Psychoanalysis, 82*: 323–345.

Leuzinger-Bohleber, M., Engels, E.M. & Tsiantis, J. (Eds.) (2008). *The Janus Face of Prenatal Diagnostics: A European Study bridging Ethics, Psychoanalysis, and Medicine.* London: Karnac.

Leuzinger-Bohleber, M., Roth, G. & Buchheim, A. (Eds.) (2008). *Psychoanalyse—Neurobiologie—Trauma.* Stuttgart: Schattauer.

Leuzinger-Bohleber, M. et al. (2008). Interviewing women and couples after prenatal and genetic diagnostics. In: Leuzinger-Bohleber, M., Engels, E.M. & Tsiantis, J. (eds.): *The Janus Face of prenatal diagnostics: A European study bridging ethics, psychoanalysis, and medicine.* (pp. 151–218) London: Karnac.

Moser, U. (2005). *Psychische Mikrowelten—Neuere Aufsätze.* Göttingen: Vandenhoeck & Ruprecht.

Perron, R. (2001). The unconscious and primal phantasies. *International Journal of Psychoanalysis, 82*: 583–595.

Roth, G. (2001). *Fühlen, Denken, Handeln.* Frankfurt a. M.: Suhrkamp.

Sandler, J. (1986). Reality and the stabilizing function of unconscious fantasy. *Bulletin of the Anna Freud Centre, 9*: 177–194.

Sandler, J. & Sandler, A. (1994). Phantasy and its transformations: A contemporary Freudian view. *International Journal of Psycho-Analysis, 75*: 387–394.

Shane, M. & Shane, E. (1990). Unconscious fantasy: Developmental and self-psychological considerations. *Journal of the American Psychoanalytic Association, 38*: 75–92.

Notes

1. In this Chapter I try to conceptualize *"unconscious fantasy systems"* in close connection with the concept of the unconscious fantasy, which I try to develop further. With this concept I describe infantile daydreams, in which already early memories of body experiences as well as primal fantasies were included. These fantasies have probably been banished into the unconscious during the Oedipal phase (becoming part of the dynamic unconscious). They have been rewritten in the sense of

"Nachträglichkeit" again and again according to later experiences and fantasies (e.g., during adolescence and late adolescence).

2. In Euripides' version the enchantress and priestess Medea lives in Colchis on the Black Sea. She is the daughter of King Aetes and the demi-goddess Hecate. According to legend, when she first sets eyes on the stranger in her father's palace, Eros is standing behind the hero and shoots his arrow right into the heart of the king's daughter. The following events correspond to the unconscious convictions of the female patients discussed here; Medea falls victim to her own passion. She struggles with all her might against her sexual and erotic feelings, cursing the stranger and his appearance, but in vain—her love for Jason finally wins the day. She is therefore unable to turn down Jason's request to ally herself with him against her father, and gives him a lotion that endows him with superhuman strength and makes him invincible. She sings the dragon to sleep, so that Jason can kill it and snatch the Golden Fleece. She tells him what he must do to tame two wild bulls and yoke them to the plough, and how to subdue the armed men who sprout from the furrows, by casting a stone quoit among them to sow dissension in their ranks and make them kill each other. Medea then flees with Jason. When the Argonauts are surrounded by their pursuers, led by Medea's brother, she lures him into a trap and delivers him up to Jason's sword. Hearing of the successful escape and of his son's death, her father tears himself to pieces in his rage. In the legend, the tragic fate of Medea that now ensues is the revenge for this double murder. Back in Greece.

Medea first rejuvenates Jason's old father, by cutting him up and boiling him with magic spells in a cauldron, and entices the daughters of Pelias to do the same with their father. However, to avenge herself she gives them the wrong herbs, so that Pelias never returns to life. Jason and Medea must then flee to Corinth. He abandons Medea and falls in love with Creusa, King Creon's daughter. When he finally leaves Medea, apparently to secure for his two sons a future in Corinth, Medea becomes suicidal at first. But then,after an impressive scene in which she conjures up the pride of a betrayed princess,she pretends to accept Jason's decision. She sends Jason's new wife an enchanted robe and diadem. When Creusa dons them, both she and her father, who rushes to her aid, are consumed by fire. But this is not enough to quench Medea's thirst for revenge. To hurt Jason completely, she finally kills both her sons and, at the end of the tragedy, flies away with their bodies in a chariot drawn by winged serpents.

CHAPTER SIX

Inside the mother's womb: the Mother-Embryo-Dialogue

Ute Auhagen-Stephanos

Abstract

More and more couples are undergoing medically assisted fertilization, a procedure that contradicts our inherent genetic preconceptions of reproduction by means of the sexual act. The very public and technological primal scene in a laboratory may considerably interfere with the natural female ability to conceive. The frozen desire, the denied sexual act of procreation and the painful instruments all prevent any erotic pro-creative or bonding urges, exacerbating mental trauma often present in the female IVF recipients. Such traumata then interfere with fertility. Building on the bonding analysis therapy methods of Hidas and Raffai (Hidas and Raffai, 2006), I have developed the Mother-Embryo-Dialogue and introduced it into the field of reproductive medicine. I integrate this as a parameter according to Eissler (Eissler, 1953) into an ongoing psychoanalysis/psychotherapy at the time of assisted fertilization. The Mother-Embryo-Dialogue reveals the insufficiencies of the woman's own pre- and perinatal experiences, and her resulting concept of motherhood. The transference created through the Dialogue enables the mother-to-be to re-experience her own earliest body memories mentally and emotionally, even before an actual conception occurs. By using the human instruments of speech and language, we are able to transform the work of the medical instruments into a communication of the soul. According to Lévinas is the nature of language friendship and hospitality. The transitional space created by the Mother-Embryo-Dialogue can biologically increase the chances of pregnancy and establish primary maternal preoccupation. Several case studies are presented in my book *Damit mein Baby bleibt. Zwiesprache mit dem Embryo von Anfang an* (Translation: So my baby will stay. Dialogue with the embryo from the first moment) (Kösel, Munich, 2009).

Background

My thirty years of psychotherapeutic experiences with involuntarily childless women have given me multi-faceted insights into the psychogenesis of so-called female sterility.

Through my work at a fertility clinic I have experienced the helplessness, suffering, frustration, failures, and fears, but also the tenaciousness of those couples who tried to conceive a child there; often over a period of several years. I also felt sadness for the loss of the many embryos; those potential children who were unable to enter life according to their biological promise.

Repeatedly I have found in my practice that the medical diagnosis of sterility is by no means final, but rather that it is often a passing phenomenon for women in certain life situations. These women have taught me that the dividing line between physical and functional infertility is a blurred one.

Fertility or infertility are far from being purely biological events. They are also states caused by deep soul conditions which are, in turn, connected with the developmental history of the woman's own childhood and even with the period when she herself was *in utero*.

We know that the soul may say "No" to a pregnancy, (even though a child is consciously wanted) if a woman is afraid of endangering herself, or if she unconsciously fears not being ready for a child. Fear works like a contraceptive pill. In some women the desire for a child is ambiguous, so that the conscious wish for a child and the unconscious fear of the child are kept in balance.

These conditions may be categorised into three main groups (of course they may also overlap):

a. Intrapersonal factors:
    These include the woman's ambivalent feelings towards having a child, her relationship with her own parents, and childhood traumas of any kind. Illnesses, excessive demands placed on the young child, lack of basic trust and, in particular, experienced states of panic may leave behind deep psychological traces which can prevent a pregnancy.

    Some women suffered from a hidden denial of all female bodily functions. Other women were entangled in a narcissistic-perfectionist, rather more male-oriented, life programme. They fell into a depressive crisis because, although they had succeeded in achieving everything else—a job, a career, marriage—they were now failing at the "simplest task", "something any cow can do", as one of my patients said.

b. Trans-generational factors: Unresolved family conflicts can be passed on to successive generations and live on, as is well known from family research (Y. Gampel, 2005; H. Faimberg, 2005). Similarly, miscarriages, terminations, or attempted terminations by the woman's own mother may cause unconscious blocks. Very often, during psychotherapeutic conversations with "infertile" women, it became clear that they unconsciously did not trust themselves to conceive and bear a child because of unresolved dependency conflicts with their own mothers.

    Fathers too play an important role during childhood. If the fathers were absent, weak, or had penetrated the bodies of their daughters, either verbally or physically, then later they cannot provide sufficient male protection in the woman's outer and inner reality.

c. Relationship conflicts: Sometimes fertility may also be blocked by partnership conflicts within the current relationship. If the role of the father was problematic (see above), then later sexual partners cannot be experienced as sufficiently protective for 'nest-building' and the raising of children.

    Thus the yearning and desire for a child can be over-shadowed by a psychological atmosphere dominated by panic, distress and sorrow. For such women, pregnancy and birth are associated with death, or with the destruction of their own bodies. Such feelings block the inner sense of security needed to allow one's own child to grow.

Prenatal research has, over the years, provided much proof that the embryo in the mother's womb already has to cope with a wide range of distressing information; even biochemical attacks on its life. The earliest, pre-language physical sensations are stored as cellular memories and may be re-activated in situations where life decisions are made. Thus a planned, or already existing pregnancy, reactivates the very earliest bodily experiences of a woman from the time when her own mother was pregnant and gave birth to her.

Once the fertilised embryo has been transferred to the womb, the high art of medically assisted reproduction reaches its limits. The future baby is now in the warm body of the mother, its first real home and the only place which will ensure its survival. But is this desired place, which is often praised as a paradise, actually safe? In the mother's body both the immune system and epigenetic factors (i.e. factors which are external to genetics) come into play. Unlike the genes themselves, these factors react to our environment and our physical state, and they influence the growth and activity of the genes.

Only one half of the embryo's genes come from the mother; the other half comes from the father and may therefore be attacked as a foreign body by the woman's immune system. Two types of immune cells that are essential for our health are formed in the thymus, a gland situated behind the breast bone. The first group is the so-called killer cells, which send out fighters in the battle against foreign bodies and germs. An increased number of killer cells in the maternal blood may therefore precipitate in the rejection and destruction of the baby in the womb. Then there are the so-called helper cells, which oppose the killer cells and prevent auto-immune reactions. During pregnancy, these helper cells protect the unborn child in the mother's body by forming a physical barrier against possible attackers from the maternal blood.

A mother-to-be requires about two hundred specifically activated genes which will "allow" the embryo to be lodged in the uterus, as has been shown by Cathy Allen (Allen, OBGYN.net Infertility, 2009). If these genes are switched off through epigenetic blocking, no pregnancy can take place, and consequently the fertilized embryo cannot survive. These genetic switches are closely connected with the immune system which is, in turn, influenced by the physical and emotional state of the woman who desires to become a mother. Modern neurobiological research has shown that our psychological states and our biological bodily reactions should be seen as a whole, constantly influencing each other and interacting in our bodies. This is also true before and during a pregnancy. The future mother's unconscious bodily processes and reactions may endanger the child by reducing the blood supply to the uterus, or creating states of excitation and stress. Her mental experiences during a pregnancy, whether positive or negative, are transformed into the biological events of the pregnancy and cannot be separated from the further development of the unborn child.

Speak to it,—to the unborn being! That is the challenge of creating a bonding analysis between the mother and the unborn child, as developed by the Hungarian psychoanalysts, Hidas and Raffai (Hidas and Raffai, 2006). Speak to the unconceived one! became my extended starting point, one which I placed even earlier in the sequence and which I introduced into the fertility clinic scenario; the place where the goal is to make a pregnancy possible, to make the female body ready for conception and to give the embryo a chance of life. Using the dialogue right from the beginning, even before conception, we are able to extend the boundaries of reproductive medicine through this mental and spiritual lens, to give the embryo a greater chance of life, and to guide the hopeful mother-to-be. This early accompaniment of the future child deepens the bond and helps to compensate for the difficulties encountered in technological fertilization. "The nature of language is friendship and hospitality" said philosopher Emmanuel Lévinas (1993, p. 444).

The Mother-Embryo-Dialogue (M-E-D)

This dialogue is a high emotionally verbal communication between the woman who wants to get pregnant and her womb, later on also with her embryo shortly before or after conception. Often I have to support the dialogue myself speaking instead of the mother-to-be, showing her how to communicate with her later child with respect and love. Through that she can identify herself with my motherly care and attitude for her womb and her future baby.

The Mother-Embryo-Dialogue is, so to speak, a mental sensing of the body, a metaphysical return to the uterus and all its capabilities. A number of women who had previously suffered unsuccessful IVF treatments or miscarriages were able to rediscover trust in their own bodies and to become pregnant after learning the Mother-Embryo-Dialogue.

If possible, I begin the treatment with a course of psychotherapy/psychoanalysis where I can accompany the woman (or the couple) and we can begin to deal with fear of failure, sorrow, pain and feelings of guilt. In this framework we can lay the foundations for trust and opening-up, for deeper understanding and insights, and for considering possible feelings of ambivalence towards having a child.

A few weeks before the insertion of the embryo into the mother's body, we start the Mother-Embryo-Dialogue as a parameter according to Eissler (Eissler, 1953). This dialogue is divided into two steps. The first step makes provision for the container of the embryo. Only in the second step does the mother-to-be address her embryo as her future child. In the dialogue, with my guidance, the woman learns to build up contact with her reproductive organs and the future child, and to develop a safe relationship with them. Under my protection she learns to find words and expressions for her emotions and physical sensations. Before the actual arrival of the embryo in her womb, the mother-to-be is communicating naturally with a part of herself, so that with her own body and soul she may physically and emotionally attune herself, with gentle care and attention, to pregnancy and motherhood. By preparing herself for becoming a mother she is also preparing the embryo to become a child of its mother and to accept and acknowledge this individual mother. According to D. W. Winnicott a baby without a mother is unthinkable, D. W. Winnicott (1965).

A woman has to learn that the doctors of reproductive medicine cannot create her offspring by themselves. They may help, with their instruments and medications, to form an embryo and to prepare the woman hormonally for a pregnancy. But the future mother must not be viewed as another instrument among other technological instruments. It is her task alone to give the child a spirit and a soul, through love and desire.

We like to use the metaphor of hospitality for the Mother-Embryo-Dialogue. The maternal body is the house, the woman is the landlady, (or perhaps the house mother) while the womb is the guest-room and the embryo the guest. In order for conception to progress towards pregnancy we need to maintain a positive mood, a state of joy as free as possible from anxiety or fear. This will in turn influence the immune system and the relevant genes to accept rather than reject the embryo. Big beginnings should always be accompanied by enthusiasm, good wishes, loving care, trust, and a positive mental attitude. Having said this, we are only really able to celebrate and internally accept the event of conception whole-heartedly if we do this as a subject, and not when we feel that we are merely an object within the field of reproductive medicine. Precisely because the procedure of medically assisted conception initially views parents and the child as objects of technology, my therapeutic starting point is aimed at fundamentally building up a relationship from one subject (the mother or the couple) to another subject (the child).

That first and decisively important step to becoming a subject has to be made by the mother-to-be, whose desire has become frozen and whose abdomen has been denied as a sight of passion. Within the Mother-Embryo-Dialogue the whole emphasis of that spiritual and emotional work lies with her. She has to begin to love her abdomen, respect it and make it ready for conception through her own powers of self-recognition. In this way she will win back her own ability to act and feel, and will be able to build up her identity as a mother from the very beginning and at the right time. A prospective mother who is unable to do this by herself needs help in order to develop a loving dialogue with her body, and to fill her abdomen with libido and the desire to bond. In this way she will be able to escape from the paralyzing passivity and dependent submission of an object undergoing IVF procedures. She will have to find her way as a subject to a creative, aware and thoughtful possession of her procreative body and her embryo.

Both the mother and the father become "subjects" through that spiritual taking-possession of the conception of their children, knowing that the really essential part is not the medical intervention but their own physical presence and their own mental and psychological attitude. The technical assistance to bring about conception is only a stopgap measure.

> The other object is the embryo conceived with the help of medical technology, a commercial, purchased product, which is given a status as a subject by its mother only after she considers herself a subject. If there can be a dialogue from the very beginning, then the mother will be in a position to give her child the status of a subject even before conception, and certainly during the pregnancy. With the help of language, the potential mother is able to transform the work of the medical instruments into soul communication. According to Freud creates language consciousness, therefore he developed the talking cure for deciphering the Unconscious (Freud, 1911b, pp. 213–226).

The purpose of the Mother-Embryo-Dialogue is therefore to create the status of an independent subject for both the mother and the unborn child. The following case studies will demonstrate specific aspects of the transference relationship.

Three Case Studies

Case 1: Tamara—the embryo as a lump of flesh without the character of a subject

Tamara, a Russian patient from an ordinary background, was sent to us as an emergency case by the Fertility Clinic. She had always conceived spontaneously but had suffered nine miscarriages, each time during the nineteenth week of pregnancy. Now, pregnant for the tenth time, and in her seventeenth week, she was experiencing early indications of an imminent miscarriage. She felt depressed and hopeless, and worthless as a woman. She could hardly stop weeping. As a young woman she had worked in a delivery room; however, she had given this up because of the "disgusting and distressing suffering", as she named it, of the birthing women at the hands of coarse, disinterested doctors and midwives. As a result, our first hypothesis was that she miscarried her foetuses prematurely because of fear of the birth process. However, we were to discover that things were not so simple.

During the first session of the Mother-Embryo-Dialogue, Tamara wanted to get up and leave. She was mentally unable to find her uterus, she did not want to concentrate and she stubbornly refused to cooperate. When asked what she wanted to do with her baby later on, she initially had only one answer, "Bring it up." In subsequent sessions, however, she became increasingly relaxed and, eventually she eyed the couch where the Mother-Embryo-Dialogue was to take place with a passionate, almost ecstatic expression. Finally she began to talk to her child and to tell it what she was intending to do when it arrived. The signs of potential miscarriage began to retreat. Tamara explained: "I used to visualize it as a lump of flesh; now I know that it is a real little human being with its own sense of Self". In due course her son was born.

Based on Tamara's statements we can assume that she herself was seen as a worthless lump of flesh by her own mother, and not as a subject. Within the therapeutic framework, she discovered that she is an individual who is perceived and accepted by others, just like the baby in her uterus is accepted by her. She experienced the birth of herself as a person and also the birth of her unborn child as a person and a subject. For Tamara and many other women, having a child provides the possibility of endowing herself and her child with an existence, so that both may become human beings. In the end, Tamara simply needed that permission to live, so that her tenth child might finally be allowed to live too.

Case 2: Christine

Christine, aged 36, came to me after six attempts at assisted reproductive therapies (ART), which she and her husband required because of the low quality of his sperm. She had previously been pregnant for eight weeks, but then a miscarriage followed. The dead baby in her body was very frightening for her. Her thoughts towards it should have come out of her together with the tiny corpse. Otherwise she had no air to breathe. During her initial sessions she kept crying and said: "Each time my hope diminishes and my anxiety grows". She felt very bad, full of anger towards the embryos and full of fear that she would never succeed in having a child. For her this would be the worst fate imaginable. Since the time of the ART procedures she had cut herself off from all the beautiful things in her life. I suggested that she write a farewell letter to her dead embryo-baby because I noticed that she had not yet separated from it, either mentally or physically. She wrote in a letter, saying Good bye to her lost embryo (without perceiving it consciously): "We wish us that you or another child come to us and enrich our life" (citation).

We worked through her separation mourning. After some weeks she made a new discovery. Christine defined it as the "aha-experience;" her realization that she could also live a good life with her husband without children. To her amazement she realized that it was more difficult for her to accept that life did not always run according to her own plans, than to accept the shattering loss of her baby.

For the next ART we prepared carefully with the Mother-Embryo-Dialogue. After having found patience and some peace during the therapy she developed a tender care for her future embryo-child. She summarized the benefits of the Dialogue as follows:

– It helps me to unburden myself, to share the sorrow. My husband, too, puts his hand on my belly and shares with me.
– I don't feel left alone as I did in the earlier attempts to get pregnant. Now we are a team, so it is easier to get a positive result.

– The uterus and the ovaries feel respected and have more motivation to support me and have fun with the new task. I really feel connected with my sexual organs.
– I feel the energy and the force which strengthen me. After the Dialogue, I feel awake, full of energy and relaxed.

Unfortunately this pregnancy had to be terminated by miscarriage because of a genetic defect of the embryo. Despite her disappointment, the Mother-Embryo-Dialogue offered her support and consolation even in this difficult farewell scene. Whilst mourning for the lost embryo, she was able to speak with her uterus, to bid farewell to the embryo and to experience all the different stages with inner peace. In contrast to her first miscarriage, she did not try to get rid of the "bad thing" in her body too quickly and ignore her emotions. Now she could remain strong and centred on herself. In this case Christine has built up in herself an inner object to which she can refer. She has learnt to worship and to trust her body, especially her sexual organs. Perhaps this is a surrogate for a good mother figure, which she has now created in her own body. A woman who wants to become a mother and contain a child now carries within herself a kind of inner mother who can offer security and help.

This case shows that the Mother-Embryo-Dialogue cannot only facilitate a pregnancy or the chance of a pregnancy, but can sometimes also offer a positive psychic effect in cases of failure to have a child. In certain cases the Mother-Embryo-Dialogue can prevent all sorts of different psychic, psychosomatic or behaviour troubles.

Case 3: Julia—an embryo fears for its life—only four egg cells

The case of Julia will show that prenatal experience is stored in the body's memory, and may unconsciously be repeated during the woman's own pregnancy. Ursula Volz calls this perception, which is focused on the patient's physical sensing, the "sensory-empathetic dimension" in psychoanalysis. (Volz, 2010, p. 87) It becomes noticeable in countertransference and is sometimes very hard to bear. In Julia's case, during my counter-transference I had to deal with and survive the terrible fears and torments of the embryo (which Julia herself had once been) fearing for its life.

Julia, thirty-one years old, is a kindergarten teacher. Her family anamnesis was quite dramatic. Julia's maternal grandparents had undergone dreadful experiences during the war and had a tendency towards physical violence. Julia's mother suffered from a range of "women's problems", such as miscarriages, uterine miomas, haemorrhages, a total hysterectomy, and "little sex". Julia herself had underwent several broken relationships before her marriage. She has now been married for three years to a man nine years older than her, who is unable to produce sperm due to an undescended testis in early childhood. This man was born with a cleft lip and palate, and consequently had his own traumatic fears and experiences. Julia has fertility issues; one blocked Fallopian tube and endometriosis. During the therapy she referred to her endometriosis as "the sweat of fear" and said, "Fear is my big issue!"

Julia's mother, a very domineering woman, had miscarried three foetuses, first a boy, in the twenty-fifth week of pregnancy, and then a set of male twins in her twenty-third week. She then became pregnant again with Julia more quickly than the doctors had advised her or "allowed". Due to renewed indications of a possible miscarriage, Julia's mother had to rest, and was often in hospital where a cerclage (a closing of the cervix) was undertaken. The entire pregnancy with Julia was characterized by her mother's fears and depressions surrounding the life of her fourth child, and the actual delivery was a life-threatening experience for Julia. She had the umbilical cord caught around her neck, one hand was pressed against her neck, and she was finally delivered, appearing blue from lack of oxygen, with the help of a suction cup and forceps. Birth and death had been experienced as being very close together. Julia was, in her own words a "total crybaby" who never slept. She frequently suffered attacks of high temperatures of up to forty-one degrees Celsius, which required a number of stays in hospital. She had often hovered between life and death. She was an over-anxious and pregnancy-scarred child. Her parents were very reticent and gave her very little physical or emotional warmth. Two years after Julia was born, her sister arrived after an uneventful pregnancy and birth. However, her mother had actually wanted to have five boys.

Julia and her husband decided from the very beginning on assisted fertilization with donated sperm. The first IVF treatment in 2008, which failed, was followed by ovarian cysts that required an operation. The second IVF attempt in 2009 resulted in a positive pregnancy test. However, this attempt produced a damaged ovum which did not develop into an embryo, because of a genetically impaired egg cell that only formed the egg sac.

Shortly before the third IVF attempt, Julia had to have an emergency appendectomy. Was this yet another psychosomatic cry for help? At this point we had been carrying out the Mother-Embryo-Dialogue in preparation for the new conception for about two months. During this time, Julia experienced her uterus as a red ballroom with soft, pulsating walls. The more she occupied herself with this, the more confident she felt. She was proud of herself: now there was so much life, where previously she had never felt anything alive. In April 2010 she underwent the egg harvesting procedure. By contrast with previous ultrasound procedures, during which eight egg cells were observed, only four egg cells could be harvested this time. In our session the next day, she told me that she had been deeply shocked by this and was in a real state of emotional turmoil. At first her reaction seemed rather exaggerated to me, and I invited her to a Mother-Embryo-Dialogue in order to understand her feelings better and calm her down. After she had laid down on the couch, before we had even spoken a word to each other, an indescribable sense of unease began to creep over me, along with a real deathly fear. Suddenly I had the feeling that I was fighting for my life. I sensed that if I could not find the right words to draw Julia out of her state of shock and to calm her down within the next few minutes, then everything would be lost, and both she and I would be lost. I spoke more intuitively than reflectively, as if I were talking or even fighting to save my own life. I knew I had to win. While concentrating fully on this battle, I used soft soothing words and a comforting tone of voice to talk to Julia's uterus and to calm it as if it were a person. Then I "talked" with her two embryos, which were still in the incubator and about be transferred the next day, and in this way I drew Julia back into our bonding relationship.

After about fifteen minutes, as if in a trance, I felt a sense of relief and relaxation rising up in me. I had succeeded; I had survived! Julia also relaxed now, smiled lovingly at me after getting up, thanked me, and said that it had been a stroke of luck that I had found time for her unexpectedly that morning. She went away relieved, but I needed another two hours to recover from the deep exhaustion of this dreadful state of fear.

Two days later I saw Julia again, and we were able to explain her state of shock. It became clear to us that the disappearance of the other four egg cells had actually been more upsetting for her than the fact that only four egg cells had survived. Three of her mother's children had disappeared from her own mother's body, although they had been visibly present beforehand. My patient,—the fourth one!—had luckily survived, but for a long time she was also threatened by disappearance and imminent death. Then Julia explained that all of her husband's sperm had disappeared, as well as the two embryos of her first IVF experience, and the empty egg of her second one. Now—again—four egg cells had disappeared! Unconsciously she had probably repeated, within the Mother-Embryo-Dialogue, the death experience of her mother's three sons and the threat to herself during her mother's pregnancy. She, whose ego was so easily shaken by anxiety and excitement, had instantly fallen into a deep depression, and in that state, in an unconscious identification with the four egg cells, she survived—yet again—that experience of death by disappearance. Within the Mother-Embryo-Dialogue she had relived something destructive from her own early life, in order to come back to life in the present once again.

In my counter-transference I took on something with which might have failed. In that projective identification I became the embryo which she wanted to reject, or rather, her mother had wanted to reject. I had to fight, just as she had had to fight as an embryo. However, I had invited her projection, had taken her (as a guest-baby) into myself, and had, so to speak, allowed death to be my guest. I succeeded in overcoming death, just as her mother had succeeded in giving life to my patient. This battle, of course, took place in a deeply unconscious communication between the two of us, within the transference and counter-transference, through my talking. I had fought for my life, for myself and for her as a person. I took on, with my energy, something that she could not take on. Such counter-transference can be seen as a compassionate invitation by the therapist to deal with certain frightening or tormenting parts of the patient.

In the final Mother-Embryo-Dialogue, after the positive pregnancy test, she was able to see her embryo, through her inner vision, as a "little crumb", lying quietly and comfortably in a fold of the mucous membrane in her uterus. She was confident that they would cope with life together. She was happy and content with the hours and days it was with her. Her husband, too, would embrace Julia every day, which was good for all three of them.

Unfortunately, I heard two weeks later that once again an "empty egg" (caused by a genetically impaired egg cell) had nested in her uterus. Although Julia was deeply saddened by this at first, she recovered from the shock much more quickly this time, following a D & C (curettage). She has not yet decided whether she will try for another pregnancy after all these difficult experiences.

In cases such as Julia's, I have to take over and work through the painful part of the patient's own earliest prenatal and perinatal phases in order to free them from their deep anxiety about having a child of their own. I would like to add that this case does not represent a typical Mother-Embryo-Dialogue. Normally the dialogue is not so overwhelming for the therapist, but a much calmer and more positive experience.

Conclusion

One could consider the Mother-Embryo-Dialogue as a kind of role-playing education or training. My presence allows the mother-to-be and her embryo to "play" at being mother and child, thus creating a new common reality and transitional space. In the course of the Mother-Embryo-Dialogue, a narrative develops which allows the patient, perhaps for the first time in her life, to build up a relationship of respect, perhaps even of worship, towards her whole body; and especially her sexual and reproductive organs. This narrative has a specific impact on the the smooth muscles and the blood vessels. It is interesting to note that we have also seen cases where women have been cured of dysmenorrhoea after having learned the dialogue with the uterus.

I should like to end with a statement by a patient, which summarizes my work very well. "It is a great good fortune to discover a new world and to live it so immediately. I feel great thankfulness in myself because, in the past, I had always had too high an expectation of my body functioning like a machine."

References

Allen, C. (2009). OBGYN.net Infertility (www.obgyn.net) 25th annual conference IVF 1 July 2009.

Auhagen-Stephanos, U. (2007), *Wenn die Seele nein sagt.* Unfruchtbarkeit: Goldmann, München.

Auhagen-Stephanos, U. (2008). Der psychoanalytische Blick auf natürliche Fortpflanzung und technische Reproduktion. In: Herzog-Schröder, G./ Gottwald, F.T. u. Walterspiel, V. (Hrsg.), Fruchtbarkeit unter Kontrolle? (pp. 249–278). Frankfurt/New York: Campus Verlag.

Auhagen-Stephanos, U. (2008). Früher Dialog und Kinderwunsch Vom Fleischklumpen zum Menschen. *Prenatal and Perinatal Psychology and Medicine*, Vol. 20, Nr. 3/4,:. 257–268.

Auhagen-Stephanos, U. (2009.). Biology without Desire-From a Transaction to a Wish. *Prenatal and Perinatal Psychology and Medicine* Vol.21, Nr. 3/4: 199–209.

Auhagen-Stephanos, U. (2009). *Damit mein Baby bleibt. Zwiesprache mit dem Embryo von Anfang an.* München: Kösel.

Auhagen-Stephanos, U. (2010). Technisch erzeugte Kinder—arme Kinder. *Journal for Theory and Practice of Child and Adolescent Psychoanalysis and Psychodynamic Psychotherapy Heft 146, XLI. Jg.* 2: 155–172.

Auhagen-Stephanos, U. (2010). Bonding takes place before conception. *Prenat Psychol Medicine, Vol. 22, 1–2*: 106–112.

Eissler, K. R. (1953). The Effect of the Structure of the Ego on Psychoanalytic Technique *J. Amer. Psychoanal. Assn 1*: 103–143.

Faimberg, H. (2005). *The Telescoping of Generations*. Routledge,: London and New York.

Freud, S. (1911b). Formulations on the Two Principles of Mental Functioning. *S.E. 12.*

Freud, S. (1914 g). Remembering, Repeating and Working- Through (Further Recommendations on the Technique of Psychoanalysis. *S.E.*

Gampel, Y. (2005). *Ces parents qui vivent á travers moi.* Librairie Arthéme Fayard.

Hidas, G. and Raffai, J. (2006). *Nabelschnur der Seele.* Psychosozial-Verlag, Gießen.

Lévinas, E. (1993). *Totalität und Unendlichkeit.* Alber, Freiburg:München.

Volz- Boers, U. (2010). *You have touched a skin inside me that lies beneath my male skin.* Int J Prenat Perinat Psychol Medicine *Vol 22,* (2010) p. 86ff. Mattes: Heidelberg

Body sensations in the counter—transference. *Prenatal Perinatal Psychol Medicine 22, 1–2*: 86–95.

Winnicott, D. W. (1965). *Maturational Processes and the Facilitating Environment.* The Hogarth Press: London.

PART III

THE BODY AS A SCENE OF CRIME

CHAPTER SEVEN

The female body as cultural playground

Marianne Springer-Kremser

Abstract

The focus of this Chapter is on the vicissitude of the disposability of the female body. After a short summary of aspects of female sexual development, the culture-specific demands and tensions arising from the interaction between cultural and psychodynamic conditions are stressed. Case vignettes from the gynecological psychosomatic outpatient's clinic will demonstrate the influence of cultural and socio-political demands on individual female suffering. Socio-political positions and regulations concerning female reproductive capacity influence pathological development, especially conflicts concerning the disposal of the female body. Finally, examples of female creativity are presented to illustrate this conflict. The process of civilisation is a modification, which the vital process experiences under the influence of a task that is set by Eros and instigated by Ananke—by the exigencies of reality; and that this task is one of uniting separate individuals into a community bound together by libidinal ties. (Freud, S.E.)

Introduction

In my capacity as a psychoanalyst, a psychiatrist for a gynecological ward, as well as head of a psychosomatic liaison service; the many facets of suffering among female patients in connection with their bodies have consistently fascinated me, just as the pain inflicted by various institutions on the female body and psyche has outraged me (Springer-Kremser, 1997). A drawing by Aloise, a long-term patient at the clinic in Lausanne was a dominant feature in my office at the clinic. Aloise had created lovely pencil and coloured pencil drawings, mainly of women, in a simple exercise book (Figure 1). In her imagination, Aloise disposes of female bodies and she re-fashions them.

> On the development of an autonomic picture of the individual person, their own body, and a conception concerning its disposability.

Freud described the ego primarily as a body-ego. Bodily functions were used as models in order to describe psychic functions. (2009) Bronstein observes, that incorporation and evacuation became models for the concepts of introjection and projection. The development of an individual coenaesthesia, (the ability to establish boundaries between oneself and others, perceptions of vulnerability and integrity, the real or symbolic meaning ascribed to individual orifices of the body (mouth, vagina, anus)), are relevant to a theory of female psychosexuality. In the following passages, such developmental processes shall be discussed in detail, as they significantly affect the perception of the bodily disposability.

Body patterns/body self

There is no doubt that primal female sexuality influences children. The fact that there is no doubt as to the primal female sexuality of the child has influence on the child. Consequently the girl in the respective society and family will develop a feeling of being female. This feeling is furthered by vaginal sensations, among other body sensations, as has been described by Greenacre (Greenacre, 1950). The child's sexual identity also comes from the manner in which main attachment figures interact with their infantile body.

A "good enough mother" (Winnicott, 1965) has the ability to correctly identify the child's needs and react to them, whilst not ascribing

Figure 1.

her own meanings to them. When the child cried, she is capable of judging whether it is hungry, suffering from wind, or simply need affection. She will understand the source of discomfort and will find a suitable remedy. If the child's needs are misinterpreted according to the mother's needs, the child develops a primal distrust. Over time, the child, being dependent on its surroundings, loses the capacity to correctly interpret its own body-signals. This re-interpretation of the child's body signals, also the mother's exploitation of the wishes for dependency, and an extreme bondage on the instinctual drive-level, as described by Stierlin (1974), help maintain in the imagination the total disposibility of the child's body by the mother.

Object relations

The smallest mental entities are unconscious fantasies, which gain special significance during adolescence. These fantasies help to establish an affective connection between an image of an object of relation, and an image of oneself. An object of relation is an object representation, even if it may be primitive and incomplete. It may include only partial-objects, for example the breast of the mother. An image of oneself can be understood as self-representation, however primitive and limited to parts. For example this may be the mouth, instead of the entire person.

The internalization of such interactions represents the initial structuring of the inner world. This inner object-relation is composed of an object-picture interacting with the self, and a self-picture interacting with the object. An affective imaging of the object picture and the self-picture under the influence of the predominant derivatives of instinctual drives at the moment of interaction.

These earliest introjections are essentially shaped by the affective conditions pervading the little girl's mind and imagination. A first internal structure emerges when entities with a similar affective valence combine. This leads to the development of good internal object images in affective connection with images of a good self, as well as to images of a bad internal object, in affective combination with a bad self, which is also consistent with a bad body self.

The positively or negatively charged self-and-object images become more and more differentiated, which makes for an increasing separation of self and object images, and a stabilization of the ego. In a further stage of development, the affective divergent images (representations, internal objects) will, by means of the synthetic function of the ego, be integrated into such images as increasingly do justice to the object of relation in its entity, as a physical and mental person.

The ego as a structure expands and improves its functions through a growing ability to use repression as a defence mechanism. Furthermore, the superego increasingly emerges as an autonomous authority with depersonalized commands, prohibitions and ideal conceptions. All this contributes to the ability to perceive and live the external world and one's own physicality with an increasing sense of reality. (Schuster, 2010)

Recognition of sexual dimorphism—the early genital phase

Between the eighteenth and the twenty-fourth month of their lives, children gradually become capable of recognizing their own sex. Boys react with an increased activity. A boy is able to touch his genitals and the penis involuntarily grows larger. It is therefore an interesting, awesome object, which needs to be protected. Girls react to the discovery of sexual dimorphism with an increasing ability to symbolize. They become creative. They are able, for example, to express themselves graphically to a greater extent (Roiphe & Galenson, 1972).

This anatomy-oriented difference may mean that little girls react with envy; they want something others have, as is often the case with children at a young age. To explore their genitals, girls have to resort to their imagination, which also explains the creative surge. The girl's envy of the penis disappears in the course of normal development; the more the girl is accepted and valued as such. The girl's fear of castration is initially related to the imagination, as the penis was taken away from the girl. Later, the fear of castration can be understood symbolically as the fear of having lost something irretrievably; to have been cut off from something indispensable. The roots of this fear reach deeply into the mother/child symbiosis, to feelings of helplessness and the possibility of being abandoned, to the dawning awareness that child and mother are separate beings. This feeling of total helplessness is an inevitable primal feeling, which originates from the long developmental period and the resulting dependency of human beings (Chasseguet-Smirgel, 1970).

The self image which emerges is not very stable; it is in a state of dynamic interaction with internal and external realities. The body also disappoints us time and again with constant changes or pain, especially in adolescence, when the integrated body experience is easily undermined (Pacteau, 1994).

Adolescence

The way the mother deals with the infantile body becomes accentuated during adolescence. If the mother mainly satisfies her own needs for contact and affection, and the child's needs are not sufficiently realized, the girl becomes fixated on this particular treatment and on this infantile body. Every change in the infantile body and therefore also of its inner representation may be experienced as disobedience requiring punishment, as the superego watches over the identification pattern with the mother (Laufer, 1981). The loss of sexual neutrality at the beginning of adolescence poses a threat. All these confusions may lead to adolescent girls hating their body. After all, the strong sexual and aggressive content of the imagination also causes intense feelings of guilt. The mother, who used to have a stimulating as well as a protective function for the girl's body, is now perceived as adversarial. Some body modifications such as exaggerated piercing might for example be perceived as self-punishment to reduce guilt-feelings.

Adolescent girls very often have the feeling that their mother knows everything about them. The menarche puts such girls in a difficult situation, because to touch their own body, especially their genitals, means to perceive that the mother has equipped them with a body whose maturity is now experienced as superfluous, troublesome and abnormal. It is exactly this sort of tension which creates a very close bond between the girl and her mother. Manipulations with the girl's body and the feeling of absolute control by the mother, play a large role in which the disposability of the body is contested.

With the end of adolescence, the sense of reality ought to be stabilized, the identification process concluded, and a conception of the body's disposability formed. The end of adolescence however, as Blos has already noted, is open. In contrast to other civilized nations—or "primitive" ones—the rituals of our western culture do not seem to have within them the power to empower children to become fully-fledged members of the "adult culture" with defined rights over their own bodies (Blos, 1973).

Puberty rituals in primitive cultures, despite their cruelty, clearly mark the beginning of adulthood and thus the disposability over the own body in a given culture, as the following digression shows.

Different forms of initiation rites on different levels of civilization for pre-adolescent children

Winterstein described these often very cruel initiation rites in his text, *Girls' puberty rites and their traces in fairy tales* (1928). In many cultures these rites, which are often brutal, mark the transition from child to sexually mature, socially adequate human being. This collection of puberty rites includes African countries, Australia, Indonesia, the North and South American Indians, and also East Asiatic peoples, as in Cambodia.

The following ceremonies/rites are schematically identified:

1. The girl is usually isolated after the first menstruation (darkness, solitude). She is looked after by an older woman, who brings her food. She is instructed by her in sexual matters, or, sometimes by a medicine man. The girl often occupies herself rehearsing domestic activities such as weaving, braiding, and spinning. She has to pass certain tests, such as being whipped or bitten by ants, which are supposed to prepare her for the pains of childbirth.
2. She is sometimes tattooed or painted.
3. Sexual operations are conducted (e.g., excision of the clitoris, circumcision of the small labia and artificial defloration).
4. Other rites connected with imagining death and reincarnation are performed. Among these are ablutions, baths, a new name, and new clothing.
5. The candidate is "freed" from the powers of a menstruation-demon (for example a snake) by certain rites.
6. Magical activities are designed to express the wish for easy childbirth.
7. Symbols of coitus may also play a role. Dances, songs, eating often conclude the initiation rite.
8. Immediately after the termination of her exile the girl is introduced to a sex life. Her first sexual experience is with an older man, usually a chieftain, or priest.

Formerly, in psychoanalytic interpretation, the father's incestuous inclination towards his daughter was staved off by the girl's exile. Interestingly, however, her defloration is entrusted to an elder or priest; in other words, a father substitute. The girl's defloration outside of wedlock, that is, before maritally sanctioned sexual intercourse, may also express the intention to relieve the bridegroom from a dangerous performance, which mobilizes fears of castration. For him defloration is part of a taboo. The real wounds of traditional culture do also have a symbolic meaning which can be connected to the individual psychodynamic.

The rituals in our culture e.g., bar mitzvah, bar minha, confirmation; in contrast to traditional culture, do not hold the power to help young people terminate adolescent development, and to feel themselves to be adequate members of the "adult" culture with clear ability to dispose of their body.

Clinical examples

Our present socio-cultural scenario seems to produce complex situations, which manifest themselves in conflicts/symptoms with which we are confronted in the psychosomatic outpatient clinic. In addition, the technical development, especially fertility technologies and cosmetic surgery, fosters self-damaging actions.

Intra-psychic and externalized dramas which revolve around the disposability of the own body and, as the case may be, its total disposability through others, are expressed, for example in the following:

- The wish of a twenty-two year old patient for a hysterectomy without somatic indication after long-lasting sexual abuse by her stepfather with her mother's apparent toleration. The experience of being totally disposed of by others, as in sexual assault, rape or incest, stimulates body-violating mechanisms. These mechanisms also could be seen as a desperate attempt to re-establish disposability over one's own body. Lemma describes different unconscious fantasies, which might underpin body modification and cosmetic surgery. The reclaiming fantasy, where one's own body could be experienced as container of other's (the mother's) hostile projections. Lemma suggests that "(R)emoval ... of a body part thus serves the function of rescuing the self from an alien presence , which is now felt to reside within the body; that is the modification (here the hysterectomy) is driven by what I am calling the reclaiming fantasy" (Lemma, 2010, p. 136).

- The wish of a thirty-eight year old female patient to continue futile in-vitro fertilizations (IVF) to heal an unexplained infertility. She had already had six failed IVF attempts with her husband's sperm and was assigned to the psychosomatic gynecological clinic. These IVF attempts had all been carried out at a private clinic in a nearby country. Because the husband worked in this country, the couple had met there solely for the IVF for longer than one year. Behind the patient's shrill and demanding manner, a deep distress and confusion were perceptible. Also evident was her distance towards her own body, and towards her body functions. Her psychic organization showed an inclination towards identity diffusion; she could neither describe her partner nor herself. Her sense of reality and reality-testing was close to borderline personality organization while her response to others was limited entirely to self-reference. The painful, humiliating insufficiency, which she tried to hide behind her demanding behaviour revealed the narcissistic wound, which Lemma described as central to the perfect match fantasy, clustering around an idealized self with an idealized object—the foetus? The mother-image?

Body-modification can be seen as an endeavour to accentuate the disposability of the body and definition of borders towards the mother, to remove the body from maternal control and to symbolize sexual maturity. In other words, to be adult. The wish for cosmetic alteration of individual body-parts in order to match an idea of beauty or maybe to fulfill other unconscious demands becomes increasingly important.

Freud himself stated "Regrettably, Psychoanalysis has not much to say about beauty". (1910)—Early female psychoanalysts also contributed to this topic and Riviere with her concept of 'femininity as a mask' captured the significance of "beauty" in a given culture (1929).

The two clinical examples clearly demonstrate the cross-linking of individual and intra-psychic structures and the socio-politically motivated right to dispose of the female body. Who disposes of the female body? Is it the individual woman? Which institutions presume to dispose of the female body; and by what means? What desperate measures are undertaken by women in order to prove; partly for themselves, partly in connection with their environment; that they are in possession of this right to dispose, that they are mistresses in their own house? Throughout the female life cycle, in connection with pregnancy and childbirth, women are directly or indirectly at the mercy of institutions, the medical system being the most obvious. The increasing medicalization and economization of the female life cycle facilitate this disposability.

The subjective image of disposability is therefore of interest. Which are the relevant fields of interaction between psycho-sexual development, and the differentiation of internal and external object relations, which cause the body's disposability, or else the helpless admission of disposability through others? The self-destructive dimension of the desperate attempts to dispose of the person's own body, together with the attempts to master the fear of their own destructive power, and attempts to avert the persecution by internalized evil, are truly shattering.

The fact that individual institutions or their representatives assume the right to dispose of bodies, especially those under their care, not only affects women. This is evident from the current dispute about sexual abuse within institutions, especially the Catholic Church.

Finally, we should remind ourselves that psychoanalysis always had a radical edge, and so have certain female artists. In works of performance art, the debate with structures of power is immanent. Female artists, who wanted to express the concern of the female sex radically, seized the possibilities, which offered Body Modification in this respect. Similar to the "Viennese Actionism"; a violent movement in 20th-century art, some female artists wanted to highlight social structures of power and suppression by symbolic and metaphoric actions, which included self-violation. The moment of substitutional actions elucidating intended shocks by confrontation with real violations has achieved considerably significance (Springer, 2010).

References

Blos, P. (1973). *Adoleszenz*. Stuttgart: Klett.

Bronstein, C. (2009). Negotiating development: corporeal reality and unconscious fantasy in adolescence. *Bulletin of the British Psychoanalytical Society*, 45: 17–26.

Chasseguet-Smirgel, J. (1970). *Female Sexuality: New Psychoanalytic Views*. Ann Arbor: University of Michigan Press.

Freud, S. (1930a). Civilization and its Discontents. S.E., 21 57–146. London: Hogarth Press.

Greenacre, P. (1950). Special problems of early female sexual development. *Psychoanalytic Study of the Child*, 5: 112–138.

Laufer, M. E. (1981). The adolescent's use of the body in object relationship and in the transference. *Psychoanalytic Study of the Child, 36*: 163–180.

Lemma, A. (2010). Copies without originals: The psychodynamics of cosmetic surgery. *Psychoanalytic Quarterly, 79, Number 1*.

Pacteau, F. (1994). *The Symptom of Beauty*. London: Reaction Books.

Riviere, J. (1929). Femininity as a Mask. In: Riviere, J. (Ed.) *The Inner World and Joan Riviere: Collected papers 1929–1958* (pp.) London: Karnac, 1991.

Roiphe, H. & Galenson, E. (1972). Object loss and early sexual development. *Psychoanalytic Quarterly, 42*: 73–90.

Schuster, P. (2010). Art, Qualität und Entwicklung der Objektbeziehungen. In: Löffler-Stastka H., Schuster P., Springer-Kremser M. (Eds.) *Psychische Funktionen in Gesundheit und Krankheit* (pp) Wien: facultas.wuv, pp 29-30, 2010.

Springer, A. (2010). Extreme body modification. In: Barkhoff, J., von Engelhardt D (Hrsg) Körperkult—Körperzwang- Körperstörung im Spiegel von Psychopathologie, Literatur und Kunst. Heidelberg: mattes-Verlag, 2010.

Springer-Kremser, M., Jandl-Jager, E. & E: Presslich-Titscher E. (Eds.). The Triage-function of a psychosomatic liaison-service for gynaecological Patients. *Journal of Psychosomatic Obstetric Gynecology, 18*: 220–228, 1997.

Stierlin, H. (1974). *Eltern und Kinder im Prozess der Ablösung*. Frankfurt: Suhrkamp.

Winnicott, D. W. (1965). *The Maturational Processes and the Facilitating Environment*. London: The Hogarth Press.

Winterstein, A. (1928). *Die Pubertätsriten der Mädchen*. Leipzig, Internationaler Psychoanalytischer Verlag, 1928.

CHAPTER EIGHT

Wetlands (Feuchtgebiete)—or: rage, body and hysteria

Thomas Ettl

"Les genous sales sont le signe d'une fille honnête."

—Brouardel, cited by Freud, 1913

Abstract

This Chapter deals with eighteen year-old Helen, protagonist of the novel *Wetlands* by Charlotte Roche, a 2008 bestseller. Helen seems the likely representation of a young, modern form of hysteria. With her licentious, permissive sexual life she is trying to solve her various problems. She looks for confirmation that she is desirable, tries to master her excitement resulting from her Oedipal phase and hopes to comfort her loneliness as a child of divorce. Moreover she wants to explore her body, to complete her body image and finally to restore the unity of the anatomic, visible body and the sensitive body (*Leib*), which was destroyed by her mother's hygiene rituals. With a very painful self-mutilation she seeks to gain control over her parents. They should re-unite as a couple, so that Helen can feel herself as a child of love, which is required for her narcissistic balance.

Medical technology and lifestyle drugs seem to make possible the separation of the anatomical body from the sensitive body (in German "*Leib*"). The *Leib* smells, becomes dirty, tired, hurts, aches, ages, shows signs of birth and illness decay. In short, the *Leib* gives the body vitality and essence. In the cult of beauty, the *Leib* is the epitome of the messy, ugly, and nasty, and will, be dispelled as incompatible with conceptions of beauty. The *Leib* becomes a faecal object and an enemy that must somehow be overcome, because it threatens the ideal of the youthful body. The plastic surgeon acts with the scalpel against the body and separates the "couple of body and *Leib*" (Böhme, 2003). Cosmetic surgery is an invasive intervention to health, a self-mutilation delegated to the surgeon. The youthful body will be exposed as a trophy, the *Leib* however displaced from the private and public awareness. As it is the *Leib* that gives the body its individuality and vibrancy, with its eradication human beings are inflicted by a body image disturbance and lose their distinguishing features and individual appearance.

The novel *Wetlands* by Charlotte Roche (2008) deals with the body, the *Leib* and self-mutilation. It is a protest against the cleanliness of the cult of beauty. In fact, the *Leib*, maligned and suppressed in the cult of beauty, returns from exile in this novel and floods the aestheticized, embellished body with its body fluid, literally until behind the ears. The "couple of body and *Leib*" is re-united.

The protagonist is Helen, a child of divorce, who states frankly, the ass belongs to her when she has sex and therefore it is subjected to compulsory modern shaving. When shaving she catches a heavily bleeding anal fissure, so she must be hospitalized. The hospital is the main setting for the novel. Helen reveals how she, lecherous, wildly and experimentally explores her wetlands, presenting to everyone her naked back. She gives men access to her rectum, which she seems to confuse with the *L'Origine du Monde* (Courbet, 1865). Soon it becomes clear: Her manic exhibition is reminiscent of an embarrassing scene from her primary school. Helen associates the airy feeling behind her back, with a childhood nightmare where she is waiting for the school bus and realizes she forgot to wear underwear. At home this would not matter as much, but in public she would rather die than be discovered as naked under her skirt. This matters more as it occurs in a time when the boys would play with girls "lift girls" skirts' (Roche, *Wetlands*, p. 23).

The shamefully child's wish to show mutually the Popo (Freud, 1908c, p. 222) the now eighteen year-old has turned to shameless lust.

She interprets an interest by men in her ass as a special attention and proof of love. Since childhood her *mons veneris* has served to reassure herself and to sleep. It was the most important part of her bodily centre, nice, warm and perfectly situated at hand. It helped her to fall asleep if she stroked it. Her *mons veneris* appears to have been her safe place ever since.

Helen's research of her body leads the reader to the basic source of that obsession, which scientists or artists in their activity must also have: a form of erotic excitement, originating in the wetlands of the body that the child explores. Freud once so offended the public with this view and until today parts of the feuilletonists still appear outraged. But Helen confirms Freud's view: Relentlessly she reports what moves children in their sexual explorations, which they are unable to communicate.

Above all, the novel provides insight into the process of appropriation of the body-*Leib*-unit, which each child has to achieve at the beginning of his life and in puberty must continue under the influence of body modification. Equipped only with an anatomical body in the beginning, the child lives in a projection of the mother long before being born and created as body *gestalt:* her "Childimago". This concept refers to the entire archive of conscious and unconscious fantasies and beliefs about her child. The Childimago comprises the history of the child in the mother, her transmissions to the child. Sometimes the name of a child implies the nature of the parents' specific Childimago, i.e. when the child gets the name of a celebrated star. It's crucial that the child in the course of its development can free itself from the maternal body projections, for the body must be produced by the infant itself in a kind of collage. Its materials are milk, porridge, snot, mucus, looks and oral fantasies, with which it takes parts from the mother's body to become a sort of collage. For this purpose the mother is touched, palpated, explored, cut into pieces; in short, she is used by the infant.

Helen describes this process from an adolescent point of view. She needs other women in order to take over parts of their bodies. For this she looked at school for female friends. If she had her period at the same time as her best friend, Irene, they exchanged their used tampons in the school toilet, carefully examined them, and then stuffed them into their own vagina. So they were connected through her "old, stinky blood" in a "blood sisterhood" (Roche, *Wetlands*, p. 114).

Helen has meanwhile learnt more about the female body with prostitutes. She doesn't dare to ask her mother or a girlfriend to spread her pussy for her, in order to get a view of it. Also she would like to change her small breasts with the big ones of her girlfriend. A plastic surgeon could cut off both their breasts and sew them on each other.

The constitutive function which other persons have in the body-image-construction, has also the mirror. Helen says her bathroom was full of useful mirrors, helping her to peek into her pussy. Obviously, by stroking her Venus hill, Helen feels exciting sensations in her genitals, but she lacks the visual representation to be able to locate the sensations. Only then the unity of body and *Leib* would be accomplished.

The mirror allows for the completion of her body image and at the same time ends the painful and alienating feeling that another would see more of her body than she does. Helen explains the emancipative function a mirror can have for a woman. She would otherwise not see her pussy if only viewed from above, unlike a man, when he is lying with his head between her legs in bed. She would see only a pile of hair and hints of her two labia. As a woman she is built so strangely: hidden from her own view.

Here she picks up what I would like to call the "mirror phase of feminism", a time during the eighties, when women were offered to overcome their limited body awareness by collective self-checks in weekend seminars. Helen wants to know how her mucus smells and tastes. Indignantly she says she refuses to make her legs wide for any-one male, and has no idea how she looks, smells and tastes. She doesn't want to be mirrored exclusively in male gaze only.

By her descriptions we can imagine what a toddler experiences when he transforms his anatomical body into his personal unit of body-*Leib*. To succeed it needs a mother's love, which wraps the child in a warm-ing narcissistic libido. If energy is missing, the child resigns, there is no narcissistic cathexis and he or she remains lifelong dependent on the narcissistic supply of the other for their body-feeling. Helen, too, is indeed not free of this narcissistic need.

Bringing the own *Leib* to life always simultaneously means to exploit the mother. She must not only offer her body, but also resign to the child's needs in order to leave her Childimago behind. Some mothers refuse to be used; others force their child into their body *gestalt,* which can create body image disorders such as anorexia. In any case, the child fails in its body-*Leib-gestalt.* The child experiences his body as foreign, and does not care what happens to it. For this reason patients with eat-ing disorders in the course of an analytic treatment usually come to a point where they look for intimate friendship with another female. The friendship may show similar erotic features to the normal early mother-daughter relationship. Helen explains that these patients want to experience the body of the girlfriend to confront their own body as female. This lesbian stage is important for patients because they return to that point of her life in which the body-*Leib* construction was disrupted. They venture towards a new beginning.

Overall Helen presents to the reader as a *Venus opened* (Didi-Huberman, 1999). In his same named study the art historian Didi-Huberman looks at the entanglement between nudity, violence, beauty and disease. He quotes the Benedictine abbot Odo of Cluny, who thinks that feminine grace is entirely in the skin. If men could look into the interior of the body, the sight of women would provoke disgust. "The feminine grace", writes Odo, "is nothing more than slime, blood and bile. Considering what the nostrils, throat, abdomen hide: Dirty all over. […] how can we desire to hug nothing more than a sack full of excrement?" (Didi-Huberman, Venus opened, p. 68). That was the strategy of a pious man hoping to escape temptation by disgust; a projective identification, as we say today. The abbot sees himself in the woman.

Helen doesn't care for this disgust. She does not want to be a beautiful Helena, in order to become kidnaped by Paris, she wants to be embraced as a bag of manure, poured out for examination, with pleasure, as she points out. She wants the inside, not the surface, to be loved. The novel gives the *Leib*, sacrificed in the cult of beauty, a place and a right of its own. It wants to bring together what under the loss of its vitality, sensuality and individuality, was once artificially separated one from the other. Unfortunately Helen misses the goal. We see the *Leib* purely as it is. Now body, beauty and grace threaten to disappear. This reversal from the inside out has further important reasons; the reversal appears again at the end of the novel, when Helen says to Robin, her male nurse, "I only sleep with you if you can suck a pony's insides out through its asshole." (Roche, Wetlands, p. 229) In *Wetland* Helen turns inside out, of parts of the feuilletonists celebrated as a new way of female sexual emancipation.

One is tempted to become blurred from the manic excursions of the protagonist in their wetlands, for what still gets to the point in the text. Who looks deeply into the vagina turns blind, warns an Arabian proverb. Helen feels lonely and is trying to expel the desolate loneliness with sexual arousal. The louder pleasure in *Wetlands* sounds, the louder shrills its true function. It is needed to comfort and to answer the nagging question: Am I valuable, am I loved by my parents, even if I am not hygienic and an easy to care for child? As young children want to have admired their faeces, which is part of their self, by Mama, so Helen. She would like to have her open body appreciated by her lovers and her readers. This has less to do with desire, but more to do with soul distress. To keep to the jargon, Helen has it not only *on the* ass, she feels herself shitty, buggered-up. She is broken. That is, her horniness does not comfort her—until the last page of the book. Then Helen emerges as a modern hysteric.

And also the public enthusiasm for the novel can be explained as a collective, hysterical defence against despair and hopelessness, a defence which victims of sexual violence often experience, except that Helen is practicing violence against herself. We are confronted with a "confusion of tongues" (Ferenczi), which occurs when a childs admission of tenderness and recognition of needs is misinterpreted by an adult as sexual seduction, and answered accordingly. Helen apparently has had experiences with such confusions, and admits she collects her tears in the cap of a water bottle. She hides it so that "none of these idiots knock it over. There's a lot of pain in that little vessel" (Roche, Wetlands, p. 175). Helen shows her tender, sensitive side that she hides behind her coarser sexuality. Her sensitivity is evident as she describes, she clings to every part of her body, even if it is hidden like the anus, from which she had to let go a piece by surgery. Helen is indignant that it was removed when she was without consciousness, and cannot see it, because it immediately ends up in the trash (ibid., p. 8). Thus she articulates a sense of loss that, for example, is mostly denied in cosmetic surgery.

Helen is so concerned with her body because she suffers from a complex trauma. Even the cover of the book in the German edition marks the way for the reader: It depicts a sticking-plaster, printed in the relief just like a Braille. Which wound is the sticking-plaster for? A summary of the fictional events, liberated from the sexual dialogue, reveals the trauma. Helen is a child of divorced parents and wishes her parents could fall in love once more. Then she could feel safe. She hopes her hospital stay can lead to the love between the parents.

However hard she tries, it will not succeed. Therefore Helen tries for an extended faked stay. She calculates that the longer she stays in hospital, the greater her chance of bringing together her parents. When she recognizes her hope is too rash, she looks for more efficient means to cheat. She injures herself by ramming the pedal steel of her bed in her already battered anus. Screaming in pain and trembling she feels exactly the pedal penetrating the wound. "It hurts like hell", says Helen. She cries; tears at the top, blood at the bottom. Nevertheless, she does not loose of sight of her calculation. "I need to lie down fast or I'm going to faint right here. That would ruin the exercise. I need to be found lying in bed so that I can pretend it just happened to me as I was lying there" (ibid., p. 174).

The reader has to imagine a deliberately induced and calculated self-mutilation. Helen's motivation is clearly her immense emotional tension. She wants to create an emergency situation to reunite her parents. Yet her self-mutilation is simultaneously an expression of her great narcissistic rage about the fact that her parents do not correspond to her wishes. She cannot influence the object.

Severe loss of blood makes an emergency operation necessary. The concern of her doctors faces Helen with her fear of death, which she herself had previously denied. That her otherwise so quiet anaesthesiologist appears panicked concerns her. Now she regrets her actions, and does not want to die just to reunite her parents.

This shows two things. First, Helen needs take the concern of the other to feel and recognize her own emotional state. Second, her self-mutilation is para-suicidal. It throws a light on Helens precarious narcissistic state. "Emergency operation, man o man, that sounds bad. But also important and exciting. As if I'm important." (ibid., p. 179). "Whether I bleed to death or not. Very defiant, Helen, but stupid. You don't want to die." (ibid., p. 180). Now we can see the risk of suicide and its typical fantasies. If she were dead, that would be a perfect reason for her parents to find each other again in their sorrow. "Great plan, Helen, except you wouldn't be able to experience their reunion. If you die, you won't be watching down from above." (ibid., pp. 180–181). Helens fantasies confirm the clinical opinion that self-mutilation is often paired with suicidal intent.

In a literary sense, the idea of marrying her parents off may be seen as a kitschy (trashy) topos. Looked at psychodynamically, the severity of her symptoms indicate a deeply distressing concern of hers, that does hurt like hell. The painful self-mutilation is an appeal to the parents, not to deny her the life-elixir of becoming a couple. The narcissistic wishes emerge. If her parents were a couple, their sexuality would be valuable, and Helen could feel she was a valuable offspring of their love.

Helen's parents, however, are not there. It has all been in vain. "Where are my parents? For fucks sake! This is not happening. They've abandoned me here. I figured … they'd be worried and come straight here. Nothing. Nobody here." (ibid., p. 190). Helen is sure other parents would be sitting in hospital or hanging on the phone in order not to miss an emergency call. She knows how better parents would be and suffers from the disinterest of her own. If the parents were "sick with worry" about her, as she says, that would be the highest amount of narcissistic attention. She would be important and thus existent. As a child of divorced parents, however, she must feel like waste.

Instead of her parents Helen's male nurse has to look after her narcissistic wound.

Helen: "I'm scared, Robin."
Robin: "Me too, for you." (ibid., p. 183)

"Understood", says Helen. "He loves me. I didn't know. Sometimes it happens that quickly." (ibid., p. 183) She takes his hand, looks into his eyes and tries to smile. Her tension releases. She has received from Robin, what she ardently desired from her parents: attention and concern.

Helen tells us that after she became eighteen she let sterilize herself despite wanting a child ever since she could remember. But the sterilization (also a self-mutilation) would have broken a recurrent pattern in her family. All female members; great-grandmother, grandmother, mother and herself were first born. They all suffered from bad nerves, and were disturbed and unhappy. She also had not wanted to give her mother a chance to dispose of her womb, because her mother would say: "How much do you want to bet that when you have your first child it's a girl?" (ibid., p. 36) This phrase is no longer threatening to Helen. The sterilization serves the same purpose as the loss of weight in anorexic patients: to ward off the maternal access to her *Leib*.

Helen's sterilization could not destroy her wish to have children. Alternatively she acts out birth with avocado pits. "I looked after that first pit for months. Had it inside me, pushed it out. And I take perfect care of all the avocado trees I've started that way. I'll never get closer to giving birth than this", says Helen (ibid., p. 35).

The novel gives reason to assume that Helen imagines the intercourse of her parents as an anal intercourse. In that case the anus would be in fact the origin of the world. She would be an intestinal birth, therefore Mother's waste and thus devalued; a fantasy which patients with eating disorders always express because they feel dirty. The fantasy may reflect the unconscious of her parents and would explain why Helen is, for her mother, the object of fanatical hygiene. "My mother placed great importance on the hygiene of my pussy but none at all on that of my brother's penis. He's allowed to piss without wiping and to let the last few drops dribble into his underwear" (ibid., p. 12). She remarks sarcastically: "Washing your pussy is considered a deadly serious science in our home." (ibid., p. 12) This suggests that she felt degraded as insignificant, and "disembodied" (exactly: ent*Leib*t) so to speak. In other words, Helen's brother may have genitals; but she and her genitals are eradicated by washing rituals. Rodulfo, an Argentinean child analyst, writes that if the child is subjected too early to a hygiene regime, it always destroys what the child has built up as its body-surface. The residues, which the water washes away, are then nothing but this body-surface in its most spontaneous dimension of subjectivity (Rodulfo, 1996, p. 158).

Helen is searching for her womb area that has been extinguished by the maternal hygiene rituals. The water has washed away her *Leib*-vagina; also her private vagina. Her vagina is only an anatomical one. In the lust, dirt and pain she hopes to detect her womb again. When she is looking for own words for her genitals (her labia she calls vanilla rolls)- then she does it in order to construct her own vagina or to recapture her *Leib*. With these metaphors she wants to bring the body playfully into the potential space in Winnicott's sense. She wants to transform the anatomical body into a personal body. When she succeeds in doing so, she can have the feeling of truly existing.

As her parents do not come to hospital, Helen starts doubting the legitimacy of her wish to reunite them. "I'm an idiot and want things nobody else wants." (Roche, Wetlands, p. 203). In her despair she finally realizes that pairing off her parents seems as hopeless as "sucking a pony's insides out through its asshole". (ibid., p. 229) She decides to stop: "Give it up, Helen. You're an adult now. You have to make your own way." (ibid., p. 150)

"Sucking a pony's insides out through its assholes" (ibid., p. 229)— what a picture! Is it meant to be a fanatic hygiene mother who penetrates her child anally and completely turns it inside out in order to clean the furthermost corners of its body? When you consider the image and its content, replacing "Pony" with "child" and "ass" with "breast", you get a reference to a problematic early relationship figure. Through this perspective, the image appears to be bold notice that Helen sees her body as a palindrome. This would mean her body could be read identically both ways, just like the name Otto. In order to capture an image of her backside, Helen arranges the mode dial of her camera to take food pictures. Sucking the ass would therefore mean the same as sucking the breast. Moving the verb "suck" into the centre, it suggests the image of an infant at the breast which must suck violently in order to turn it inside out to get milk. That sounds like a strained, desperate sucking. By this futile sucking thirst would become greed; like the sexuality later on. The breast in the experience would be a bad breast, a process which can come to an end only by exhaustion. Helen would therefore intuitively have recognized her problem and taken the image as a self-interpretation, as it were: If you want something, you have to try hard, but it will not help. This turns the image into a significant life history marker. She got no milk at that time just as she gets no visits today, despite all her efforts.

Helen is not aware of her breast-feeding-trauma, but her body seems to remember the desperate sucking. Sometimes she feels as if her shoulder muscles were getting shorter and shorter. The shoulder wanders to the ears and grows down. This always happens when she realizes that everything is meaningless. The whole novel is about senselessness. One of Helen's last words are: "I'm too tired" (ibid., p. 229).

In all the traces of deprivation we see the result of early childhood deprivation due to lack of attention and concern. Apparently Helen was frequently left alone emotionally by her obsessive and depressive mother. Or her mother was just an answering machine: "I pick up the phone. I dial mom's number. Nobody answers. Answering machine. "Hi, it's me. When is somebody to come visit me? I'm in pain and I have to stay here longer …" I hang up. Slam it down … on an answering machine you can't tell the difference between a friendly hang up and an angry one" (ibid., p. 202). Helen is in despair over her mother machine: "I lift the handset again and ask the dialling tone Mom? Are you sick? What's wrong?" (ibid., p. 202).

We can assume what happens to her in hospital has also occured at home. The dry, cold and unvarying diet Helen receives in hospital is a symbol for the emotionally barren, dry and disinterested atmosphere which she experienced at home. Helen is told that the other patients

WETLANDS (FEUCHTGEBIETE)   193

eat roast, peas, potatoes and sauce. "Sounds like paradise. For one thing because it is warm. I only get cold food; and after a while it leaves you cold inside, too." (ibid., p. 215) The title *Wetlands* tells us what Helen longs for; emotionally dried out she longs for some warmth and humidity.

Important for the sadomasochistic use of her body is the following memory which Helen defines as "distinct". Sitting on the edge of the bathtub, she gets her ears cleaned with a cotton pad dipped in warm water by her mother. "A nice tingling feeling that immediately turns to pain if you go in too far", says Helen. (ibid., p. 121) She feels the same pleasure and pain when she brushes her ears with cotton pads today. This "go in too far", this pain is an expression of the *Leib*; threatened to be lost by hygienic measures. The pain is a memory of the anal-intrusive mother, experienced as inflicted pain, but pleasurable. This is of utmost importance in order to understand the pain as a bodily reminiscence of a scene with a significant other. That is, the pain represents an important relationship figure. „ Helen says unmistakably: "I have to do something .... Doesn't matter what. The main thing is not to think about my parents or the pain in my asshole" (ibid., p. 198). Parents and pain are linked by association.

If Helen called this her strongest memory, it must have been influential. This means, she has introjected her intrusive mother. In fact, intrusion is the plot of the novel. The painful cotton pad in the ear, the shower head she puts into the vagina, the pedal steel in the rectum, the sterilization; all are variants of intrusion. Male relationships are no exception. The self-mutilation and the intrusive scenes are the re-enactment of a traumatically experienced mother-child scene, the re-enactment of violence experienced as an intrusion into the body orifices by a fanatically hygienic mother. Such performances have a re-traumatising effect. Helen directed the ensuing narcissistic rage specifically against herself. In the self-mutilation is enacted towards her parents who refuse to meet her need; a need, which like body needs, tolerates no delay. Even now the anger is directed, at least *prima vista*, against Helen's own body. But we shall see that Helen's body is the body of her mother, and therefore the angry self-attack is aimed at her mother's body. Unconsciously, the self-mutilation is a violation of the object.

The cleaning scene is perhaps one with the greatest impact because Helen's mother was emotionally present, as the "warm water" indicates. A depressed, suicidal mother however, is emotionally more often absent. Presumably Helen turns so extensively towards her own body, because she needs it as a substitute for the missed mother. Her body has object-qualities. It is as if she flees from an anaclitic that is an objectless depression into her wetlands, which she substitutes for the lost idealized early mother.

Helen comforts herself not only with her physical body, but also with her secretions: from the nose, eyes, the skin and the wetlands. "I stick my middle finger deep into my pussy and leave it in the warmth for a moment before taking it back out. I open my mouth and stick my finger all the way in. I close my lips around my finger and pull it out slowly. I lick and suck as hard as I can in order to get as much of the taste of the slime on my tongue as possible" (ibid., p. 46). Here Helen re-enacts her feeding-trauma. The finger is the nipple, the mucus the milk and the word "firm", (also used in the Pony picture) refers to the hopeless effort. Helen finds use for everything from her body, including her vomit. Fittingly she thinks she is her own "garbage disposal, a bodily-secretion-recycler" (ibid., p. 121) which means, Helen can feel self-sufficient and omnipotent. She feels as pseudo-autonomic as patients with eating disorders do. However, like them Helen remains fixed to incorporating and eliminating, and circles continuously in the oral-anal mode. She calls that her "second life in the bathroom" (ibid., p. 121). Helen turns her whole body into a breast, but this breast is devalued, including only waste. Helen said that after drinking red wine and taking pills she had to puke, "first Corinna, then me …. In a big white bucket. The puke looked like blood, because of the red wine. … And … there were undigested pills floating around. This seemed like a terrible waste to us" (ibid., p. 59). She drank litres of the puke from her friend, mixed with her own, until the bucket was empty. The vomiting shows it is nothing but (mentally) undigested stuff; beta elements. When the bucket was empty, Helen was again filled with undigested elements, which had to be externalized again. The recycler finds no redemption from its vicious circle.

We can sympathise with Helen. She is missing a mother who gives her the ability to deal with worries, fears and loneliness, and helps by calming and processing all the indigestible in its interior (the beta-elements). The lack of alpha-function drives Helen into object regression. From the scene where two people merge in a liquid with each other, we conclude that her girl friend has become a mother figure. In the genital fusion of the tampons the girl friend was still a blood sister. Now we have an oral fusion, in which the indigestible in the mother becomes the indigestible in the child. Mother and child become united in the vomit. It is also a re-enactment of a pathological fusion of the two partners in undigested, beta-elements; vomit laced with alcohol and drugs. For a foetus it would mean a risk of being poisoned. It is difficult to decide whether Helen is talking about milk or intestinal contents (she is an intestinal birth). Both ways, however, Helen has to save the indigestible, the bad, by making it something precious, otherwise it would be a waste and her mother would be completely lost. She would rather have a bad mother than none at all. It becomes obvious why Helen feels herself as waste, as you are what you eat.

Waste is found everywhere. Helen tries to combat her loneliness through self-entertainment. Since she fears to be alone, she tells herself stories from earlier times again and again, stories long since done with. In the absence of another person she talks to herself. She is ruminating. She is a story-recycler. For Helen, this is better than sitting helplessly in bed and hoping someone will come. Conversation with oneself acts as an antidepressant. Furthermore, just as she consoles herself with stories she consoles herself with men. She would go to bed with "any idiot" (ibid., p. 102), she would not sleep alone a whole night long. Each of them was better than none, says Helen. Her life is reduced to waste. These "afflictions of being a child of divorce" (ibid., p. 102) were not intended by her parents when they separated. No adult thinks so far ahead, in Helen's opinion. *Wetlands* can be viewed as a guide for parents; and as a case history for analysts. Rarely do we find put into word and image such obviously regressive layers of a subject-object merger, so therapeutically difficult to navigate, but in this novel.

Repeatedly we witness the metamorphosis of traumatic experiences into desire. Helen openly shows her traumatophilia. To make it work, Helen must dissociate the disgust. The dissociation takes place through the idealization of body fluids. The reader feels disgusted with her. Literarily speaking, the feelings are with the reader, but clinically speaking Helen is not allowed to feel disgust. Otherwise she should have to distance herself from her body, which is the substitute for her mother. The loneliness would be unbearable.

In this bleak early traumatic childhood another traumatic scene attacks Helen. One day when she comes home from primary school, she finds her mother and her little brother in the kitchen lying hand in hand on the floor and sleeping. The stove is opened. It smells like gas. "What to do? I saw a movie once where somebody struck a match and the whole house blew up. So, nice and slow, I carefully creep over to the oven—there are people sleeping here—and turn off the gas. Then I open the windows and call the fire departments … both are on the way … yes, they're still sleeping … I can ride with them … They have their stomachs pumped at the hospital and dad comes directly from work" (ibid., p. 60).

The rest is well known. The family does not talk about the suicide attempt. Irritated, Helen responds with a failure of reality testing. She doubts her perceptions; has she invented the scene or talked herself into it? For years, she is tortured by questions to her mother: "Did you try to kill yourself along with my brother?" (ibid., p. 61). Even more hurtful is the agonizing question: "Why didn't you want to take me with you?" (ibid., p. 61) This question evokes her deep disappointment; her mother prefers her brother and wants to have him with her dying. Helen however, is excluded, rejected, left alone. Here we find the parallel to the subsequent self-mutilation in hospital, where her father does not come immediately to her. A small remark makes clear how deeply Helen is wounded. Slowly and cautiously she crept to the stove, because "there are people sleeping here." (ibid., p. 60). To be able to distance herself from them, she turns them into anonymous figures. This softens the deep pain. From this point onwards, Helen is haunted by flashbacks. She smells and hears constantly emitting gas. But there is nothing to smell. No gas, nothing is wrong. ".. I had fooled myself again" (ibid., p. 85).

Certainly anal pleasure, which provides the occasional literary bad smell in the novel, may contribute to these flashbacks. The flashbacks reveal her death wish against the couple mother and brother. In her gas-delusion she fantasizes both were dead: "I stood on the sidewalk in my nightgown, lit up by the only street lamp on our block, and looked at the tomb of my mother and my brother" (ibid., p. 85). Her destructive desires manifested themselves in the cynical and triumphant remark about the gas: "It's actually a pleasant smell" (ibid., p. 85).

Disappointed by her mother, Helen turns to her father, looking for what she had missed in her. With him she could not talk about real feelings and problems, only about replacement issues. He had never learned. He just says nothing apart from when she asks him question, though he would not look unfriendly. When her father finally comes to hospital, he brings her an inflatable air cushion for her sick behind.

Helen is pleased; "oh, thanks, Dad. He's obviously spent a lot of time thinking about me in pain and wondering what he could do to help. My father has feelings. And feelings for me. Nice" (ibid., p. 167). Now it is Helen who has created a "confusion of tongues". Shakily, she turns her joy on her father's attention immediately into incestuous fantasies. When inflating the cushion she let a lot of spit hang on the nipple. Her Dad puts it in his mouth without wiping it. Helen smugly says that would be "the precursor to a French kiss. Wouldn't it be considered that?" (ibid., p. 168). Then she frankly admits that she could imagine having sex with her father, and begins to narrate it. When she was very small, in the morning her parents went naked from the bedroom to the bathroom. Her father had carried a "big club growing from his groin" (ibid., p. 168). Already had she been very fascinated. "They thought I didn't notice. But I did. And how" (ibid., p. 168). This is the excited and the exciting father with his puff-nipples. However, the oral quality of her father-longing can be easily seen from the context. Helen seeks a *père maternel*. That is while she does not know in what profession her father works in. A mother has to have no job. Moreover, her father remains untouched by gases. Zeus, father of the beautiful Helena, is simply immortal, Helen thought, if she would come out alive from the house she had with her father, fortunately no longer living in this house of death. This is the only advantage of divorced parents in Helen's opinion. It is an important one, for it allows the Oedipal triumph over her mother.

Let us examine Helen's family. Father and brother seem to be the representative of the *Leib*. According to Helen's mother each disease comes from the father and no interest was paid at all to the penis-hygiene of the brother. He is dirty. In the cult of beauty the *Leib* is dirty, sick and ugly. Is it the *Leib* that is male? The fanatically hygienic mother represents the aestheticized body. This could be an interpretation of beauty and hygiene delusion, which the novel explores, but only what is pure can be soiled. Does it mean that women clean or aestheticize their bodies so they can be spoiled by men? Should that be the internal logic of beauty or the hygiene craze? It would include an old fantasy in a new performance. If Helen's parents represent the "couple of body and *Leib*," it would not be a coincidence that this novel is about a divorced couple. After all, in the beauty cult, the "couple of body and *Leib*" are also divorced.

It remains to be said that *Wetlands* is a case history of a virtual girl which can safely be taken for countless others as a varied blueprint; whether it is connected with self-mutilation, eating disorders, cosmetic surgery or risky sports. The psychopathology of the protagonist is understood in the modern way treated with the plaster of lasciviousness (i.e. the hysterical defences). Modern symptoms such as self-mutilation, eating disorders or body image disorders report a similar uprise in "edition" like *"Wetlands"*.

One last point remains to be made. After her release from hospital, Robin takes Helen home with him. Helen secretly hopes for a lifelong connection with him, in contrast to her divorced parents. She hands raisins over to him soaked with her tears. "If someone eats a woman's tears, the two of them are forever bound to each other." (ibid., p. 201) Robin knows nothing of a long-term relationship. In fact, Helen had soaked the raisins with her tears without his knowledge. On the way home Robin hesitated, stopped and considerately buttoned Helen's back open hospital shirt, so that no one sees her naked back. "He wants to cover me up in public. Good sign," Helen says (ibid., p. 229). Robin signalled to her that she is mistaken when she thinks everybody would be interested in her backside.

It is important to note that this returning home scene reminds us too much of the childhood scene at the bus stop where Helen was waiting naked underneath. Does that mean the entire hospital stay is the re-enactment of a childhood wish to expose herself, starting with a beauty work, the Lady Shaven? That would mean the novel that started to shake the fragile stature of the aestheticized body ends exactly where it did not want to end, in the exhibitionism of the beauty cult.

It seems too early for Robin to have sex with Helen. He protects Helen against a further career as an intruded upon victim.

Helen
asks him: "If I'm living with you, I guess you'll want to sleep with me?"

Robin: "Yeah, but I won't do you up the ass for now."

Helen: "I will sleep with you only if you can suck a pony's insides out through its asshole."

Robin: "Is that even possible—or do you not want to sleep with me?"

Helen: "I just always wanted to say that to a guy. Now I have. And I do want to. But not today. I'm too tired." (ibid., p. 229)

What an amazing character. She has managed to create a relationship with Robin. She sets limits, says "no" and takes time to grow. She needs the time. First of all she must say goodbye to the diapers and the paediatrician she still visits, as she tells us. We know she must overcome her early trauma embodied in her pony-fantasy first. Perhaps after that erotic play between the two can begin, but maybe it never will. The pony-fantasy involves an insurmountable barrier. It is the barrier between parent and child; the generation barrier that protects incest. To deny it would have consequences. However, perhaps in later stages of her life, thanks to her thirst for knowledge, Helen may become a scientist or a land-art-artist as she gives birth to avocado trees. This keeps the future enclosed in her womb. Perhaps she is also threatened by deep confusion.

Overall, no romantic happy ending, but at least a hopeful end. However, unquestionably a rather disappointing finale for all those who where taken in by the lasciviousness.

Bibliography

Böhme, G. (2003). *Leibsein als Aufgabe. Leibphilosophie in pragmatischer Sicht.* Kusterdingen: Die Graue Edition.

Courbet, G. (1865): *L'Origine du Monde.* Musée D'Orsay, Paris.

Didi-Huberman, G. (1999). *Ouvrir Venus. Nudité, rêve, cruauté.* Paris: Éditions Gallimard.

Freud, S. (1908c). *On the Sexual Theories of Children.* S.E., Vol. 9, 209–226.

Freud, S. (1913k). *Preface to Bourke's Scatologic Rites of all Nations.* S.E. Vol.12, p. 333.

Roche, C. (2008). *Feuchtgebiete.* Köln: DuMont.

Roche, C. (2009). *Wetlands* (translated by Tim Mohr). London: Harper Collins.

Rodulfo, R. (1996). *Kinder—gibt es die? Die lange Geburt des Subjekts.* Freiburg i. Br.: Kore.

CHAPTER NINE

Vicissitudes of female revenge

Elina Reenkola

Abstract

Revenge is a reaction to insults and humiliation. In revenge, a person intends to regain narcissistic balance after damage to their self-esteem. Fueled by the death instinct revenge aims at inflicting harm and damage upon an object. Freud considered revenge as an adequate psychical reflex to an insulting experience. Revenge may be manifested in fantasies or deeds, conscious or unconscious. I will discuss female revenge that has been traditionally a tabu. Women have been idealized as life-givers and mothers and a cruel avenger does not easily fit into this image. Women themselves feel shame and guilt about their aggressions. I argue that female retaliation is therefore often expressed indirectly. I will discuss how woman's separation process and Oedipal configuration are reflected in revenge. I will further consider how feminine libido and the feminine inner space shape her revenge. Spesific forms of female revenge will be addressed; indirect revenge with her suffering, revenge with her body and her children, revenge on a man. The story of Lena, who took unconscious revenge on me in the course of her psychoanalysis, will be described. The crucial role of shame and shame-rage will be also discussed.

Introduction

Like love, aggression and revenge are significant forces. Love and revenge are in a constant dialectical relationship, creating tension and conflict. The beast is in all of us, and it needs to be tamed. Traditionally, there has been little discussion of female revenge and aggression. It is hard to accept the idea that woman, the one who gives life, could be a cruel avenger. For a woman it is difficult to admit her vengeful strivings due to shame and guilt they evoke. I argue that female revenge is expressed most often in indirect ways and unconsciously. In women revenge is often directed against themselves, either against their bodies or against objects they see as parts of themselves, their children. The specific feature of female revenge is that the object is not usually directly the humiliator. Explicit violent revenge is rare for women. Female revenge is often silent and invisible. I consider the woman as a subject, not merely an object or a victim. I shall focus on the psychic factors, not on the violent or cultural factors of revenge.

This essay grows out of my experiences with women in psychoanalysis who have described how difficult it is to recognize revenge and aggression in themselves and how revitalizing it can be to get in touch with these feelings and verbalize them. This essay attempts to shed light on the darker areas of a woman's soul.

I will first discuss revenge in general and Freud's thoughts on revenge. I will consider how feminine libido, the woman's inner space as well as the girl's separation process and her Oedipal configuration are reflected in revenge. I will describe forms of revenge specific to women: indirect revenge, revenge on a man, and revenge through motherhood. I will tell the story of Lena, who took revenge through suffering in the course of analysis.

The expression "revenge is sweet" is evocative. According to dictionary definitions, revenge means "to inflict harm upon someone in return for injustice, injury, insult, humiliation etc. by that someone to either oneself or another, in order to thus get satisfaction or requital to one's hurt sense of justice." In revenge, a person strives to restore narcissistic balance after his/her self-esteem has been hurt and humiliated. Revenge can mean an act or a fantasy, it can be conscious or unconscious, and it contains the feeling of vindictiveness. Powered by the Death instinct, revenge involves inflicting harm upon the object. Revenge can feel fully justified. It can be experienced as the repair of a wrongdoing or humiliation one has suffered. In Greek mythology, Nemesis is the goddess of retribution but also the goddess of justice. Revenge follows revenge and thus the vicious circle of revenge emerges.

Freud refers to revenge in many of his cases. In his early writing (1893, pp. 205–207), from the time before he developed his dualistic theory of drives, he describes revenge as a powerful instinct which civilization attempts to disguise rather than repress. He wrote about revenge as an adequate psychical reflex to an insulting experience. Vengeful affects may increase if the excitation cannot be released. This can lead to various symptoms, such as hysteria.

Observing the *fort-da* play of his one-and-a-half year old grandchild, Freud (1920q, pp. 16–17) describes how the boy processes the temporary absence of his mother by throwing a wooden reel with a piece of string and pulling it back. By throwing the object away the child can satisfy his impulse to revenge himself on his mother, who went away. The child can process this unpleasant experience by turning his mother's absence into the act of throwing away, thus being able to take revenge on the mother symbolically, through play. Revenge often includes the defence mechanism of reversing roles from passive to active. Freud thus determined that even children as young as eighteen months can experience the need to revenge evoked by separation anxiety.

In the case of Dora, Freud (1905e) described the young woman's pathological vengefulness towards Mr. K. after his advances. In his postscript to the case, he still reflects upon Dora's revenge on men: "Men are so detestable that I would rather not marry. This is my revenge," Dora had said. After the treatment had been terminated, Dora consulted Freud about neuralgic pain she had developed in the right side of her face. Freud interpreted this pain as self-punishment for feelings of revenge on Mr. K. and himself. He also wondered whether the patient could take a more effective revenge than by demonstrating upon her own person the incapacity of the physician who has treated her. Freud clearly observed Dora's revenge using her own body as the weapon.

Freud (1920q, pp. 162–164) also identified revenge in the case of a young homosexual woman. This eighteen year-old woman wanted to revenge her hurt on her father by turning away from men in enraged resentment and bitterness by seeking another target for her libido. She wished to take revenge on her mother for having a baby with her father rather than getting to have his baby herself. She had many other reasons for harbouring vindictive thoughts about her mother. Her mother had favoured her three younger brothers, had limited her independence and prevented her from developing a close relationship with her father. The girl had previously attempted suicide, when her father had happened upon her and her female lover in the street. Freud interpreted this woman's self-punishment as follows: suicide signifies both murdering the object of identification and turning the death wish towards oneself instead of directing it at the object. Here, Freud presents a mechanism by which death wishes, aggression and revenge are turned towards oneself. Indeed, especially for women this is a common mechanism for dealing with aggression as well as revenge.

In this case the revenge was also fueled by the jealousy created in the early triangular setting between the siblings in their rivalry for their mother's love, as well as the strivings in the negative Oedipal stage to be the mother's partner. When discussing this case, Freud failed to grasp the girl's wish to be her mother's companion. In the therapy process, Freud could not stand the girl's aggression towards him, so he terminated treatment and recommended she continue therapy with a female therapist. He did not understand the girl's vindictiveness and hatred towards men, so instead of dealing with the girl's negative transference he terminated therapy. The girl did not admire Freud but was instead very arrogant. In his view, Freud had presented important theoretical insights about the girl's psychodynamics, and she had reacted to them with scorn. Freud's decision to terminate therapy was probably influenced by his own hurt and unconscious vindictiveness towards the girl who treated his theories with contempt. He did not name this case, perhaps an act of his own revenge.

Shame and revenge

Experiences of shame are the fuel of revenge. The core of shame is the exposure of one's separate self and the threat of not being acceptable or lovable when expressing one's innermost desires, feelings and thoughts. The three partial factors of the rapprochement phase; weakness, dirtiness and defectiveness; are the genetic triad of shame (Wurmser, 1994).

Disappointments in love and reciprocity make one susceptible to shame. Feelings of insufficiency and defeat in the Oedipal strivings are the landscape of shame. Earlier defeats and humiliations with her siblings in the pursuit of mother's love evoke shame and revengeful wishes. In addition to painful feelings, shame always contains different kinds of shame fantasies. They may carry ideas of an audience with laughter, ridicule, humiliation or contempt. The significance of the gaze and being looked at are essential in shame fantasies.

The role of the superego is central in both shame and guilt. The rift between the self and the ego ideal plays an essential role in the emergence of shame. The unattainability of one's ideals exposes one to shame. A woman's ego ideal is bisexual, whereby shame fantasies can be aroused from two directions. In terms of a woman's masculine ideals, feelings of shame can emerge if a woman's work or professional performance is criticized. In terms of the feminine ego ideal, one threat is exposure as an imperfect mother or woman. In the area of motherhood, the woman may be especially sensitive to comments criticizing her mothering skills. Another aspect of the feminine ego ideal may be the wish to be considered attractive or perfectly beautiful. Insults to her looks can hurt a woman and foster a wish to revenge. In short, shame arising from either sexual dimension can kindle vindictiveness in a woman.

Loving and being lovable are often crucial female ideals. The threat of being unlovable for a woman is intensive because of her specific Oedipal configuration and narcissistic hurt, where she is rejected by her two love objects, mother and father, more clearly than males.

Shame can lead to burning feelings of rage, and shame and rage together stir up the desire for revenge. Shame-rage can arise especially if one is insulted and subsequently treated with contempt, if one is abandoned or excluded, and cast far from the goals set by the ego ideal (Lewis, 1971). In revenge fantasies, feelings of utmost helplessness and worthlessness can be turned into strength and power.

For women, vindictiveness evokes shame along with guilt. Expressing vengeance can feel like losing control, even more shameful than childhood incontinence. A woman might think that if she takes revenge, others might ridicule her as "an angry bitch," "a Fury" or "a wicked avengeress," thus evoking powerful feelings of shame. Male revenge, by contrast, is associated with power, as can be seen using the example of honour killings.

Woman's inner space and revenge

Feminine and masculine creativity and destructivity have partly distinctive features. The vicissitudes of female revenge are shaped by the woman's bodily reality, although the female anatomy does not directly explain them. A woman's body and the meanings she gives it are an essential component of a woman's personality. The invisible inner space, its pleasure and the potential for interiority shape her experience of separateness.

Pregnant women, in particular, continuously experience both unity and separateness with the foetus. The foetus is inside the woman, as a part of her body, but at the same time it is a separate individual with its own genome (Reenkola, 1997). Only women can experience a baby as being of the same flesh as the mother but simultaneously also a separate being. She can feel another heart beat beside her own, inside her body. Ogden (1992, p. 117) emphasizes how "oneness and separateness, reality and fantasy, me and not-me coexist with one another, each creating, preserving, and negating the other," in a dialectical relationship.

In the female body, there are intermediate states such as the placenta, the umbilical cord or the amniotic fluid. The ambiguous separateness experienced by women as "umbilical cord and placenta logic," a logic which facilitates "both-and" type of thinking. In this logic, separateness does not have absolutely clear boundaries (Reenkola, 2004). Raphael-Leff (1993) has written about the placental paradigm meaning the fact that the "bidirectional placental system can serve as a metaphor for the imagined give-and-take within the acffectively colored exchange" between a pregnant woman and her foetus. The experience of being pregnant, bearing another being inside her, can activate fantasies of merger. Placental paradigm involves blurring of boundaries the nature of which varies with the maternal emotional state. French philosopher Derrida (1981) writes about "the logic of the hymen." The hymen is situated between the internal and the external, it is neither but simultaneously both, existing between desire and fulfillment. According to Derrida, the hymen thus challenges the idea that separateness and oneness are split into separate polarities. For a woman, separateness is not as clear-cut as it is for a man, and this also applies to revenge. As I will discuss more fully below, in indirect revenge females can demonstrate their revenge through their own suffering, thus turning the revenge towards herself. Revenge on the mother can take place through female bodily suffering and symptoms.

A woman can experience her inner space as a treasure or as trash. Inner-space strivings can be either life-protecting or life-destroying. They can be manifested as receptiveness and the fostering of new growth. The woman may protect the potential of her inner space to carry new life and thus refrain from violent revenge. Inner-space aggressions are destructive wishes typical of women. They focus on another person's fertility and babies, but also on symbolic fertility, productivity, and thought-babies. They can be manifested as tendencies to smother the separateness of the other.

A woman can experience damage to her inner space as mortally shameful. A rape victim can experience her body as filthy, penetrated, shamed; far from the intact and beautiful body of her ideals. Possible pleasure felt in incestuous relationships can evoke deep shame and suicidal ideation in a girl. Shame experienced by the victim of rape or sexual abuse can flame up murderous revenge towards the abuser. Losing one's virginity, having the hymen broken against one's wishes is a traumatic and shameful experience that can also evoke vindictive thoughts.

The miscarriage of a desired pregnancy, loss of a baby or loss of fertility are painful for a woman. This is especially so in cases where these are caused by someone else, and a woman might harbour revengeful feelings towards that person. Since the foetus is a part of the woman's body and often also part of herself, losing a baby is uniquely painful to a woman.

The many faces of female revenge

Indirect aggression is typical of women. In one sense this means that women turn inwards, targeting their aggression and revenge towards themselves unconsciously as depression, self-destructive behaviour and suffering. They can also channel aggression in their bodies as psychosomatic, anorexic and bulimic symptoms, or cutting, as we have found in long-term therapies. Casual sexual relationships where the girl does not protect her body can be a way of taking revenge on her mother.

Indirect aggression can also mean damaging the object without using direct verbal or physical attacks but rather through circuitous routes. It can be carried out without a single bad word or gesture. Using indirect revenge, the woman can appear innocent, thereby avoiding shame and guilt. Indirect aggression is invisible.

Why would a woman use indirect revenge? One motive comes from the unique relationship between mother and daughter. The daughter's task is to separate from her mother, who is similar to herself as well as being her first object of love, desire and identification. Strivings for separateness, however, can be the earliest sources of guilt for a girl.

Separating from the mother can feel mortally dangerous to the mother or to oneself. Symbolic matricide as a separation from the mother and Oedipal rivalry with her is hard work for the girl and evokes fears in her of mother's revenge. The ambivalence of love and hate towards the mother arouses immense guilt in a girl, having a powerful impact on the vicissitudes of aggression in women (Reenkola, 2002). The girl directs her hatred and revenge towards the mother into indirect channels or represses them in order to secure the mother's vitally important love, as well as to avoid the mother's revenge.

Revenge, like aggression in general, can be either constructive or destructive. When love is only minimally mixed with aggression and revenge to lessen their force, vindictiveness will attempt to destroy its object and the death instinct reigns. When love dilutes aggression and revenge, the strivings are not as forcefully focused on destruction. In constructive revenge, the woman may revenge with superior achievement or attempt to improve women's status and rights. Revenge can be manifested, for example, by doing well in one's studies, career, creative undertakings, by amassing wealth, or through fertility.

Creativity always involves breaking boundaries, a transgression which requires aggression as a driving force. Revenge can thus be a driving force in creativity. It can then evoke guilt for one's success. It is possible to process vengeance symbolically in one's mind in the transitional state Winnicott (1971) discusses. In creativity one can make reparation for one's fantasized destructiveness (McDougall, 1995).

The female hippocampus is like an elephant; it remembers insults and romances longer than men do (Brizendine, 2006). Revengeful wishes for the insults may be harboured for a long time in the woman's mind.

Revenge and motherhood

Motherly love has traditionally been viewed as sacred, as has loving one's own mother. It is therefore difficult for a woman to tolerate ambivalence between love and aggression towards her own children and her own mother. In the unconscious, fertility and destructiveness are often linked.

A woman may take revenge on her mother for childhood humiliations and insults as well as her Oedipal defeat. She may invalidate maternality or other symbolical properties of the inner space. She may choose not to have children. She may turn her back on her mother, and assume the position of "the womb's enemy". She may turn to idealizing masculinity and phallic qualities such as power, toughness and visible achievements. The Electra myth (Sophocles, 1986) describes a daughter's ultimate revenge on her mother; matricide carried out by the brother, Orestes. At the same time, Electra also kills her femininity and the value of her inner space. By contrast, Electra idolizes her father Agamemnon, and forgives him all his evil deeds. Casual sexual relationships and unprotected sex where the girl subjects herself to risk of damage to her inner space may reflect unconscious revenge on her mother.

Using clothing to take revenge is a feminine form of indirect revenge that requires a lot of skill. It calls for a cultivated eye and can make the target of revenge feel like a failure. By dressing with overwhelming style and elegance, the woman can revenge the Oedipal rivalry on her mother by turning defeat, in her fantasies, into a crushing victory. The mother can feel invalidated and crushed, being cast as an aging woman. Using the opposite strategy, by dressing poorly and un-femininely, the daughter can demonstrate her disdain and contempt for her mother and for femininity. Like Snow White's evil stepmother, a mother does not always tolerate her daughter's growing into an attractive woman, one who is more beautiful than herself. The mother may revenge the daughter's awakening sexuality and strivings for independence by preventing her from dressing in her own style or in the current youth fashion. She may force the daughter to wear clothes similar to her own. A mother may unconsciously not be able to tolerate her daughter's separateness, and may even destroy or hide her sexy or beautiful clothes. On the other hand, the mother may also wish for her daughter to be her mannequin, her calling card, her source of pride and honour. Dressing her daughter beautifully may not only manifest caring but also be a manifestation of a narcissistic wish to use the daughter as a vehicle for self-esteem. Being placed (or placing herself) in the position of one who brings honour to the mother gives the daughter safety and her mother's esteem, but also undermines her separate selfhood. The daughter's hatred and revenge for having been abused by her mother and having been turned into her mother's appendage can emerge; especially during the rebellion of adolescence.

The mother may be an avenger. It is difficult to combine vengeful thoughts or anger towards the beloved baby with the experience of pleasurable fusing love with the baby. They elicit feelings of guilt and shame. They may be turned inwards as depression and self-punishment, as is seen in post-partum depression.

Inside the family the woman has limitless power, like in a dictatorship. By identifying with her cruel mother, the woman can have revenge by tormenting her own children. The mother may revenge herself on a child if she or he does not fulfill the mother's symbiotic longings but instead separates from the mother; or if the child expresses emotions intolerable to her, like aggression or defiance. She may avenge by physical violence; hitting, pinching or pulling the child's hair. She may use food as the instrument of revenge, forcing the child to eat, by cooking bad-tasting food or leaving the child hungry. In adolescent rebellion, the mother may sever contact with the child. The mother may retaliate if the child does not fulfill her narcissistic wishes of perfection or brilliant achievement. The vicious circle of revenge starts here. Children may identify with the tormentor mother and start tormenting other children in kindergarten and school. As parents, they may torment their own children without being aware of it.

Women may have the fantasy of a revengeful and murderous mother in at least three versions:

- she might be a mother murdering her children like Medea (Leuzinger-Bohleber, 2001)
- her mother might murder her if she grows up to be a beautiful woman like Snow White or if she has babies
- she might murder her old menopause mother with her fertility and pregnancy (Reenkola, 2006)

Being abandoned by one's mother is an utmost insult that may evoke retaliation wishes.

Revenge on man

The woman is often depicted as representing the symbolical attempt to create new entities out of the life instinct, *Eros*, while the man represents the attempts of the death instinct to break these bonds of life. We project onto man the image of violent attacker, while onto woman that of innocent victim. This is a common primal scene fantasy which permeates our entire culture and media. However, splitting aggression away from the woman and placing it on the man reduces woman and makes her unreal. A mirror image of women as good and devoid of destructive strivings, provides a tempting image, but one that does not reflect reality. Revengeful feelings arise as a logical consequence for oppression of women, physical violence towards them, unequal rights, rape, and sexual abuse; but where do we see female revenge?

Vengeance on men is often directed inwards as suffering or towards their sons and other boys. Mothers, kindergarten and elementary school teachers have unlimited power to treat boys cruelly in an invisible way, without anybody knowing it. They can crush and suppress boys, snuff out their rambunctious play and force them to participate in typically female cute craft activities without heeding their specific needs and phallic strivings. They can humiliate boys discreetly, ridicule them or be contemptuous of their masculinity. In reaction to this boys may harbour vindictive fantasies and feelings towards women. The vicious circle of revenge is thus created. Boys start to carry out their revengeful strivings and oppress women when they grow up and gain power.

Vengeance on men may also arise in the inner world of women as a consequence of psychological factors. The first time a woman has intercourse defines her way of relating to men. The first time can be a loss and experienced as castration, as implied in the phrases "losing her virginity" or "piercing the hymen." According to Freud (1918), the loss of virginity evokes vengeance towards the woman's first sexual partner, even if he is a beloved husband. As an example, he takes the Biblical story of Judith and Holophernes. According to Freud, Judith seduced Holophernes to take her virginity so that she could then direct her hatred and revenge over losing her virginity towards the enemy chief and cut the man's head off. The revengeful castration wish evoked by the piercing of the hymen was directed at the enemy. Thus, the men of her people could remain good.

Contrary to Freud, for many women the first time can be an experience full of pleasure and love, a milestone and an achievement in the growth from girl to woman. It certainly means the entry into adult female genital sexuality as Holtzman and Kulish (1997) have described. Freud does, however, perceptively describe how the woman can split love and sexual desire apart. Even if she loves her husband, sexuality can evoke hatred and revenge in her. This setting depicts the splitting apart of the "good" and the "bad" phallus in the woman's mind. In the fantasy of the bad phallus, the penis is piercing, violently penetrating and destructive.

In fairy tales, it is symbolized by a monster, a bear or a disgusting toad that, in the end, turns into a prince. The fantasy of the good phallus in the woman's mind contains power, the construction of something new, and fertility. In her fantasies, a woman may split apart the good and the bad phallus. The integration of the fantasies of the good and the bad phallus is a demanding task for the woman and calls for psychic work. The woman's archaic primal scene is reflected in the thought about the evil phallus and vengefulness towards the man. The evil or envied phallus lives powerfully in the unconscious, alongside love and the fantasy of the good phallus. The girl's defeat to the father in the negative Oedipal constellation may fuel retribution towards men. The girl's fantasies of the father as the winner, who can satisfy the mother's desire, may evoke vengeance in her and colour her experience of the loss of virginity.

The woman may take revenge on the man by psychologically castrating his masculinity. Revenge may be concealed in subtle forms of belittlement, contempt and humiliation. In the area of parenting, the woman has many weapons. She may place herself morally above the man and accuse him of shirking his familial duties. As a self-sacrificing martyr-mother she can take revenge by elevating herself above the man. A woman may nullify the significance of the father and fatherhood. The mother may withhold information about the child's origins and paternity, and even destroy it. Thus, the woman can use her children as a tool in her revenge. In the Greek myth Medea, an immigrant, took vengeance on her husband, Jason, by killing their children because she was abandoned and left without her status. Being abandoned by a man may indeed evoke intense revengeful wishes in a woman. Sex may also be a weapon in revenge.

The evil mother is often projected onto the man. I shall describe this mechanism in Lena's case. Taking revenge on the earliest power-figure and oppressor, the mother, is experienced as mortally dangerous to the woman. She is horrified by the thought of the mother's taking revenge on the treasures of her inner space. Therefore, it feels safer to vent her anger on the man and accuse him of subjugation and oppression. After all, it is easy enough to find just reasons for doing so.

Symbolic vengeance

A woman may also turn to art as a tool for revenge in a symbolic way. Artemisia Gentileschi was a seventeenth century Italian artist, the daughter of the famous artist, Orazio Gentileschi. When she was eighteen, Artemisia was raped by her father's pupil Agostino Tassi. A trial ensued, which became an exceedingly insulting and humiliating seven-month public scandal and disgrace. Tassi was found guilty and sentenced to jail (Garrard, 1989). Gentileschi worked through the humiliation and vengeance towards Tassi evoked by the trial, by painting the Biblical theme of Judith and Holophernes. In the painting, Judith is calmly and resolutely cutting off Holophernes's head with his own sword (Gentileschi 2008a). Standing by her, as her support and ally, is her handmaiden Abra. Gentileschi thus depicts a strong, active woman executing revenge. In the Biblical story, Judith first charms the enemy chieftain, Holophernes, then lures him into his tent and kills him. She takes the severed head to her home town, where she is celebrated as a heroine. Thus the rape victim Artemisia was able to turn her experience of being victimized into its opposite—a symbolic execution of power and revenge—by painting a woman cutting the head off a man.

Some time later, Artemisia painted a series of paintings depicting a repentant and melancholy Mary Magdalene (Gentileschi 2008b). In the Bible, Magdalene was a prostitute who repented her immoral ways and became a close friend of Jesus. It is possible that guilt and repentance in Artemisia was evoked not only by her vengeful feelings and fantasies but also her own sexual desires. After the rape, the sexual relationship between Artemisia and Tassi had continued, since Artemisia expected Tassi to propose to marry her in order to salvage her reputation. The painting of the melancholy Magdalene is the inverse side of the painting of the aggressively revenging Judith. In the former, the revenge and aggression are turned inwards towards the woman herself, as repentance and depression, as guilt over one's own feelings and desires. In the figure of Magdalene, there is not only melancholy but also sorrow.

Apparently, Artemisia was able to deal creatively with her vengeance and mourn the overwhelming insult and humiliation by expressing it symbolically in her paintings. She was an esteemed painter in her time, and eventually married another artist and had children.

The story of Lena: revenge with one's own life

Lena started in psychoanalysis when she was in the fourth week of her first pregnancy. The analysis, four sessions a week, lasted a total of six and a half years, interrupted once for ten months due to my own maternity leave. She was a twenty-nine year old student who lived with Ari, the "man of her dreams." Lena had ambivalent feelings about being pregnant and expecting a baby, so sessions were devoted to talking about these issues. She admired and also envied the presumed freedom and independence of male life.

Lena hid her pregnancy from her parents for as long as possible so that "nobody would take it away." She needed to closely guard the baby and her innermost core. Lena was afraid of her mother's revenge, which would be directed at her baby. Beginning in puberty Lena would have confusing fantasies and dreams about having sex with her father. Her incestuous wishes towards her father elicited strong concerns in her about her mother's revenge towards her baby (i.e. she had feminine castration anxiety parallel to phallic castration anxiety).

With the approach of the due date approaching in mid-September, Lena was filled with many worries and fears. Then, in early September, she gave birth via an emergency Cesarean section. The experience was traumatic and shocking to her, worse than she had feared.

Lena's analysis resumed two weeks after her delivery, and around the same time she began attending an advanced level seminar for students working on their master's theses. She enjoyed breast-feeding and would have orgasmic sensations while nursing, which she mentioned in a secretive and embarrassed way. She also enjoyed studying and the intellectual efforts it called for.

After the graduate seminar Lena had a nightmare where she was attempting to rescue her baby from a fire. In another dream, she almost drove the wheel of a car over her baby's head. These dreams reflected her ambivalence towards the baby. Alongside love, hatred and vengeance as well as death wishes towards the baby were evoked in her.

Two days later, Lena contracted a breast infection with a high fever. At night she had a dream where she walked past an open coffin. The body lying in it was not dead but alive, scabby, swollen and naked. She associated the body with her swollen and sore breast. The body then morphed into her mother. She thought the dream was like her mother revenging herself on Lena, for the previous day she had expressed some disparaging thoughts about her mother. In her mind, she was also taking revenge on her mother for her childhood disappointments by disparaging her and her "horrible mothering." In Lena's dream the mother, in turn, was taking revenge on her with the breast infection and by using coffin symbols to remind her of the possibility of death. For Lena, the breast infection was punishment for having harboured vengeful thoughts about her mother, for invalidating and disparaging her.

Lena was invalidating maternal qualities in herself even though she was deriving enjoyment from them as well. Was she allowed to enjoy maternity without her mother's revenge and punishment? Her harsh and vengeful superego made it difficult to do so.

The early roots of revenge

After a year of Lena's analysis, I took maternity leave that lasted ten months. Lena was both surprised and shocked by my pregnancy. It provoked in her hatred and feelings of having been sidelined, and she wished to revenge herself on me. As my maternity leave approached, Lena started to accuse me more openly and believed I was abandoning her. She felt that I no longer cared at all about her agony over the duties, worries and conflicts of motherhood. In the transference, I started to represent her mother, who had left Lena in the countryside for the month of July from age one onwards, to be taken care of by her grand-mother; the first time also abruptly weaning her from the breast. The mother had gone to work in July, staying in the city with the father. Lena's blissful love relationship with her mother was interrupted. She had experienced the one-month separation from her mother alternately as her mother's death or her own. It was this that Lena now began to remember. I was no longer an ally or an idealized analyst to her, but cold and abandoning, just like her mother, who was unable to be sensitive enough to consider her little girl's longings. Powerful vengeance towards me arose in Lena, and since it was evoking guilt in her, it began to manifest itself only gradually as the analysis progressed. She was raging at Ari, not at me.

Taking care of the baby began to feel overwhelming, burdensome, exploitative, and a manifestation of gender inequality, whilst before she had found mothering pleasurable. We were able to uncover some feelings of how humiliating and shameful it would be to be angry at me without having any influence on my life and my decisions. Her Oedipal desires and longings for her mother were combined with her earlier longings for fusional love. The man, her husband Ari, was the target of her rage and accusations at this stage.

After my maternity leave, Lena returned angry about the break and reluctant to continue analysis. Violent men threatening women had been haunting her in her dreams. Lena's symptoms became more severe; she would get attacks of vertigo, her headaches became worse, the bouts of pain in the left side of her body grew more intense and her fears of getting breast cancer intensified. She quarreled with her husband. She would also fly into fits of rage at her son, Topi, if he did not obey her at once. After such fits, she would suffer from deep guilt. She had finished her degree and found a job in her field, but her work felt overwhelming. Her whole life seemed marked by suffering and feeling overwhelmed. The sessions began to be heavy and exhausting as well. She started to whine. Her analysis felt stalled and dead. I began to feel helpless, unable to help her, and worried that I was a bad psychoanalyst. I began to think that with her whole life and bodily symptoms she was demonstrating a kind of suffering that analysis was powerless to alleviate. I wondered whether she desired to show me just how bad an analyst I was. Was she taking revenge on me for being abandoned? I began to actively talk to her about this.

The experiences of separation, so intolerable to a young child, now came alive in the analysis, and we began to understand the reactions evoked by my maternity leave and summer vacation breaks. She was now able to get into more vivid contact with the emotions triggered by the break. Deep hurt, powerlessness and rage emerged in the sessions. The pressure from her harsh superego, and her feelings of guilt and shame had prevented her from getting in touch with these emotions. She had expressed them indirectly, through the sufferings of her son, her body and her life. She concluded:

> "I had taken all my revenge out on Topi, and it's all your fault. You are like my mother who left me in the countryside every July. I have sealed off my core, I will no longer show it to my mother or to you. That will be my way of revenge, I do not know how to be angry directly." Her mother had also not contained her little girl's silent hatred. I felt like a poor analyst/mother, for I understood how badly it had felt for Lena to lose trust and be left alone. "I will avenge everything on my mother! I will not become an adult, married woman like my mother did! I will also take revenge on you for always leaving me, with your husband. I will not get well—I shall not let you help me—that will be my revenge. As an analyst you are incapable of helping me! I will show that to you and have my revenge!"

The failure of the analysis would also be an attempt to humiliate me and bring shame on me as an analyst.

An important turning point for Lena was to get in touch with her vengeful feelings towards me, as well as with her desire to harass me sadistically with her suffering and to prove that I was unable to help her. It was essential to get in touch with the feelings of smallness and humiliation behind them, as they had been fueling her vengeance. Now Lena had the strength to process these intolerable affects and experiences.

Lena began to reflect upon the treasures in her mother's life, the finely furnished house and its pretty garden. Her mother cooked delicious food and wore feminine clothes and jewelry. The first year of Lena's life, while she was being breast-fed, had been full of mother's love and of her loving her mother. Hurt at being abandoned, however, Lena had turned her back on her mother as her revenge. Lena now experienced a shameful longing for her mother. "To be over thirty and start longing for your mother even though I've never done that before!" Lena managed to say, holding back tears. She now began to rediscover in herself identifications with her mother's loving motherliness and sexual femininity. Soon Lena started to make plans to end analysis in a year. She changed to a more pleasant job, and also started to dress femininely.

Blueberry twigs

During the last year of analysis, two weeks after Christmas vacation, Lena told me that I looked tired and worn out. She continued that she had finally decided to pick blueberry twigs and put them in a vase. She had been admiring how the twigs on my windowsill gradually budded with light green leaves and then rose-colored flowers. In the woods she had assured herself that, "It's okay to pick blueberry twigs, especially if I only pick one here and another there in order to not destroy nature and take all of next summer's blueberries." Remorseful, Lena felt that she was stealing, as well as destroying nature. The frozen blueberry twigs; coming alive, sprouting leaves and flowers in the heart of winter; to her symbolized fertility and new growth. By doing as I had done, she feared she had stolen an idea of mine. To her it signified stealing new growth, robbing "all of next summer's blueberries," robbing the babies and the fertility of Mother Nature/mother-analyst. In Lena's mind, this could result in severe punishment from her mother, according to the principle "a baby for a baby." She had fantasies about getting pregnant again, and feared that it would magically destroy my vitality, or that I would in turn take revenge on her by destroying her fertility. Lena became pregnant a couple of weeks after this session.

Lena had an unconscious fantasy of a revengeful and murderous mother in which her becoming a mother would bring death and destruction to her own mother/analyst (Reenkola, 2006). Another version of the murderous mother fantasy was the fear that her mother would destroy or kill her baby at the beginning of her first pregnancy, when she kept her pregnancy a secret from her mother for a long time. In her associations and her dreams, her baby was the product of her forbidden relationship with her father and therefore punishable.

Lena was tempted to return to revenge fantasies during the closing phase of the therapy. The stage of revenge was played out often in her inner space. In April, after Easter vacation, a month before ending analysis, Lena had a dream where she was with a therapist who resembled her unpleasant kindergarten teacher, Rita. At the time, Lena was in her third month of pregnancy. Rita was examining her with a contraption that resembled the metal detectors used at airports. The instrument was inserted into her, into her vagina, all the way into the womb.

As if they were searching for bombs! It was awful! They are searching for bombs, for hatred and destruction inside of me. Hidden! Towards you! The bomb and the baby cannot both fit inside the same womb! How can one unite motherhood and destructivity? Even having a baby is an act of aggression towards you and therefore punishable. Revenge and hatred—how can I give them up? I'm furious with Ari. I'm disappointed and furious with you. At our last session, I am going to announce that I have cancer and am going to die. However, that revenge would be powerless, as I myself would be the only one to suffer.

In addition to her painful experiences of separation, Lena's vengeance was fueled by her humiliating defeat by her mother in her love-wishes towards her father. Lena's Oedipal love wishes towards her father were manifested in her retreat to guilt filled suffering. Happiness and success had signified danger for Lena, as they were associated with enchanting her father and attaining a crushing victory over her mother. Regressing into sado-masochistic reacting had been a safer choice for her.

Lena ended analysis in May, pregnant. Her vengeance and fear of her mother's revenge had been significantly reduced. As a gift she brought me a flowering African violet that she had grown herself. Previously she had loathed African violets because her mother had grown them.

But now, however, Lena could find in herself early identifications with and love for her mother. I found the gift touching.

Mourning and forgiveness

Mourning is necessary for becoming free of the shackles of revenge. A person brooding on revenge is not able to mourn his/her narcissistic injuries. In *Mourning and Melancholia* (1917) Freud proposed that pathological grief is caused by ambivalence towards the lost object.

"The self-tormenting in melancholia, which is without doubt enjoyable, signifies ... a satisfaction of trends of sadism and hate which relate to an object and which have been turned round upon the subject's own self..."

The loss can also be an ideal of the integrity of one's self-esteem and body. In normal mourning, the person gradually detaches the ties of love from the lost object by repeatedly remembering the experiences in which the ties were forged. Thus she or he can gradually remove these ties to the lost object, even as love and hate vie with one another. In revenge the ties of hate towards the object are prevalent.

Giving up revenge requires mourning the shame and insults one has suffered. This is possible if one gets in touch with one's revengeful emotions and fantasies. Relinquishing one's striving for omnipotent control of the object may be difficult. The process can be powerfully liberating for a woman and free her from revenge turned inwards. It may open the way for forgiveness, though it is not always possible to forgive the deepest narcissistic injuries.

References

Brizendine, L. (2006). *The Female Brain*. New York: Morgan Road Books.
Derrida, J. (1981). The double session. In: B. Johnson, (Ed.), *Dissemination*, Chicago: University of Chicago Press.
Freud, S. (1893a). On the Psychical Mechanism of Hysterical Phenomena: Preliminary Communication. *S.E., 2*.
Freud, S. (1905e). Fragment of an Analysis of a Case of Hysteria. *S.E., 7*.
Freud, S. (1917e). Mourning and Melancholia. *S.E., 14*: p. 251.
Freud, S. (1918a). The Taboo of Virginity. *S.E., 11*.
Freud, S. (1920 g). Beyond the Pleasure Principle. *S.E., 18*, pp. 16–17.
Freud, S. (1929a). The Psychogenesis of a Case of Female Homosexuality. *S.E., 18*, pp. 162–164.

Garrard, M. (1989). *Artemisia Gentileschi*. Princeton: Princeton University Press.

Gentileschi, A. (2008a) (http://www.artemisia-gentileschi.com/judith4.html)

Gentileschi, A. (2008b). (http://www.artemisia-gentileschi.com/magdalen 2.html)

Holtzmann, D. & Kulish, N. (1997). *Nevermore: The Hymen and the Loss of Virginity*. Northvale: Aronson.

Leuzinger-Bohleber, M. (2001). The "Medea fantasy": An unconscious determinant of psychogenic sterility. *International Journal of Psychoanalysis, 82*: 323–345.

Lewis, H. B. (1971). *Shame and Guilt in Neurosis*. New York: International Universities Press.

McDougall, J. (1995). *The Many Faces of Eros*. London: Free Association Books.

Ogden, T. H. (1992). *The Primitive Edge of Experience*. London: Karnac.

Raphael-Leff, J. (1993). *Pregnancy: the Inside Story*. London: Sheldon Press.

Reenkola, E. (Mäenpää-Reenkola, E) (1997). *Naisen verhottu sisin*. Helsinki: Yliopistopaino.

Reenkola, E. (2002). *The Veiled Female Core*. New York. Other Press.

Reenkola, E. (2004). *Intohimoinen nainen*. (The Passionate Woman) Helsinki: Yliopistopaino.

Reenkola, E. (2006). Schwangerschaft, Depression und Psychoanalyse. (Pregnancy, Depression and Psychoanalysis) In *Die vielen Gesichter der Depression: "Trauer und Melancholie"* Deutsche Psychoanalytische Vereiningung.

Sophocles. (1986) *Electra*. In: (Watling, E. F.) *Electra and other Plays* (pp.). New York: Penguin Classics, 1986.

Winnicott, D. (1971). *Playing and Reality*. London: Tavistock.

Wurmser, L. (1994). *The Mask of Shame*. New York. Aronson.

PART IV

SEXUALITY AND THE FEMALE BODY
IN THE LIFE CYCLE

CHAPTER TEN

Female sexuality beyond gender dichotomy

Ilka Quindeau

Abstract

The commonplace classification of male and female sexuality is not self-evident from a psychoanalytical standpoint. If we want to define sexuality beyond the reproductive function the dichotomy of male-female sexuality needs to be transcended. The recourse to the classic concept of bisexuality enables a wider notion of a sexuality in which fantasies and unconscious memories are as important for sexual arousal as physiological functions. In lieu of a genuine female sexuality I therefore want to develop the concept of a comprehensive sexuality that is not gender-specific. In each individual the sexual experience oscillates consciously and unconsciously on many different levels between positions of femininity and masculinity.

The variation between men and women is rarely more obvious than in the area of sexuality. Initially it may appear evident that gender-specific differences in female and male sexuality exist. However, if we endeavour to describe these differences in more detail, or even define them, things immediately become more difficult. Intuitive certainty slips away.

223

Let us examine the psychoanalytical concept of sexuality. We remain a long way from any final answer to the question of female sexuality from this perspective. Even in Sigmund Freud's *Three Essays on the Theory of Sexuality* (1905), two concepts which are difficult to reconcile stand side by side. These are the concept of genital primacy and the concept of infantile, polymorphous-perverse sexuality. Whereas genital primacy, established in adolescence, infers a gender-specific structured sexuality; polymorphous sexuality is not aimed towards reproduction but is defined as a perverse, childlike sexuality, which contradicts the notion of a polarized two-gender structure. In addition, this infantile development does not remain restricted to childhood but goes on to present a characteristic feature of human sexuality in adulthood. Let us add to this Freud's basic assumption of constitutional, innate bisexuality, in which cross- or trans-gender identifications fall victim to repression along with the formation of a heterosexual gender identity. Cross-gender identifications nevertheless remain in the unconscious. Beside these ground-breaking concepts, Freud's ideas of female sexuality which he developed based on a model of male sexuality, and which he saw as characterized by a "lack" or "deficit" are highly problematic. He believed that in the genital stage a kind of "involution" (Freud, 1905d, p. 207) occurred in the female psyche, since in puberty clitoral sexuality (seen as a part of "male sexuality") would fall victim to repression. The clitoris as the erotogenic *Leitzone*, the source for sexual arousal, would be replaced by the vagina. This view was sharply criticized in the 1920s and 1930s, and replaced by the assumption of independent, genuine female desire, which integrated both genital zones.

Before I discuss female desire in detail, I would like to briefly describe my academic perspective. I intend to highlight the primacy of the other (*alter*), in contrast to different perspectives, such as the object relations theory, classic Freudian or Kleinian psychoanalysis, or even inter-subjective, relational psychoanalysis, all of which are based on the notion of a subject.

This focus on the subject can be understood as a legacy of the Enlightenment, as well as coming from the German Idealism movement. However, by conceptualizing the unconscious as a central motivating system, Freud has already de-centralized the subject, even though he himself and many of his followers consistently returned to it. Jean Laplanche picked out these re-centric movements in psychoanalytical thought and tried to overcome them with his General Seduction Theory. (Laplanche, 1989) He developed a concept (as a fundamental anthropological situation) of an asymmetrical relationship between the adult (with an already fully formed unconscious) and the infant, with its developing psychological structure. With this idea of the primacy of the other, he reversed the idea of the subject as a "producer of his or her develop-ment" (Lerner & Ross-Buschnagel , 1981). This idea has been the central paradigm of academic developmental psychology in the last decades— but also often in psychoanalysis. Laplanche replaced it in favour of the idea that the subject is sub-jected to the other in the process of his or her development (in the original sense of the Latin word *sub-iectum*). The subject is thereby constituted by the other. The paradigmatic situa-tion for the primacy of the other is represented by the so-called General Seduction Theory. The infant is confronted by the adult, in the form of a mysterious, unconscious message, permeated with sexual desire. The infant is not able to withdraw from this message, nor can it integrate it. Rather, this message forms the nucleus of the child's unconscious and is constantly pushing for translation and understanding. A demand is sent out from the unconscious sexual desire of the adult which the child is forced to deal with, and which it must respond to, yet without being able to do so. In dealing with this conflict, the psychological structure of the child is formed. This theoretical approach is my point of departure for the conceptualization of sexuality; the central issue is the uncon-scious sexual desire on which the gender-specific structured sexuality of the adult is founded.

Now I will proceed to a psychoanalytical gender discourse. Put sim-ply, there are two different views. First, the view of phallic monism in classical psychoanalysis and second, a differentiation theory in feminist-oriented psychoanalysis from the 1970s and 1980s (which forms the mainstream of psychoanalytical theory). As we know, the concept of phallic monism operates with only one gender. Masculinity functions as the implicit norm, while femininity represents the deviation, a lack or a deficit. The approach of differentiation theory is to create a posi-tive concept of femininity through criticism of phallic monism. Thus femininity is placed as the other opposite masculinity. The significant contribution of differentiation theory is that it has overcome the concept of deficit and has provided femininity with aspects which were hitherto reserved only for masculinity (such as aggression, although in a specifi-cally female form).

I would now like to go a step further in this direction by replacing a reductionist dichotomy of masculinity and femininity with gender ten-sion, a conflict-laden status of male and female identifications within each individual (see Quindeau, 2013). Sexuality offers this gender ambiguity an excellent *locus*; not between the individual persons concerned, as was suggested by the cultural primacy of heterosexuality, but in every individual. My central thesis is that the sexual experience and behaviour of women is the place or *locus* where the generally accepted gender dichotomy is subverted. This offers modes of pleasurable sexual expression, based both on conscious, female receptive satisfaction modalities, as well as modalities that are generally unconscious, repressed, male and penetrative. This return of the repressed elements constitutes, in a very special way, sexual pleasure. With this idea I refer to Freud. In his writing *Jokes and the relation to the unconscious* (1905c) he described how the return of repressed elements generates a feeling of pleasure. He shows this by explaining the mode of humour. I would like to suggest that sexual pleasure as well comes out of the return of the repressed.

In order to develop my argument, I would like to go back to a range of tried and tested psychoanalytical concepts. I will begin with Freud and his concepts of constitutional bisexuality and polymorphous-perverse infantile sexuality. These are contrasted with the notion of an Oedipus-complex and genital primacy. Freud's view is at the same time connected, even if not entirely without contradiction, with phallic monism. I will expand my thesis on female sexuality as a *locus* for phallic (male) identifications with a short review of the concept of transference, which Freud is known to have viewed as a playground for repressed elements, in order to define psychodynamically the process of the gain of sexual pleasure through the discovery of repressed elements.

I will discuss Irene Fast and her integrative perspective as a prominent representation of the differentiation theory, as well as the continued development of the latter through Donna Bassin's gender theory from the field of inter-subjective, relational psychoanalysis. Finally Reimut Reiche's work is introduced along with the term gender tension.

Freud's concepts of gender, bisexuality and genital primacy

Freud's remarks on masculinity and femininity are among the most controversial passages of his work. There is no doubt that phallic monism, the paradigmatic orientation of sexual development toward the male gender, should be criticized. According to that point of view, femininity does not constitute an independent gender, but is built upon a fundamental lack; a woman becomes a woman because she does not possess a penis.

However, even in Freud's work complex views of masculinity and femininity can be found. There the terms male and female do not only describe characteristics that can be assigned to either men or women, but also elements which can be found in varying degrees in every human being. Freud attributes this mingling of masculine and feminine character traits in the individual to the concept of bisexuality. He writes:

> Such observation shows that in human beings pure masculinity or femininity is not to be found either in a psychological or a biological sense. Every individual on the contrary displays a mixture of the character-traits belonging to his own and to the opposite sex; and he shows a combination of activity and passivity whether or not these last character-traits tally with his biological ones. (Freud, 1905d, p. 219)

What we can see in this definition is that Freud has created a remarkably sophisticated concept of gender, in which commonly held clear differences are dissolved. However, he does not maintain this view consistently throughout his work, but falls back into traditional conceptualization. Nevertheless, these formulations provide the basis to develop new psychoanalytical thinking about gender. This carries on with Freud's questioning of the seemingly clear differentiation between male and female, and he does not assign this distinction to concrete individuals, but understands them in the sense of positions within each person. The core of such a gender concept is bisexuality and thereby, the resulting variety of gender identifications and of psychological, as well as bodily dispositions.

Such a concept of gender can also be found in recent developments in socio-cultural gender discourse, from which psychoanalytical theory has benefited from for many years. In particular, post-structuralist deconstruction of differences between men and women serves as a model for new psychoanalytical thinking based on the Freudian concept of bisexuality.

Freud's central concern was an expanded understanding of sexuality; he believed it should neither be restricted to adulthood nor reduced to genitality, but should encompass a wide spectrum of sexual pleasure. For Freud, sexuality possesses a so-called "polymorphous-perverse" character; and begins with the very first life experiences of a child, for example, while breast-feeding. The expression "polymorphous-perverse" may sound pejorative in this sense.

However, Freud employed the term perverse, taking the Latin word *pervertere*, to describe forms of sexual activity which do not merely serve the purpose of procreation. The word polymorphous describes the many different forms of expression of infantile sexuality.

Before turning to the problems arising from Freud's argumentation, let us first look at what we might gain from it. With the concept of infantile sexuality we are making a connection between child and adult behaviour. This opens up a view, on the one hand, of a continuum of sexual experience and behaviour and, on the other hand, of its very varied forms. Sexuality is not restricted to biological procreation, but is experienced in different, psychologically equally valid forms. This applies both to hetero- and homosexual object choices and to the so-called perversions. This sexual concept, found in the first two of the *Three Esssays* was originally broad, non-normative, and not hierarchical. However, in the third of the *Three Essays* as well as in other parts of his work, Freud reverted to the common sense view of his time and created the concept of genital primacy, which re-establishes procreation as the central function of sexuality. Despite this, the broad concepts presented in the first two essays do offer a range of advantages, particularly regarding the development of a new sexual theory, and should be reconsidered developed further. The concept of genital primacy would, therefore, be seen in another light.

It seems especially important that the model of infantile sexuality is based on a trans-gender concept and avoids judging sexual experience and behaviour based on normative standards. In order to conceptualize psychologically equal forms of sexuality, it is essential to see that sexuality begins before puberty (sexual maturity. Focusing solely on genital primacy, which is established in puberty, inevitably results in a corresponding primacy of the procreative function; which implies that other forms of sexuality are subordinate to it.

For my further argumentation, it is not necessary to dwell on the particular forms of infantile sexuality; Freud's conceptualized forms of oral-, anal-, and urethral eroticism, as well as of phallicism and genitality, have remained unchanged in psychoanalytic theory. The central notion of the concept of infantile sexuality, in my opinion, is its ability to emphasize the infantile, polymorphous nature of adult sexuality, rather than its description of child behaviour.

In Freudian sexual theory the polymorphous, trans-gender variety of pleasure and satisfaction modalities stand in contrast to the structuring and normative principles of the Oedipus complex and genital primacy. According to Freud, in the process of resolving the Oedipus complex, gender differences are firmly established, along with a clear designation to one of two genders, while the other-gender parts are displaced into the unconscious. I consider it important to note that along with the Oedipus complex socializing, ordering principles such as gender dichotomy are imposed on the individual's psychic structure. Pursuing my argumentation further, I will now address the question of what happens to the repressed male aspects of the innate bisexuality of a woman. Additionally, I will question what happens to the polymorphous, perverse infantile sexuality at the juncture of puberty where the individual experiences sexual maturity. As in establishment of gender identity, a similar process of disambiguation can be found in the establishment of genital primacy. The great variety of polymorphous-perverse infantile sexualities is subordinated to the dominance of genitality. This creates a construction of gender-specific structured sexuality, as well as a hierarchical order of the various forms of sexuality in which heterosexuality is dominant. A whole range of modes of infantile desire and satisfaction are thereby repressed. In our culture this refers, for example, to anal, possibly coprophile, or urethral modalities (i.e. what is seen as pathologically perverse).

Gender identity—gender ambiguity

Now I should like to turn to the question of the development of female gender identity and by referring to two key psychoanalytical concepts. In her work *Gender identity: a differentiation model* (1984), Irene Fast presents a thesis, now widely known in the field of psychoanalytical discourse, regarding the conceptualization of gender identity, which diametrically opposes the concept of bisexuality. The differentiation paradigm assumes an undifferentiated condition with respect to gender at the beginning of life, which means that the earliest experiences of small children are not yet gender- differentiated. Rather, children at an early age are within "an undifferentiated and overinclusive ... matrix" (Fast 1984: 13). Children do not become aware of gender difference until they are about two years old. This awareness is conceptualized as an ubiquitous offense or insult, which requires an intense internal conflict in order to cope with the limitations of the child's own gender. However, with this conceptualization a heavy burden is put on the representation of gender difference as it is based on the experience of offense or insult. The envy of the other gender represents the crucial experience in the development of the person's gender identity.

Fast refers to typical difficulties which generally occur in connection with the perception of gender difference. Thus the transition from undifferentiated experience of unlimited possibilities to the acknowledgement of gender difference is experienced as loss or deprivation. These painful experiences may arise in varying degrees of acuteness; maybe as an absolute loss (for example, if not omnipotent, then powerless) or even as personal deprivation, which others are not subjected to (op cit 44 f). In the normal case these difficulties will be temporary, and in their place comes a feeling of personal belief, a delimited, complex self-esteem. Referring to the development of a girl, Fast writes:

> A delimited feeling of self as a specifically female being who is able to identify with other women, experiences herself as specifically female in her relationship with other women, and develops a productive relationship with men, who she understands in their own maleness and sees as independent of herself. (ibid., p. 25)

Fast is essentially unclear about how the transition from loss proceeds psycho-dynamically to a positive gender identity. She merely remarks that a girl, at the moment at which she becomes aware of the gender difference, would identify earlier cross-gender representations and identifications as no longer compatible with her own gender.

These denials are referred to by Judith Butler (1997), following Lacan, as foreclosure which lies at the basis of melancholy gender development. Thus it seems more appropriate to link the process of acquisition of gender difference to grieving or sadness, rather than to look at it as a defence process (Quindeau, 2004). It remains to be noted that those cross-gender identifications do not simply disappear, as Fast's theory appears to state.

This is also one point of criticism by Donna Bassin (1996), who is of the opinion that the comprehensive cross-gender representations could not be replaced by a simple acceptance of limitations of outer reality.

The fact is, that in contrast to Fast's epigenetic developmental model (orientated on Piaget), the repressed, rejected representations remain active and operant in the unconscious. A further problematical feature is Fast's conceptualizing of "gender-inadequate attitudes." Here I believe her argumentation rests on the un-reflected assumption of heteronormative gender roles that appear to be deeply rooted in North-American thought; these norms are the standard against which ideas of psychological health, as well as the sentencing of delinquents are measured (May, 1986).

The assumption that it is possible to define what is masculine and what is feminine, as revealed in such attempts depicted above, ignores the inherently conflicting nature of identity that can be seen in every individual development and encountered in every psychoanalysis. In spite of all intentions, the differentiation theory merely follows a biological or essentialist understanding of gender. In contrast to Irene Fast, Donna Bassin (1996) presents arguments against a polarization of genders, and she states that her aim is the reconciliation of male and female. I consider this approach to be extremely interesting, and a potentially productive further development of psychoanalytical conceptualizing of gender. I would like to discuss it in more depth. Instead of a two-sexed gender dichotomy, Bassin presents a theory in the field of the psyche with diverse sexual identities, mingling of active versus passive, male versus female, subject versus object. She criticizes the one-sided attribution of the term phallic to male genitalia. The phallic mode, including curiosity, penetrating (both in the physical and intellectual sense), and much more, is accessible to both genders. She presents the limitations of assigning phallicity only to the male gender, which results in serious limitations of experience and expression for both genders. The phallic mode, per definition masculine, is seen as unfeminine and incompatible with the female gender role, In the same way, receptiveness is seen as feminine, and incompatible with the male gender role. This restriction of variability creates a normative gender identity through polarization and repression.

Bassin contrasts phallicity with the notion of genitality; following Abraham, who as early as 1926 described a resolution of the Oedipal phase as the end of gender polarity. Bassin once again takes up his concept of a genital character. She considers the latter to be the ability to focus on a love object, which would make it possible (through far-reaching surmounting of narcissism and ambivalence) to enter into a relationship with another person. The reconciliation of masculinity and femininity in the genital phase, according to Bassin, depends on the Self opening up a transitory space (*locus*) and utilizing cross-gender representations as symbols. Those symbolic representations serve to overcome the dichotomy between the genders. Such an integration of cross-gender representations is clearly distinct from the repression and rejection suggested by Fast, as well as from the problematic holding on to the illusion of unlimited possibilities, which is often referred to in connection with bisexuality (see Blos, 1962).

Instead, the cross-gender representations in Bassin's approach serve the development of the Ego and support it in its function of "internal and external control" (Bassin, 1996, p. 116). This aspect of fortifying the Ego, in turn, refers to working through the grief, as mentioned above. This point is not, however, taken further by Bassin. At the same time, her focus on the "ego"-function, offers another opportunity to empha- size the essential changes which have been undertaken by the inter- subjective, relational approach of psychoanalysis over against classical psychoanalysis. Those cross-gender representations are not understood as unconscious (drives) desires, that is, as *modi* of desire; but rather within their function for the ego or self. According to Bassin, those cross-gender aspects encourage the ability of the Self to acknowledge the other as a "subject on equal terms". An assimilation of the other in one's own self makes this acknowledgement and acceptance possible. Bassin demonstrates this with the example of the psychological real- ity of a woman; as long as a woman is determined exclusively by her vaginal world, her internal generative space, and can find no access to her early over-inclusive body-ego-representations, she is unable to enter into a genuine object-relationship with a man. (It could be added here that this is obviously the same for a man.)

Although I consider the afore-mentioned individual aspects in Bassin's approach to be appropriate, I should like to refer again to the very different paradigms which are the basis of our approaches. While the acknowledgement theorem aims at acknowledging the other as a "subject on equal terms" (that is, as the same kind of subject as myself) in my "alterity-theoretical" view, it is all about acknowledgement of the other as an other.

To put it succinctly, it could be formulated as follows; I am concerned here with an acknowledgement of the other side of the subject, that is, specifically not about the area which the subject autonomously controls and of which it is aware (as the term subject provides for in present-day psychoanalysis); rather I would like to concentrate on the unknown, the other, the inaccessible, and the unconscious. Referring to the generative space of the woman, that means that I would not place an emphasis on making an object-relationship possible, as Bassin does, but rather see that space as the *locus*, where bisexual, same-sex and cross-sex representations, as well as various pleasure modalities and phantasies have a place and can remain side by side without delimiting and rejecting the unknown or the other in the sense of a clear dichotomous gender identity and/or sexual identity. Generative space stands for the acknowledgement (recognition) of the other in the self. This makes it possible to have a more relaxed attitude towards dealing with those "other parts", both in oneself, as well as in others, and not to devalue them or fight them.

Beside Donna Bassin's gender conceptualization, I consider Reimut Reiche's approach (1990) as very constructive for a psychoanalytic understanding of gender and sexuality, which arises from the primacy of the other; even though Reiche shares my alterity-theoretical paradigm as little as Bassin does. With his concept of gender ambiguity Reiche (unlike Bassin) emphasizes the unconscious drive dimension of gender identity and gendered relationships as a central aspect of psychoanalytical theory. As one of the first in the German-speaking field of psychoanalytical discourse, he questions gender dichotomy:

> Even the term "two genders" is incorrect and leads one to thinking in terms of bipolar opposites and binary models. The correct formulation should be as follows: gender can be found in two forms (= dimorphic)" (Reiche, 1990, p. 46).

This emphasizes difference within unity. In contrast to his American colleagues, his questioning of gender dichotomy is not based on sociological criticism of societal ideas of heteronormative gender order, but is, on the whole, based on a biological argumentation. It is interesting to note how different approaches with completely different reasoning arrive at similar views. For my own argumentation the important point, beside Reiche's consistent account of the unconscious, is his basic understanding of bisexuality, for which he uses the term gender tension. This does not refer to a form of relating between humans, but to the tension-laden state within a man, or within a woman, which results from the two-sidedness of gender, or the difference between masculinity and femininity.

Sexual experience as a place of repressed transgender modalities of pleasure

This concludes my thoughts on gender discourse. In my view, innate bisexuality is critically important as it overcomes the dichotomy of the sexes and posits the resulting gender tension in every man and every woman. I want to now develop my thesis that repressed trans-gender modalities of pleasure find their expressive shape in sexual experience. Pleasure is derived from the return of the repressed (i.e. the very mechanism known to us from humour).

Initially, let me distinguish two dimensions of sexuality. The first is the realm of conscious behaviour and experience, including sexual phantasies and wishes. The second is the realm of unconscious desire, and unconscious phantasies. In this context, Fritz Morgenthaler has distinguished organized sexuality from the sexual (1987, p. 140 forward). In his view, the sexual is an unspecific energetic potential that follows the primary process. The development of libido and identity channel the sexual toward specific objects thus transforming it into organized sexuality: "When we speak of sexuality in contrast to the sexual, we are speaking of that which the secondary process has made of the instinctual impulses in the Id" (ibid., p. 146).

Unfortunately, Morgenthaler then separates this interesting distinction into a very superficial binary opposition of good and evil; he speaks of the dictatorship of sexuality which behaves towards the sexual like a military junta. By contrast, I would like to focus on how the sexual, the unconscious, repressed modalities of desire and pleasure, express themselves in manifest sexuality. Thus, I see manifest, organized sexuality less as a dictatorial oppressor and more as a mode within which repressed aspects can be expressed. Indeed, it is the return of the repressed that in my view generates the specific pleasure.

In order to allow for transgender aspects, it is important that the construction of gender not be overly normative but rather maintains some level of openness for trans-gender identifications. Therefore, I prefer the image of gender tension, of a continuum with masculine and feminine poles, to that of a gender dichotomy.

In the course of developing a gender identity during childhood, transgender identities are repressed, as Irene Fast explains in her integration theory. We know, however, that the repressed aspects are not lost; instead, they continue to have effects in the unconscious. Furthermore, they push into the conscious, an obvious point which is often ignored. Certain conditions favour this emergence of the repressed. Freud identifies regression which, for example, enables dreaming during sleep. The daydream, the parapraxis and humour are all descendants of the unconscious which are enabled through regression. A similar process appears to be engaged in sexual experiences during which regression occurs. This central point deserves further elaboration, particularly with a view to recalling Freud's concept from *The Interpretation of Dreams* (1899).

There, the process of regression is described as a transformation of ideas into sensory images. Freud emphasizes that regression does not only occur in dreams but also in the context of other psychological processes; Freud gives hallucinations, psychic symptoms, but also conscious remembering as examples (Freud, 1900a, p. 540 and p. 548). I would like to add sexual experiences to this list. It would exceed the scope of this Chapter to retrace the complex reasoning Freud provides in Chapter Seven of *The Interpretation of Dreams*; instead, I merely refer to his conclusion. Regression occurs as a reversal of the direction of an arc of perception from the sensory organ to the brain. The reflex arc serves as its example for all psychic processes; it has a sensitive and a motor end. Freud puts the unconscious and the preconscious at the motor end. Thus, dreams are not caused by external sensory stimuli but by unconscious latent dream thoughts which are in turn transformed into sensory images.

When we apply this pattern to sexuality, we find an interesting foundation for the concept of psycho-sexuality. The idea of a psycho-sexuality emphasizes the importance of unconscious phantasies which play a significant part in sexual arousal alongside physical sources of arousal. Just as dreams result from a reversal of the arc of perception and as latent dream thoughts excite the sensory organs, the arousal of the genitalia occurs not only through external stimuli but also through latent thoughts, and through unconscious phantasies.

The primary pleasure experience, which Freud also introduces in Chapter Seven of *The Interpretation of Dreams*, provides the paradigm for these unconscious phantasies (Freud, 1900). The memory trace of this experience is inscribed in the body and there establishes the proto-type of pleasure. This prototype is subsequently never reached again, but it becomes the engine of all future desire. In the course of the psy-cho-sexual development, these experiences of pleasure are continually rewritten resulting in individual constellations of the various modali-ties of desire and pleasure in their oral, anal, urethral, phallic and genital expressions. Such individual constellations can be understood as sexual scripts (see Gagnon & Simon, 2005) which are at the base of individual sexual behaviour and experience. During an orgasm, both dimensions of the genital expression (the phallic-masculine and the receptive-feminine) combine to enable the oceanic feeling of melding together (Freud, 1927c).

The repressed masculine identifications that find their expression in the sexual experiences of women are apparent both at the immediate physical level and at the level of phantasies. For this, I am drawing on a conceptualization by Otto Kernberg (2011). In this study about the sexual couple, he articulates the following properties of erotic desire. First, the strive towards pleasure, which is always aimed at another person, at an object that can be penetrated, or at an object from whom penetration is desired. This longing for closeness and melding together is thought to contain both aspects of violent transgression and union with another person. It seems particularly important to me that pen-etration and reception are not understood as the properties of a man or a woman. Instead, what is contemplated is a fluid interplay of penetra-tion and reception at the physical and phantasy levels. Kernberg adopts an important component of Freud's concept of *Trieb* (drive), when he emphasizes that phantasies of active incorporation and passive pen-etration are experienced together with those of active penetration and passive incorporation (ibid., p. 867). Active and passive modalities of pleasure interact and cannot be divided between the sexes.

The second important point of this interplay of phallic and receptive elements is that it is not restricted to the sphere of phantasy, but that it is directly physically present. In this context, it is critical to think of the body holistically and not to solely focus on the primary sexual organs. Phallic elements cannot only be ascribed to the penis, but also to fingers and tongue; similarly, not only the vagina but also mouth and anus are *loci* of receptive modalities of pleasure. In this conceptualization, we can see not only the direct physical origin of phantasy, but also that the polymorphous modalities of desire and pleasure are not restricted to the genitalia.

Kernberg considers the psychic bisexuality as evident in sexual experiences universal among all men and women. He attributes it to the mutual identification of both participants in the sexual relationship. This explanation seems somewhat problematic, invoking, as it does, the cultural norm of heterosexuality as foundational for his entire theory of the sexual couple. This is not theoretically necessary. One can conceive of a psychoanalytical theory of sexuality which places different forms of sexual orientation on an equal plane. For the question of universal bisexuality, this means that its origin is ascribed less to the identification with the sexual partner and more to the infantile identifications with both parents and the resulting gender tension internal to the psychic structure of men and women.

There is one further aspect where I would distinguish my own thought on gender tension from Kernberg's conceptualization. He points to the feeling in sexual experiences of becoming both sexes at once, to briefly transcend the sexual divide, together with the feeling of mutual completion in the pleasure of penetration and incorporation as well as being penetrated and incorporated. Even though I share this description of sexual experience without restriction, I would not limit tracing this experience back to the transcending of the mother-child divide during the oral phase which is replayed unconsciously in orgasm. Rather, I would to like to point to a developmentally later stage and to refer to gender difference. This difference is overcome not through the physical union with a male partner, but instead through the temporary reversal of the repression of trans-gender, masculine aspects that a girl had to relinquish in the course of developing an unambiguous gender identity.

Looking to the future

Given that the intuitive divide between a female (and male) sexuality could not be maintained on closer inspection, I want to conclude my argument by speaking about overcoming gender difference in psychoanalytical sexual theory. Overcoming does not mean negation or denial of existing difference. Rather, I am arguing a Hegelian dialectic mode of reasoning that at the same time sustains the difference between men and women and transcends it, resulting in its elevation to a higher plane. Even though we are not dealing with questions relating to the philosophy of history, I associate with this transcendence a moderately optimistic expectation of progress, viz. that the relationship between the sexes will gain a new quality in the future, more relaxed, liberated and less pre-occupied with boundaries. This may be the appropriate place for summarizing my main argument.

Beginning in puberty, the difference between the sexes gains central importance. Physical and affective changes cause the infantile sexuality to transform into its adult form. Adolescence, as a phase of accelerated and condensed developmental processes, offers a second chance for the processing of psycho-sexual conflicts of early childhood, particularly of the Oedipus complex. The lens of the general theory of seduction, which forms the base of my argument, offers an alternative to Freud's thesis of the dual temporal nature of human sexual development. Adolescence is not a new beginning, not a second starting point of sexual development; rather, it is a specific constellation, a node in the developmental process where various re-inscriptions on various levels are bundled. Infantile desire and pleasure modes (partial drives) are re-inscribed and dislodged from their primary love objects. As was the case in prior developmental stages, new answers come forth to respond to those enigmatic messages. The newly acquired genital maturity and capacity for reproduction plays an outstanding role for these answers. This is evident from the target which is set, prescribing that individuals in adolescence be particularly subjected to social ideas of ordering. The polymorphous-perverse sexuality is socially regulated and subjugated under genital primacy and heterosexuality. Freud's thesis of genital primacy under which the partial drives are subjugated has frequently been criticized as a conventionalization of psychoanalytical sexual theory; with justification, at least if this primacy makes the reproductive function the focal point. This would necessarily imply a normative hierarchy of homosexuality and heterosexuality. However, one could conceptualize a different reading. I understand the psychological representation of the genitals as a projection screen, as a place where the individual partial drives can be integrated into a cohesive whole. This development is, of course, not merely restrictive, but rather an integrative concept of genital primacy that can explain the altered quality of sexual pleasure that begins with sexual maturity. Not only are the modalities of pleasure for the first time connected to the possibility of pregnancy, (at least in the case of heterosexuality) but the quality of orgasm in adults is significantly different from that of children. The interior genitals gain significance in puberty, a central task lies in their connection with external genitals to achieve an encompassing whole (Kestenberg, 1968).

This connection is a pre-requisite for the phantasy interplay between internalization and externalization during sexual experiences. Finally, the integration of the partial drives is connected to the integration of trans-gender aspects; thus, the phallic mode of pleasure is not limited to men and the receptive mode to women. Instead, both infantile modes are available to the love life of men and women, albeit in different ways. The transcendence of gender difference occurs in sexual experiences through the transcendence of partial drives which are elevated, integrated and therefore preserved. Infantile modes of desire and pleasure are not disconnected from the genitalia in the course of this re-inscription, but are reshaped and transformed under the genital influence.

These considerations lead me to question a decades-old consensus in psychoanalytical discourse. Freud, Melanie Klein, Irene Fast and many others in between were in agreement that the unlimited capacity of women for sexual pleasure was predicated on the repression of masculinity, male identifications and introjections. Observations during psychoanalysis with female patients have caused me to question this viewpoint. Therefore, I have attempted to show that the reverse is true; only integration, not repression, of the trans-gender aspects results in pleasurable sexual experiences. I do not understand this integration to be an intentional, conscious process, but rather unconscious psychic work. The idea of integration is posited in antithesis to the common psychoanalytical concept of differentiation, according to which trans-gender childhood identifications have to be discarded in the course of developing gender identity. This apparent need to discard is the result of a cultural primacy of gender dichotomy. This dichotomy conceptualizes gender not as a unified notion with two forms. Rather, the unity is dissolved and two separate genders are contemplated, genders that are thought of as mutually exclusive, polarized and hierarchical. My critique is aimed at the notion of a dichotomy of the sexes, at the conceptualization of a polarity as well as the normative descriptors of masculinity and femininity. According to traditional theory, gender identity develops through the drawing of boundaries and not through integration of the other. In psychoanalytical terms, this means it develops through denial or discarding and projection of trans-gender elements. Identity thus constituted necessarily brings restrictions of one's behaviour and experiences as well as a devaluation of the other.

Questioning gender dichotomy and the thesis that we achieve deep sexual pleasure only through integration of trans-gender elements ultimately leads to the recognition that the conventional distinction between male and female sexuality cannot be psychoanalytically upheld. My model of a gender-inclusive human sexuality that overcomes the polarity of masculinity and femininity, seeks to delineate a new path for a psychoanalytical discourse on gender. In the meantime, a wealth of studies on femininity has been conducted and thus the still valid criticism of Freud's femininity concepts has been integrated into mainstream psychoanalytical theory. Now, the time has come to no longer emphasize the differences between men and women, but to conceptualize what they have in common. The notion of difference remains of central importance for psychoanalytical thought; by talking about the primacy of the other, which is essential for my approach, I am emphasizing the difference of the other. This refers not only to the relationships between the sexes, but is valid for any relationship between humans and is also fundamental for the relationship of each individual with themselves. In this sense my argumentation does not undermine feminist insights. On the contrary, it is an attempt to carry on thinking about concerns for equality. Emphasizing the difference between men and women inevitably means reaffirming the hierarchy between the genders. I am attempting to describe the psychological conditions that must be understood, if one wishes to put an end to the continuing replication of this hierarchical order.

References

Abraham, Karl (1926). Character formation on the genital level of libido development. *International Journal of Psychoanalysis, 7*: 214–232.

Bassin, Donna (1996). Beyond the He and the She: Toward the reconciliation of masculinity and femininity in the postoedipal female mind. *Journal of the American Psychoanalytic Association, 44S*: 157–190.

Blos, Peter (1962). *On Adolescence. A Psychoanalytic Interpretation*. New York: Free Press.

Butler, Judith (1997). Melancholic gender. Refused identification. In: Butler, J. & Salih, S., *The Judith Butler Reader*. Malden, MA: Wiley-Blackwell, 2004.

Fast, Irene (1984). *Gender Identity: A Differentiation Model.* Hillsdale, NJ: Analytic Press.

Freud, Sigmund (1900a). The Interpretation of Dreams. *S.E.5.*

Freud, Sigmund (1905c). Jokes and the relation to the unconscious. *S.E., 8.*

Freud, Sigmund (1905d). Three essays on the theory of sexuality. *S.E., 7.*

Freud, Sigmund (1916–17). Introductory Lectures on psycho-analysis. *S.E., 15, 16.*

Freud, Sigmund (1927c). The future of an illusion. *S.E., 21.*

Gagnon, John H. & Simon, William. (2005). *Sexual Conduct. The Social Sources of Human Sexuality.* New Brunswick, N. J.: Aldine Transaction.

Kernberg, Otto F. (1991). Aggression and love in the relationship of the couple. *Journal of the American Psychoanalytic Association, 39*: 45–70.

Kernberg, Otto F. (2011). The Sexual Couple: A Psychoanalytic Exploration. *Psychoanalytic Review, 98*: 217–245.

Kestenberg, Judith. (1968). Outside and inside – male and female. *Journal of the American Psychoanalytic Association, 16*: 457–519.

Laplanche, Jean (1989). *New Foundations for Psychoanalysis.* Oxford: Basil Blackwell

Lerner, R.M. & Busch-Rossnagel, N.A. (eds.) (1981). *Individuals as Producer of their Development : A Life-Span Perspective.* New York : Academic Press.

May, Robert. (1986). Maleness from a psychoanalytic perspective. In: Friedman, Robert & Lerner, Leila (Eds.) Toward a new psychology of men. *Psychoanalytic Review, 73*, 4.

Mitchell, Stephen A. (2004). *Can Love Last? The Fate of Romance over Time.* New York: Norton.

Morgenthaler, Fritz. (1987). *Homosexualität, Heterosexualität, Perversion* (Homosexuality, heterosexuality, perversion). Frankfurt am Main: Fischer.

Quindeau, Ilka. (2004). Melancholie und Geschlecht (Melancholy and gender). *Zeitschrift für Sexualforschung. 17*, pp. 1–10.

Quindeau, Ilka. (2013). Seduction and desire – a psychoanalytical sexual theory beyond Freud. London: Karnac.

Reiche, Reimut. (1990). *Geschlechterspannung* (Gender tension). Frankfurt am Main: Fischer.

Sherfey, Mary Jane. (1966). The evolution and nature of female sexuality in relation to psychoanalytic theory. *Journal of the American Psychoanalytical Association, 14*, 28–128.

CHAPTER ELEVEN

Change and renewal in a woman's life

Mariam Alizade

Given that science and reflection leave the enigma of the concrete world intact, we are invited to explore it without any presuppositions[1].

—Merleau-Ponty, 1964, p. 207

Our life is more, however—unlike that suggested in Erikson´s phase model—than chronological time, more than numerical age; it contains likewise the ¨eon¨, the rhythmic, cyclical instinctive arc from birth to our conclusion, the time of contradictions.

—Schlesinger, 2003, p. 42

Introduction

The main objective of this Chapter is to deconstruct the signifier "woman" and to explore the interaction between linear time and unconscious time in the context of the life cycle of a woman. Derrida uses this term deconstruction (*Abbau* in German) and refers to it as an operation similar to taking apart a building to see how it is constituted or de-constituted. Deconstruction, in some way, is present in Freud's complemental series. More recently, Bleger (1963, pp. 116–134) studied the phenomena of reciprocal interactions, distinct forms of causality and determinism in the complemental series. I proposed a fourth complemental series constituted by the presence of cultural and historical factors which are internalized in distinct strata of the mind (Alizade, 2004a). This interrelates with the three series postulated by Freud in 1916. The inclusion of this fourth series highlights the principle of relativism, and is closely connected to the ideas which I will put forward in this Chapter.

Let us imagine life as an immense ocean which each human person is submerged in for a brief time, where each generation is constantly renewed and where people are born and die with their wishes, expectations and the experience of their own individual lives. Let us think in terms of transience and diversity. Diversity is mentioned by Freud (1912e) when he wrote:

> The extraordinary diversity of the psychical constellations concerned, the plasticity of all mental processes and the wealth of determining factors oppose any mechanization of the technique; and they bring it about that a course of action that is as a rule justified may at times prove ineffective, whilst one that is usually mistaken may once in a while lead to the desired end. (ibid., p. 123)

Morin (1974), in his in-depth studies on complex thought, claims to account for interactions among different fields of knowledge from a multidimensional viewpoint. If we acknowledge from the start that "complete knowledge is impossible" (ibid., p. 11), Morin urges us to avoid an abstract and one-dimensional view while denouncing the simplification paradigm that pervades current thinking. Simplification makes use of the disjunction, reduction and abstraction principles. In his opinion, hyperspecialization has fragmented the complex network of realities and has produced the illusion that one small chunk of reality constitutes reality itself. He has coined the term "blind intelligence" to express a way of thinking that does not take into account the inseparable relationship between the observer and what is observed, with the subsequent disintegration of realities. To his mind, the prevailing methodology gives rise to an increasing obscurantism in as much as science does not think about or reflect upon itself" (Alizade, 2004b). It is important that we do not fall into the trap of "blind intelligence", and that we endeavour to adopt a pluralistic viewpoint and to have an open-minded approach.

Time, change and renewal

Time moves along different axes. First, we have linear time, subject to chronology, and second, the timelessness dimension of the unconscious, where contradictions exist side by side.

Change and renewal interact with both chronology and timelessness. As described in different dictionaries, change is to alter the condition or the appearance of something and renewal means to make something new, via a process of transformation. Renewal consists of a kind of metamorphosis through which the psyche gives new meaning to representations and affects. The concept of psychic renewal is closely linked to mental health and explains the youthful, vigorous attitude in those in their later years, as well as those who seem old before their time.

This Chapter considers mental renewal as an element which enables an individual to modify and reach different conclusions regarding the different events in their life time. To renew oneself means to move away from chronology, and to come closer to the timelessness of the unconscious. Renewal is inextricably linked to death and resurrection, to loss and gain; and is inherent in our existence. It is not subject to the laws of chronology and the different stages of life. It functions at an individual level, or at a group or relational level. In the latter case, the other becomes an agent of renewal.

As Schlesinger (2003) points out, the chronological stages of life, brilliantly described by Erikson (1997), possess a high degree of relativism. Chodorov (1999, p. 17) begins her book by insisting that "it is important to question the excessive confidence in traditional psychoanalytical theories about development which are based on the past to explain the present, or which assume the existence of a universal psychosexual trajectory of development."

Any classification of the stages of life will always be tentative and subject to exceptions. Renovation challenges the established criteria and/or the static character of the stages of existence.

In his brief text on transience (1916a), Freud writes:

> Transience value is scarcity value in time. Limitation in the possibility of an enjoyment raises the value of the enjoyment. ... As regards

the beauty of Nature, each time it is destroyed by winter it comes
again next year, so that in relation to the length of our lives it can in
fact be regarded as eternal. The beauty of the human form and face
vanish forever in the course of our own lives, but their evanescence
only lends them a fresh charm. (Freud, 1916a, p. 305)[2]

What is this fresh charm he refers to? Evidently he means the charm
inherent in the capturing of this transience. "The burning life of the
ephemeral", writes Bachelard (1932, p. 24) when referring to the phenomenon of seizing the eternity of the instant. A lucid process of work-
ing-through liberates the life-force. The human being manages to detach
themselves from the psychic burden of the duration and conventions of
chronological time, and succeeds in becoming a person who lives in
a timeless, ever-changing present. This small recess within their mind
which is outside-time is a guarantee of a lively and playful approach to
life, which enhances an individual's quality of life by freeing them from
the weight of a reality which may be overloaded with meaning.

Kristeva (1998) lucidly explains that in all analysis there is a
combination of conscious, linear time and a time "outside-of-time"
(*hors-temps*) of the unconscious. This author asks herself:

> What do we do with time which, by definition, is conscious, if we
> postulate an unconscious psyche? Therefore, what sort of psychic
> apparatus is this that operates between both time and "outside-
> time? Such is the scandal of Homo analyticus, which Freud invites
> us to contemplate, confessing (with excessive modesty, as was his
> custom) his own difficulty in surmounting this difficult task which
> he has bequeathed to us. (ibid., pp. 276–277)

Renewal is linked to this dimension of timelessness, to Freudian *Zeitlos*,
and provides the conditions for a psychic eternity which is revitalising
and restorative. The new raises an important philosophical question; is
there anything new which did not already exist beforehand? For some,
the new is something that already existed but which reveals itself at a
specific moment; for others, it arises from nothingness, a vacuum, and
is closely linked to the creative process. That is, it is "creatio ex nihilo"
(Ferrater Mora, 1999, pp. 2593–2594).

Newness appears in both forms. The element which illuminates the
new and furthers confusion surrounding it emerges from the depths
of the pre-existing unconscious, and also from a void full of creative

potential. This creativity originates in a way which is imperceptible and unknowable. These adjectives reflect the undeveloped creative potential of each individual. The creative process is a catalyst, preparing the ground for psychic renewal and for the transgression of the normative discipline of the "facts of life", which is assumed to be absolute and unquestionable. We know all too well that chronic, stagnated states of mourning and psychic structural rigidity are obstacles to the free-flow of energy. Reaching the end of the mourning process enables the subject to enjoy good mental health. When this minor state of mourning cannot be positively sustained, the mourning process intensifies and new lost objects impose a burden on the ego.

The most important feelings which hinder renovative psychic movements are fear and hatred. To rid oneself of hate is to improve the quality of individual life. Phobias and negative sentiments inhibit thought and prevent the subject from generating new representations and new links. I have suggested a particular type of phobia, (Alizade, 2001) the phobia of oneself. This is the fear of the development of one's own potential with the consequent psychic refuge in the mechanisms constructed by habits and conventions.

Those elements which are conducive to renewal are sensuality, plasticity of defence mechanisms and the ability to mourn.

The human being

Human identity includes the whole of human beings within a primary asexual or non-gendered order. These early identifying features are mental organizers that co-exist with gender identities. Human gender is the central pillar from which the diversity of genders stems.

> The binary division laid down by social rules does not eliminate the human character of the species. The human dimension is sustained as an on-going quality and continues to be present over the course of the human being's life. (Alizade, 2009)

This powerful affirmation will doubtless provoke controversy in gender studies for those who feel that the human universe is based on the principle of gender and sexualization. As I wrote:

> Freud dealt tangentially with the human aspect of the psyche. He wrote (1933a): "However, we find enough to study in those human

individuals who, through the possession of female genitals, are characterized as manifestly or predominantly feminine." (p. 116) And a little later: "… but we do not overlook the fact that an individual woman may be a human being in other respects as well." (ibid. p. 136).

In his metapsychology, he referred more specifically to this issue when dealing with the primary identification. He wrote:

> The effects of the first identifications made in earliest childhood will be general and lasting. This leads us back to the origin of the ego ideal; for behind it there lies hidden an individual's first and most important identification, his identification with the father in his own personal prehistory. (Freud, 1923b, p. 31)

I would like to draw attention to the footnote which follows:

> Perhaps it would be safer to say "with the parents"; for before a child has arrived at definite knowledge of the difference between the sexes, the lack of a penis, it does not distinguish in value between its father and its mother. … In order to simplify my presentation I shall discuss only identification with the father. (ibid., p. 31)

I proposed that the notion of a psychic world, outside the sex-gender system, be considered as a transitional concept which, by definition, "suggests a territory which is able to admit contradictions," and which maintains" concepts of judgement in suspension while their heuristic value seems irreplaceable" (Green, 1990, p. 418). A human being is not permanently the product of their sex or the multiple facets of their gender. The set of possibilities deriving from the sex-gender system (nuclear identity, momentary feelings of being a man or a woman, feminine or masculine representations) do not constitute the totality of the field of representations.

There are mental processes which lie outside the dominion of psychosexuality. The universals of existence constitute a common backdrop to our journey through life. These universals are laws or general conditions which make up the basic life matrix of experiences and events. Helplessness, finitude, the need for the other in order to survive, are universal elements inherent in the human condition which are not dictated by sexual or gender differences (Alizade, 2009).

On women's lives

When we talk about women, who are we referring to exactly? Is there anything specific to a woman's life?

The concept of penis-no penis with all its symbolic derivations (phallus-castration) establishes a primary dissimilarity between the sexes that marks the generic sets of men and women. This difference inaugurates an initial phase of comparison and rivalry between the sexes. The onset of menstrual periods inaugurates a new order and a second difference, this time based on having/not having blood. The red coloured fluid that returns again and again with its rhythmic singularity in each woman establishes the bloodied difference. This difference divides the sexes in a way that is based on antithesis, blood versus no blood. The passage through a woman's life is made up of stages marked by the cyclical flow of blood, the interruptions in menstruation, pregnancy and menopause (Alizade, 2002, p. 29).

Physiology is not sufficient to bring women together into one uniform category. The subjective dimension of the body prevails over anatomy and physiology, breaking boundaries and creating multiple scenarios (Alizade, 2007). Feminine heterogeneity embraces masculine facets of women; asexual women, maternal women, transvestite women, transsexual women, ill women, well women, erotic women, women who are simply people, and many others. The constitution of the ego, ego interest, identifications, and unconscious internal rules, among other psychoanalytic parameters, are all generators of different facets of identity. Benoist insists that:

> An identity which is crude, immediate, and superficial, must give way to an investigation of the profound structures which mould identity in their relational aspect: the question of the Other appears as a constitutive factor of identity. (Benoist, 1977, p. 15)

We need to have a keen awareness of the culturally-bound character codes connected to the body. Each culture and each stage of history influences behaviour, functions and relational meaning with respect to the body. Public opinion, internalized in the super-ego, dictates aesthetic criteria, erotic gestures, and rituals of love. The socio-cultural context interprets meta-verbal body language and assigns values to specific movements and expressions.

The sexuality of women also lies within the realm of diversity. In the same way in which there is no one way of living life, there is no one way of experiencing sexual enjoyment of the body. In *Feminine Sensuality* (1999), I have drawn attention to the plurality of pleasures and the potential for pleasure which may or may not derive from a woman's body. In an erotic relationship, a human being who was born a woman, may on occasion discard their original gender and temporarily metamorphose into another, partially or totally. The interactions of a partial drive and the projections of different objects both onto oneself and onto the other, generate an enormous variety of imaginary fields. In his fascinating essay *Thalassa*, Ferenczi (1924) introduced us to what he termed the anfimixis of eroticism, that is to say, the fusion of distinct types of eroticism between two subjects. At no point does he draw a clear distinction between man and woman. Likewise, Bataille (1957) in his study on eroticism explores sexuality from a purely human perspective.

The fundamental metamorphoses are not those which depend on the exterior transformation of the body during the course of linear time but rather those which take place invisibly within the interior of the mind. It is here that I would like to place emphasis on the potential for renewal that each woman possesses when she is able to step outside the conventional structures of the stages of life. The mind is the generative source of representations and affects which organize the psychic interpretation of each experience.

From the perspective of positivity (Alizade, 2010), renewal is a challenge through which woman, whatever their sexual orientation, their identification, their wishes, their quality of life, the moment in their lives; can succeed in transforming their thoughts about themselves. They are capable of converting *thanatos* into the erotic and attenuating their fear of those stages of life which will lead them to decrepitude and death. This psychic process is a genuine liberation in which the power of consciousness intervenes. Each life is a unique adventure with the potential for creativity.

Binary dimension and complexity

Two basic elements underline identification conflicts in sex and gender; belonging and recognition. The binary nature of the sexes is ingrained in our culture as an indisputable fact. Feminists position themselves strictly as women whereas transgendered people claim the right to belong to a stable binary sexual identity (man-woman). In contrast, queer groups challenge this binary perspective and defend the right to multiform gender and sexuality outside all socio-cultural norms.

Butler (2009) highlights the suffering and the controversies among feminists, members of the queer movement and transsexual groups. This great diversity of identification which queer people aim for contrasts with the desire of a transgendered person to belong to a specific gender. The complexity of the notion of object in psychoanalysis is in line with this identification diversity. Psychoanalysis has emphasised the importance of the projection of an object onto the other.

> Freud described the unconscious projection of a mother into her husband. He wrote. "Perhaps the real fact is that the attachment to the mother is bound to perish, precisely because it was the first and was so intense, just as one can often see happen in the first marriages of young women which they have entered into when they were most passionately in love. In both situations the attitude of love probably comes to grief from the disappointments that are unavoidable and from the accumulation of occasions for aggression. As a rule second marriages turn out much better." (Freud, SE, 1931b, p. 234)

This quotation indicates the presence of an invisible and affective object projected into a manifest relationship. Psychoanalysis sails on a sea of undiscovered meaning, in a way similar to that of new hieroglyphics and codes that expect to be deciphered as if they were dreams. The same happens in the analysis of the positive and negative Oedipus complex and in the interplay of identifications. Butler stated that:

> To become culturally assimilated into the world, individuals create an active gender project which they constantly act out and which *seems* to be a natural fact. (Femenias, 2003, p. 35)

The italics of the word "seems" emphasize the appearance of female homogeneity and the cultural error of considering this to be natural. Butler challenges the idea of two natural sexes by exploring the social and historical roots of determination and the binary division of human beings into men and women. As Butler clearly states, even sex is determined culturally, and everything which seems natural is merely appearance.

Gender studies, investigations into neo-sexuality, intersexes, transexuality, same-sex parenting, interdisciplinary studies, and queer studies among others have opened up new areas of investigation. Heterogeneity, relativism, deconstruction, subjectivity and link interactions have been converted into conceptual models which have provided answers to many questions and which have generated theoretical and clinical uncertainties (Alizade, 2004b).

Feminists position themselves strictly as women whereas transgendered people claim the right to belong to a stable binary sexual identity (man-woman) and queer groups challenge this binary perspective.

Due to the incorporation of different identification and socio-cultural problems in clinical practice, psychoanalysis should consider reviewing certain theories and their psychic consequences. Berlin (2004) distinguishes between psychoanalytic listening and gender listening and explains different interpretive styles according to the theoretical framework and the training of the analyst.

Theory sustains clinical practice as long as its hypotheses are flexible enough to accommodate new findings. New paradigms emerge, some tentatively and others more boldly.

Clinical vignette

A patient sought treatment due to a conflict in which chronology and the process of renewal were at odds with each other. She had just turned thirty nine. She had been an accountant for an important company and had retired four years previously as she had wanted to explore new avenues, and to study philosophy and drama. Life had been kind to her had it not been for the fact that chronological time was making her suffer. Menopause and maternity approached as two important events on the horizon of her life. Menopause did not worry her.

In contrast, pregnancy and bringing up a child were conflictive representations. She began to feel pressured by the cultural expectation that, in terms of her age (linear time) she should be a mother. "If only I had more time biologically to decide what I want to do", she sighed in one session. She put pressure on her partner, often aggressively, to agree to have a child. She was, however, ambivalent about having a child. The idea of becoming a mother depressed her as well as the prospect of the physiological demands to which she would be submitted. Her gynaecologist had warned her that, after forty, having a baby could pose risks. The patient felt dependent on the other (husband/child) as a limiting internal mandate. For her, this period of new life-projects ran counter to bringing up a child and the managing of a household. Maternity was something unchangeable, rigid, which conformed to social norms. Her conscious awareness of not wishing to have a child produced feelings of sadness and guilt. The falseness of her happiness and smiles could be felt when, during the session, she said how wonderful it would be to become pregnant, and how she hoped this would happen. Her face would then show signs of tiredness and a lack of enthusiasm. She would lower her gaze and remain silent.

Should an analyst think that sound mental health depends on the enthusiastic acceptance of maternity? Should they consider that true renewal is based on becoming pregnant, giving birth, breast feeding, the profound bond between mother and child, the total devotion to the infant? Should the analyst turn back the clock with interpretations so that the patient will get married and will become pregnant? Does there exist only one, correct psychoanalytical way of leading one's life? These moments in clinical practice, rooted in mistaken notions about the relationship between nature and culture, require the suspension of ideologies and theoretical assumptions. What is needed is a willingness to explore new clinical perspectives regarding factors which influence mental health.

Conclusions

As mentioned before, the deconstruction of the human being as a woman brings into play a multiplicity of psychic alternatives and avatars of identity which question the conventional shared beliefs about age and the stages of life.

The detection of turning points, contradictions and paradoxes in the observation of many women requires an element of creativity when listening. A positive, healthy combination of temporality and culture, of classical and emerging theories, should be coupled with scientific awareness of the complexity of variables involved.

The analyst can detect different levels of well-being and pathology both in the adherence to the laws of chronology and the pseudo-renovative defence mechanisms which deny the passage of time. Pathology can be observed in the desire to have a child whilst a sound state of mind can be seen in the rejection of maternity. Pathology is evident in her compulsion to have a partner whereas good mental health can be seen in her enjoyment of being alone. The parameters regarding mental health need to be reconsidered.

The psychosexual world of women gives rise to a dialogue between psyche and soma, which provides the signifiers for different life experiences. This dialogue is neither univocal nor stereotypical. The suspension of the chronological dimension is the necessary condition for renewal and psychic rejuvenation. I consider that the capacity for renewal goes beyond biological cycles in those women who enjoy good mental health.

I would like to propose some key criteria for a healthy psyche. These include the development of goodness within the human being (life drive), the joy of living and the integrative harmony of the inner world; whatever an individual's choice of objects or sexual orientation, or whatever form their mental map of identifications and identities may take. Each human being has the right to develop from the basis of psychic and cultural diversity, which will facilitate their individual passage through the different stages of their life.

Abstract

The main objective of this Chapter is to deconstruct the concept of a woman, and to explore the interaction between linear and unconscious time in the context of the life cycle of a woman. Change and renewal interact with both chronology and timelessness. This Chapter considers mental renewal as an element which enables an individual to modify and reach different conclusions regarding the events in their life time. It states that it is important not to fall into the trap of "blind intelligence", following Morin´s concept (1974), and to adopt a pluralistic viewpoint and an open-minded approach.

The Chapter develops the importance of human identity which includes the whole of human beings within a primary asexual or non-gendered order. These early identifying features coexist with gender identities.It also raises crucial questions such as: When we talk about women, who are we referring to exactly? Is there anything specific to a woman's life?

The sexuality of women lies within the realm of diversity. There is no one way of experiencing sexual enjoyment of the body. In the last part, the Chapter considers the binary dimension and recognition, as two fundamental pillars that intervene in gender identities. This Chapter also includes a clinical vignette and states that the deconstruction of the female human being brings into play a multiplicity of psychic alternatives and avatars of identity which question conventional shared beliefs about age and the stages of life.

References

Alizade, M. (1999). *Feminine Sensuality*. London: Karnac. (1992). *La Sensualidad Femenina*. Buenos Aires, Amorrortu Editores.

Alizade, M. (2001). La fobia a uno mismo. Paper presented at the XXIII Simposium y Congreso interno de APdeBA 1, 2 y 3 de noviembre 2001. Unpublished manuscript.

Alizade, M. (2002). The fluidity of the female universe and its psychic consequences. In: Alizade, A. (Ed.), *The Embodied Female* (pp. 25–36). London: Karnac, 2002.

Alizade, M. (2010). *Psychoanalysis and Positivity*. London: Karnac. (2010).

Alizade, M. *Lo positivo en psicoanálisis*. Buenos Aires: Lumen (2002).

Alizade, M. (2004a). La cuarta serie complementaria. (Unpublished manuscript).

Alizade, M. (2004b). Relaciones Lógicas y Controversias entre Género y Psicoanálisis. In: (Alizade, M., Lartigue T. Ed.) *Psicoanálisis y Relaciones de Género*, (pp. 17–32). Buenos Aires: Lumen, 2004.

Alizade, M. (2007). Paper presented in Río de Janeiro march 2007 at the VI-COWAP Latinamerican Dialogue (Cuerpo y Subjetividad: Castración y Finitud.) (Unpublished manuscript).

Alizade, M. (2009). Femininity and the human dimension. In: Glocer Fiorini, L., Abelin-Sas, G. (Eds.), *On Freud´s ¨Femininity* (pp. 198–211) London: Karnac.

Bachelard, G. (1932). *La intuición del instante*. Mexico: Fondo de Cultura Económica.

Bataille, G. (1957). *L´Erotisme*. Paris: Les Editions de Minuit.

Benoist, J. M. (1977). Facetas de la Identidad. In: (1981). *La Identidad* (pp. 11–21). Seminar chaired by Lévi-Strauss, España, Ediciones Petrel.

Berlin, D. (2004). Escucha del efecto del género en el paciente psicoanalítico. In: Alizade, A., Silveira, M., Gus, M. (Eds.) *Masculino-Femenino. Cuestiones Psicoanalíticas Contemporáneas* (pp. 58–65). Buenos Aires: Lumen, 2004.

Bleger, J. (1963). *Psicología de la Conducta*. Buenos Aires: Eudeba.

Butler, J. (2009). El transgénero y la actitud de la revuelta. *Rev. De Psicoan. LXVI, 3*, 2009, pp. 731–748.

Chodorow, N. (1999). *The Power of Feelings*. Yale University Press: New Haven-London.

Erikson, E. (1997). *The Life Cycle Completed*. Norton and Company: New York, London.

Femenías, M. L. (2003). *Judith Butler: Introducción a su lectura*. Buenos Aires: Catálogos.

Ferenczi, S. (1924). *Thálassa, una teoría de la genitalidad*. Buenos Aires: Letra Viva.

Ferrater Mora, J. (1999). *Diccionario de Filosofía*. Barcelona: Editorial Ariel.

Freud, S. (1912e). On beginning the treatment. Further recommendations on the technique of psychoanalysis. *S.E., 12*: 123–144.

Freud, S. (1916a). On transience. *S.E., 14*: 303–307.

Freud, S. (1916b). Introductory Lectures on Psycho-analysis. Lecture XXII *S.E.16: 346–7*

Freud, S. (1923b). The Ego and the Id. *S.E., 19*.

Freud, S. (1931b). Female Sexuality. *S.E., 21*: p. 234.

Freud, S. (1933a). Femininity in New Introductory Lectures in Psycho-Analysis. *S.E., 22*.

Green, A. (1990). Lo originario en Psicoanálisis, *Rev. De Psicoan, XLVII*, 3: 413–418.

Kristeva, J. (1998). El escándalo de lo fuera-del-tiempo. *Rev. De psicoan.*, T LV, 2, pp. 269–285.

Merleau-Ponty, M. (1964). *Le visible et l´invisible*. Paris: Gallimard.

Morin, E. (1990). L´intelligence aveugle. In: Name of editors, *Introduction à la pensée complexe* (pp. 15–24). Paris: ESF, 1990. L´intelligence aveugle is the first chapter of Morin´s book.

Schlesinger. G. (2003). A ¨pause¨ for changing life: climacteric change and menopause. In: Alizade (Ed.) *Studies on Femininity* (pp. 41–51). London, Karnac, 2003.

Notes

1. Puisque la science et la réflexion laissent finalement intacte l´énigme du monde brut, nous sommes invités à l´interroger sans rien présupposer.
2. Freud, 1915, GW, X, p. 359. ¨Der Vergänglichkeitswert ist ein Seltenheitswert in der Zeit. Die Beschränkung in der Möglichkeit des Genusses erhöht dessen Kostbarkeit. Was die Schönheit der Natur bertrifft, so kommt sie nach jeder Zerstörung durch den Winter im nächsten Jahre wieder, und diese Wiederkehr darf im Verhältnis zu unserer Lebensdauer als eine ewige bezeichnet werden. Die Schönheit des menschlichen Körpers und Angesichts sehen wir innerhalb unseres eigenen Lebens für immer schwinden, aber diese Kurzlebigkeit fügt zu ihren Reizen einen neuen hinzu.

CHAPTER TWELVE

Menopause dreams

Teresa Rocha Leite Haudenschild

But all things that come to an end,
much more than being beautiful,
these, will stay …

—Drummond de Andrade, 1951

Abstract

The author suggests (Benedek, 1950) that facing the losses of the menopause in positive terms (Meyer, 2002) depends on the capacity constructed in preceding life for working through mourning; including primary, Oedipal, puberty and single-life mourning, and also that experienced in everyday life. This requires a constant contact with internal and external reality, and therefore contact with psychic pain and a capacity for coping with it. The mourning dreams of a fifty-five year old analysand are presented here, in which she mourns the loss of her young body and sexuality, of biological fertility, and of the children who have left home to form their own family. Among these dreams there is one of recapitulation (Guillaumin, 1979) in which she integrates various periods of her life.

Introduction

Menopause dreams may be of mourning or of a greater or lesser denial of internal and external reality (Segal, 1993), as the result of escape from psychic pain originating from the awareness that the body grows old. These are dreams which highlight the passage through this very important time in her life in which the hormonal changes are as intense as in puberty. In puberty there is a hormonal increase, whereas here we see a drop in hormonal activity. Deutsch (1944) suggested that everything that a woman gains in puberty she loses in the menopause. The psychoanalyst and endocrinologist, Benedek (1927), disagreed with this point of view, stating that a woman who has sufficiently realized her motherhood and sexual life will not experience psychic disturbance in the menopause, since here, as in puberty, there is a new edition of the Oedipal conflict; and the mature woman may confront this from a position of greater serenity and without intense ambivalence. Laci Fessler (1950), in research involving 100 women, relates that fifteen did not present physical or psychic symptoms and faced the menopause in a positive way. This was also proposed by Meyers (2002), in the sense of constituting "a new, better integrated, better functioning, whole self, invested with an increased self-esteem and capacity for new pleasures, and a sense of freedom" (ibid., p. 99). The patient I present in this Chapter belongs to this latter group and her dreams are of mourning, one of which is a "dream of recapitulation" (Guillaumin, 1981).

Dream work and mourning work

Guillaumin (1981) writes that since the dream is a child of the day and of the night and of love between the Id and the Ego, it can be maintained at the disposition of diurnal memory, seeing perhaps a posterior complementary elaboration which will send it to a waking life, after which it will be submitted to the world following the reality principle, of which it is the nocturnal emissary adulterated by the desire to sleep (ibid., p. 283).

The analyst as a paternal representative connected to the secondary process and the diurnal reality helps the patient to leave the maternal oneiric envelope of the work of the dream (Green, 1972), to leave the scene of the dream, essentially visual, to comprehend what was dreamed.

For Bion (1963) the capacity to dream presupposes a psychic apparatus for thinking thoughts (alpha function) capable of transforming the sensitive data of internal and external reality into alpha elements originating from an emotional experience (capable of being stored in the memory). These are the elements which will be articulated in the production of dreams by the "ineffable subject of the Unconscious" (Grotestein, 2000). Therefore, despite being the fruit of unconscious primary processes, the dream already presupposes a basis of representations constructed from secondary processes of contact with reality which are stored in the Unconscious.

The mourning consists in renunciation of investment in certain objects and demands the work of a complete ego, not functioning solely on the primary process as in dreams. The objects lost by women during menopause are the body and the sexuality of youth, biological fertility, the relationship with their own young children and the family constituted with them. However, some mourning dreams are like artistic creations which prepare new investments of objects in the reality of waking life. Among these dreams, we may think of "dreams of recapitulation" (Guillaumin, 1979) that remember the investments of periods of a life, or of a complete life, like "turning a page" (Quinodoz, 1999) in order to bring to light other possibilities of investment and object relations.

Menopause dreams of mourning

Mrs. A.

I now present the dreams of mourning of a fifty-five year old analysand, a professional photographer, who had just stopped menstruating, despite having been told two months previously during an ultrasound examination that her ovaries were still productive. Her doctor informed her that her menstrual cycle had stopped as a result of a loss of elasticity in her Fallopian tubes. After much deliberation, she opted not to take hormonal supplements. Having experienced a regular cycle from the age of eleven, menstruation had now stopped, never to return. She did not experience the hot flushes associated with menopause and only a few instances of insomnia, which were tackled without stress, as she took advantage of the time to read something of interest. She has four children, two of whom are married, five grandchildren and she maintains an active and pleasurable sexual life with her husband of more than thirty years.

She comments that the arrival of the menopause brought a serenity she had never previously experienced. It was like a well-deserved retirement. She tells me that she would wake in the morning at the same time each day, but since it was a Saturday she had decided to sleep a little longer. She awoke again, with this dream fresh in her mind and wrote it down.

I ask her to tell me the dream, but instead she reads it to me:

Path

I am on a wide dirt track, the colour of sand, looking at tall dry grasses swaying in the wind. It's very early in the morning, the sun is shining brightly and the sky is clear blue, like in an Italian film, beautiful ....

Suddenly, from nowhere, within the tall grasses emerge a young bride and groom. The long forked veil, secured by a ring of flowers on her head, flows like the transparent wings of a white butterfly fluttering in the wind.

He is joyful, arm in arm with her, beaming, both walking to the sound of music driven by drums and a hurdy gurdy (a medieval instrument).

Behind them, a procession of youngsters.

When they all reach the track where I am, they turn left and follow it, turning their backs to me, without noticing me ....

The music becomes quieter and quieter until I can't hear it any longer.

Faster music suddenly becomes audible, now driven by flutes, and again from nowhere, in the grasses more to the right, come children, jumping playfully.

The smallest are in front, holding each other's little hands. The girls' heads adorned with flowers. The boys are in short trousers revealing their chubby little legs.

The different ages pass, the last being almost the age of the couple who have gone.

The children also come to my path and also head to the left, as if they don't see me.

I see them bobbing up and down until they disappear over the horizon.

Unexpectedly, melancholic flutes play, slower. And, from among the tall grasses appears a humble funeral procession. The few followers bear a simple coffin of light red wood. And sad, heavy, and slow, they take my path to the left, like the others.

I realize that it is already late, almost night, I must go. But to where?

Dream of Recapitulation

She relates that what most impressed her about the dream was the feeling of being outside of the dream, as an observer, and the surprising scenes that came to pass. She also observes that the dream was punctuated with music driven by repetitive percussion, with a rhythm appropriate to each period of life.

Her own admission of not being present in the dream confirms her absence from the scene, but that at a certain moment she remembers standing in the path, by saying "my path", just exactly when she is not seen by the children.

She responds to me with a tone of sadness: "Yes. They were captivating. I really wanted to be seen by them …."

I tell her that the dream seems to speak of various life cycles; youth, infancy, maturity (represented by her position in the middle of the path) and death.

I ask her for associations, and so we begin the work of elaborating the scenes of the dream. She relates the veil of the bride, forked in two, to her own wedding veil, matching with the Renaissance style dress. The kindness of the groom she relates to the way in which her husband treated her. The long dry grasses are like those in autumn on their farm, where the couple would often spend the weekends, each of them attending to their work in their own area. The wind indicates the breath ever present in each passing moment of life. The wind among the grasses reminds her of the sea, as with the movement of the waves, continuous.

I say to her that this path where she stands in the dream is like the firm ground of her intimate life. This ground is constructed in the primary intimate relationship with the mother, and is the basis for all of the marriages to come, starting with the marriage or reconciliation with oneself, and present also in our relationships in the analytical field. This image reveals that her unconscious was telling her to take account of the situation in which she found herself; in the middle of life's path, contemplating what she has already lived and what remains of these life cycles; in order to be able to proceed. She can proceed with the support of her husband, both of them being reborn into a new life, each with their own creative work. After a pause, she says to me; "Did you know that psyche in Greek means both the soul and butterfly?" referring to the Renaissance style veil which appeared from the grasses like a huge butterfly.

"So it's as if an enormous newly born butterfly had taken off, fluttering over the head of the bride? As if her psyche might protect her in new marriages to come?" I say.

She falls silent, as if in thought, and says that in each scene there were details that really impressed her. She notes that the hurdy gurdy is an instrument from the Middle Ages whose sound had always attracted her, as if marking the rhythm of her life. And that even from the perspective of non-participant observer, each scene provoked a great deal of emotion and surprise.

"In middle age, you can stop in the middle of the path and watch life go on around you, continuing, without end" I offer.

She tells me that when the bride and groom go, the appearance of the children captures all her attention, enchanting her.

I say that the girls of varying ages show their bodies coming into bloom, and also a blossoming mental life, indicated by the flowers in their hair. Flowers that we can correlate to the flower and the veil-butterfly flying on the head of the bride.

She says that the children were very graceful and seemed to be full of joy, each one in their own particular way. As a counterpoint to their happiness, this was the moment in the dream in which she felt the most sadness.

I remind her that this was a goodbye to the possibility of her being a mother again and therefore the most difficult and saddest farewell; however, she would continue to enjoy the sexual life of a couple.

She agrees and adds that the aspect of the scene with the children that had the most impact on her was seeing the young legs of the boys.

I remind her that she enjoys doing the things she does in her own particular way, just like the children. She had lamented just a few weeks previously the fact that her husband could no longer dance with her the way he had always done, since his legs were becoming older and weaker.

She comments that her own legs were like this too: "I think it's the part of the body that suffers age the most. My breasts are still firm, but my legs are full of fatty parts, and are getting old". She remembers that when she met her husband, still a boy at the time, he wore shorts that showed his knees, like the boys in the dream.

I comment that this says that, just like her husband, she also does not have a young girl's legs, such as those of her grandchildren.

She says: "At least I can still dance."

Yes, I say. At least you can still move your body and in your mind: you have inside you a happy child who can still dance, and even jump.

She laughs and becomes silent for a while.

We reach the end of the session and in the following sessions she does not return to talk about the subject of the dream until about a month later, when having just arrived, she says:

I was thinking of the saying of Mies Van Der Rohe: "Less is more".

What reminded you of that?

The simple wooden coffin in the dream, without golden handles and ornamentation …. It was of light red wood, and very well made, like those boxes handmade by craftsmen. It seemed light: the bearers were slow and heavy because they were sad, not because of the weight of the coffin.

You are speaking of the sadness of your losses due to the menopause and due to the awareness of not having as many years ahead of you in life as you had in your youth. But if we confront all this in a simple manner, everything becomes much lighter.

The music was sad. The flutes were slow. It reminded me of the procession for Psyche, when her parents take her to marry an unknown groom and leave her on the edge of a precipice where Zephyr will come to take her to Eros. The music was funereal and not happy, like that of a wedding procession.

Like Psyche, you feel you have to face your unknown destiny alone, carried by life's wind, the path of an unknown partner, with the hope of retribution through love (Eros).

I did some work recently for a magazine aimed at women which is celebrating its 50th anniversary and the Art Director loved it.

If you can't have any more children you can create in a partnership: in your work, with your husband, here with me.

What is impressive about "Psyche" is the loneliness, and the surprises that arise in each moment of the story. Have you read it?

You would like to know if I can be close to you in your thoughts of having to confront your new life. But on the other hand, I think you are saying, through what you say to me about Psyche, that you also have your internal parents who accompany you on this course in the direction of your future life. However, you realize that every day that passes, you will have to face surprises alone.

Yes. Psyche's parents go to where the path and the land end. Since they can't stay to see who will come for her, they leave her there dressed as a bride. But they are certain that she will have a good marriage.

Your internal parents seem to guarantee you that you will make good partnerships with those who produce creative objects. But I was thinking of the sadness of Psyche at saying goodbye to her parents who leave her to the sound of flutes that seem to cry.

Yes. It was a sound that penetrated us.

Recapitulation of the affective history of the dreamer

This dream dramatizes the affective history of Mrs A. Her dream performs a diachronic synthesis of a long period of time, "as if (she) had a real source of documentation of (her) affective history, that escapes the conscious" (Guillaumin, 1979). Furthermore, beyond this dream there is a prospective dimension, as if it is preparing the analysand for what is to come; growing old, and death.

Guillaumin suggests that the dramatization and the secondary figurative narrative forces us to "ask, at least in certain cases, whether or not the dream Ego is, in various aspects, more mature and integrated than that in waking life" (1979, p. 299) with a very different power of organization than the waking ego.

We are not surprised in analysis that this power (of the dream Ego) should be particularly invested, erupting in the conscious in the moment of the memory of the dream, which resends to the awakened person objects which are far more complete and with much more elaborate contents, of which the person manipulates in the direct transference". I think that this ego is the "ineffable subject of the Unconscious. (Grotstein, 2001)

Guillaumin draws our attention to the function of the para-excitation of dreams of recapitulation, which defends the analysand from the persecution of partial objects, since it integrates situations of loss with scenes that (as in the case of Mrs A.) are integrated with the analysand's entire life. Therefore they favour mourning and not melancholic or pathological solutions.

Quinodoz (2008) points out that people who grow old have to rethink their own histories. "A person realizes that the presence of death is in the frame of their life, which grants them another mode of self-awareness" (ibid., p. 80); and indeed of knowing others, in inter-subjective relationships.

Museums

Two months later Mrs. A brought me the following dream: I am with my husband in a foreign country, staying in the luxurious house of an Arabic couple, and my husband is there to carry out some work for them. The woman is young and kind, and comes to my room while I am getting dressed to go out and suggests more appropriate clothes for the street in her country: skirts which cover the legs and comfortable flat shoes.

We leave and make our way along the streets to the museum, lying in a kind of hammock carried by servants; she lies between my husband and I. Some streets are covered by arcades, richly adorned with reliefs and paintings which I follow with my eyes, fascinated. They are scenes from everyday life, like the Japanese prints from the eighteenth century, but the scenes are Arabic (Note 2). We arrive at the museum which is situated below street level, accessible via some narrow steps. After moving through various rooms, we arrive in a room with great slabs of stones exhibiting fossils: small animals, some cut through the middle, showing graciously designed insides, revealed forever.... I spend a long time in this room and when I reach the end I can't find my husband and the young woman. I walk through the other rooms alone and when I arrive at the last, I don't find them there either, as I had hoped. I leave and ask on the street where the nearest museum is (which we were also due to visit). It is becoming dark as I make my way there. I climb a small hill and encounter a group of teenage girls surrounding a sweet stall which belongs to one of them. I ask her for the museum and she gestures to her left extending her hand, and I see it illuminated, atop a higher hill. She tells me that I have to go down to a stream (showing me the way down the hill, continuing my path), then cross it and climb up to the museum. And she adds: "It's not far". But it is dark and I think it is dangerous, and it would be better to go the following day. So I ask her where I can find a taxi. She indicates, behind her, to the right, and I see a street below busy with traffic. I go down and I resolve to wait for a taxi however long until one passes. At this point I realize that I don't know where I am going: I don't have the address, nor do I remember the name of the foreign couple with whom we are staying.

I wake up and my husband is not by my side in bed. I call him and he answers. He is reading and I go to him and give him a hug.

When I go back to sleep, I am back in the house with my husband in some sort of bar (like those we sit in when are waiting for a place in a restaurant) and the man of the house suddenly appears smiling with his brother. Both are very alike and dark skinned, and the owner introduces his brother to my husband, recommending my husband's services. I awake reconciled.

When she finishes, I ask her how she feels in this foreign country.

I've always been curious to know how they lived, at least the Arabs of old who lived in Alhambra, for example. They must have been sophisticated and have lived a good life. The house was beautiful and the woman, very sweet. They made us feel at home. She advised me thoughtfully to put on some comfortable shoes because we were going to walk a lot. As regards the skirt, I already had one.

I say: "With a skirt like that, you don't have to show your legs which are getting older."

That's it. (Pause) And then suddenly the three of us were in the hammock, my husband, her and I, in the middle of the street and the scenes followed: the blue sky, the arcades … .

I say to her that this young woman could be her when she was young and sexy, lying at her husband's side as if she were both women—marking the sexualized relationship and the strong, mature bond that she had with him.

In the dream it didn't seem strange, it was really natural. I only felt a little jealous afterwards, when I left the museum alone to look for them. I thought: "Where have they gone?" (Silence) The forms of the stones were beautiful, they were forms of life eternalized in stone. They had the red tone of the wood of the coffin.

You seem to be mourning the loss of your fertile body, young and alive like the woman in the dream. Could it be that your husband could leave you to form a relationship with a girl who one day you once were?

She says: Oh sweet bird of youth! (reminiscent of Williams, 1959, play. (Pause). The feeling, when I couldn't find them, was of abandonment, loneliness. But I didn't give up the hope that I would find them and kept on going. When the girl at the sweet stand showed me the way, I imagined myself walking alone as night fell and the little river that she said I would have to cross shone like a silver cord. There above, the museum was lit up. But I didn't have the courage to go on my way in the dark and I decided to return home.

You say that while looking for the couple, you kept on going, and you climb and see "sweet" young girls, like the one who was with your husband. To continue your journey you would have to leave these girls and go alone, going down to the little river and after climbing up to the museum. But you decide to "leave until tomorrow" this climb to the museum, perhaps this time accompanied. As you are now, by me.

I was scared. I was in a foreign land. I didn't want to take risks. I went down the hill quickly, behind the girl, and suddenly I was in a fantastically brightly lit street, full of traffic and noise. But I felt safe. I only felt 'up in the air' when I realized I didn't know the address of where we were staying. That's when I woke up.

In the dream you work through your anguish facing the awareness that your body has become "petrified" to pregnancy, just as the little creatures preserved in the reddened stone, which once were alive. Men continue to be able to procreate, and I think that this is implicit in the couple formed between your husband and the younger woman, whom you put in the dream. The mourning for your fertile body can only be done by you alone and this is why you see yourself alone in the fossil room and alone on your way through the elaboration of this grief.

(Silence) Do you know that song: "Young woman, beautiful and loving, makes a man moan without pain".... It's a man who sings it.

You wish to preserve the "sweetness" and the love of this woman, to make your husband moan.

I would. (Pause) I don't want to face old age alone.

You could face the unknown museum alone which may reveal what it means to grow old, but you want the guarantee of being accompanied.

From afar the museum looked like the Acropolis, lit up. But it looked dangerous to go up there alone at that time, between day and night.

So you preferred to return to your busy life, filling your mind with obligations and noise, like the street you arrive on so quickly.

This is really what happens. It's difficult to look at what you have lost. Even if the memories are beautiful.

The important thing is that you realize there is no way you can return.

I see. But it had such an impact that I awoke.

It's as if you had escaped from the situation.

I escaped. And I checked my husband was there, available.

So much so that you could continue to dream.

In this last part, he played the principal role, someone so special that the owner of the house insisted on introducing his brother to him. They were very dark haired, like my mother: she looks Arabic—it must be Portuguese ancestry, Moorish.

I think that the strong and healthy relationship you have had with your mother, who always valorized you, could be fundamental to this affair with your husband, showing that it could be productive for you both, just as in the dream, business being done by him with both brothers. (I think to myself (cf. Meltzer, 1986) that the two very similar dark skinned brothers may refer to two firm maternal breasts and therefore to the primary maternal relationship, fundamental to the constitution of future relationships. It reminds me that she had commented previously that her own breasts were still "firm". It is also interesting that, when she relates the dream, she says she was in a bar, like those we wait in when we are in line for a table at a restaurant.)

I ask her for associations to the little silver river which she would have to cross.

It was a stream of life, but I would pass over it and it would go on its way.

And while it goes on to fertilize and nurture other pastures, you have to pass over it, leave it behind and head in a different direction, the way of the museum, which may contain forms of life, petrified … .

Did you know that there is a hypothesis that the ancient Greeks stored their treasures in the Parthenon? Each family had a safe, like in banks today?

So, when you arrived at the Acropolis you would find your resources stored, to be used in facing the life ahead of you?

She remains silent for a long time and then says: I had never thought of that. I wanted to go but I thought that at another time, perhaps the next day, it would be easier. I might even enjoy the walk, sit at the river's edge a little, and afterwards head on.

You tell me that you need time to metabolize the anguish and sadness which attack your mind, as you were afraid to risk being assaulted as night fell. Now, in daylight, along with me, we can think about this unknown path, with less risk.

Goodbye to biological procreativity and grown up children

For six months Mrs. A. had various dreams about her children as babies that had grown up. She appeared singing lullabies to send them to sleep, showing them how to walk. In the dream that ended this series, one of her children (a thirty year-old) appeared at the age of eighteen months, in a half-light in the doorway that opened out to the garden of her mother's house, saying goodbye and smiling to her, and walking alone in the direction of flower beds full of blossoming flowers.

It appeared as though in her youth she said goodbye to her parents (in the previous association about Psyche), and she is now able to say goodbye not only to her capacity to have children, but also to accept having grown up children, walking on their own two feet away from her, in the direction of a fertile life; like the garden full of flowers at her mother's house.

When writing this, I also thought that she had transmitted the stability and fertility of the earth-soil of the maternal home, a trans-generational transmission that could be passed on to her grandchildren (the youngest of whom was the age of the child in the dream.

Growing old in company

Recently, with a gap of two years between the previous dreams, Mrs. A brought me the following dream:

> I was at home and D. arrived, a colleague from University whom I hadn't seen for many years. She was young, with wonderful skin. She's really dark skinned and dark skin doesn't age so fast. I looked at my husband (who looked like William Hurt in the dream, and I think this because he smiles with his eyes while he talks) and I realized that the skin on his forehead was covered in spots. It had the same red tone of the stones in the museum, with the asymmetrical

marks of life. And he was incredibly animated showing off to our friend some of our "treasures" which were some old plates. He was telling her the age of the plates, and where we had got them from …. I thought, our skin isn't like this old porcelain, which seemed to have the same shine and seemed even more beautiful, since it is rare.

I say that she is growing old with her husband, who remains enthusiastic and who values what they have built together. And, if we are alive and not inanimate, like the old plates, then it is good that we have lively company who grows old with us, like the marks of life on a forehead.

Have you seen "Doctor" (Note 3) with William Hurt? (Note 4) He was a doctor and had to have surgery on his head, and didn't know how it would turn out. He became closer to his patients.

You feel that I am closer to you perhaps because we have had to cope with the same farewells. There are many operations that we have to go through in our heads ….

Farewell

To finish I would like to share a dream which I had whilst writing this Chapter. I dreamt that I received a present in the post; a little red handkerchief with little coloured lines around the edges that crossed each other almost in the corners.

Just three weeks later, on reopening "Adiós a la sangre" (*Goodbye to blood*, Alizade, 2005), I was able to take account of what I was unconsciously elaborating in this dream; a living farewell, shared among friends of my generation. The life that passes inexorably, as shown by the coloured stripes that cut each other, crossing (Tustin, 1981), indicating a limit a few centimetres from the edges. The little lines are identical to those that appear every day on the screen of my old computer, which has served me well throughout its many years of service. Little lines like wrinkles appear with each day that passes. They are multicoloured, and so they are marks of life that will help us to receive the experiences of young generations to come (as in Raphael-Leff's (2010) concept of "generative identity", formed from the beginning of life, through the relationship with the primary objects, matrix of creativity). And to carry out our work with our creative mind despite the aging body, the fruit of our psychic fertility ….

References

Alizade, M. (2005). *Adiós a la sangre*. Buenos Aires: Lumen.

Benedek, T. (1927). Climaterium: a developmental phase. *Psychoanalytical Quartely*, *19*: 1–27.

Bion, W. (1963). *Elements of Psycho-analysis*. London: Heinemann.

Deutsch, H. (1923). The menopause. *International Journal of Psycho-Analysis*, *65*: 55–62.

Drummond de Andrade, C. (1951). Memória. In: *Claro Enigma*. Rio de Janeiro: Companhia das Letras.

Fessler, L. (1950). The psychopatology of climacteric depression. *The Psychoanalytic Quartely*, *19*.

Green, A. (1972). De l'esquisse a l'interprétation des rêves: coupure et clôture. *Nouvelle Revue Psychanalyse*, v.5, pp. 155–80.

Grotstein, J. (2001). *Who is the Dreamer who Dreams the Dream?* Hillsdale: The Analytic Press.

Guillaumin, Jean (1979). Le rêveur et son rêve. In: Grunberg, B. & Sasseguet-Smirgel, J. (Eds.) *Les rêves: la voie royale de l'inconscient* (pp. 265–304). Paris: Tchou, 1979.

Guillaumin, Jean (1981). Le travail du rêve comme deuil des objets de la veille. *RevueFrançaise Psychanalytique*, 1: pp. 6–185.

Haines, Randa. (1991)."*The Doctor*", Touchstone Pictures.

Hashimoto, M. (2002). *Pintura e escritura do mundo flutuante*. Rio de Janeiro: Hedra.

Meltzer, D. (1986). *Studies in Extended Metapsychology*. Perthshire: Clunie Press.

Meyers, H. (2002). The challenges and options of menopause. In: Alizade, A.M. (Ed.), *The embodied female*. London : Karnac).

Quinodoz, D. (2008). *Vieillir: une découverte*. Paris: PUF.

Quinodoz, J-M. (1999). Dreams that turn over a page: integration dreams with paradoxical regressive content. *International Journal of Psycho-Analysis*, *80*: 225–238.

Raphael-Leff, J. (2010). The "dreamer" by day life - imaginative play, creativity, and generative identity. *The Psychoanalytic Study of the Child*, Vol. 64: 14–53.

Rosenbaum, E. (1988) *A taste of my own medicine: When the doctor is the patient*. New York: Random House.

Segal, H. (1993). *The Function of Dreams. The Dream Discourse today*. London: Routledge.

Tennessee, W. (1959). *Sweet Bird of Youth*. New York: New Directions Publishing.

Tustin, F. (1981). *Autistic States in Children*. London: Routledge.

Notes

1. Translated by Christopher Mack.
2. I think she refers to the Japanese woodcut prints of the seventh, eighteenth and nineteenth century, that portray everyday life, the most well known exponents of the period being: Moronobu (1682–1753), Harunobu (1724–1770), Utamaro (1756–1806), Hokusai (1760–1849), Kunisada (1786–1865), Hiroshige (1797–1858), and others. Their motto was *"floating on the current of life, like a gourd down a river"*. (Hashimoto, 2002).
3. "The Doctor" (1991) Touchstone Pictures, directed by Randa Haines, based on the autobiography of Dr. Edward E. Rosenbaum (1988). *A Taste Of My Own Medicine: When the Doctor Is the Patient*, New York: Random House.
4. William Hurt: these losses will hurt.

AFTERWORD

We dedicate this book to Mariam Alizade.

With deep sadness we heard of the sudden premature death of Mariam Alizade, an author in this book, the second overall Chair of COWAP (Committee on Women and Psychoanalysis), a warm and tireless promoter of all COWAP activities and those related to COWAP. Mariam died in March 2013, shortly before this book, which she supported with great passion, was published. She was a valued theoretical thinker in feminine sexuality and gender issues, a friend, a positive person, warm and supportive but also a fighter.

It is my deepest wish to join Frances Thomson Salo in thanking the contributors of this book for their enrichment as well as to thank the IPA publication committee for their kind support.

It is my concern also to thank the other members of the German COWAP group which made possible this project in the tradition of women groups with enthusiasm and patience: Ursula Reiser-Mumme, Ute Auhagen-Stephanos, Brigitte Filor, Herta H.Harsch, Gudrun Hess, Renate Hoehfeld, Annegret Mahler-Bungers, Eva Reichelt, Gertraud Schlesinger-Kipp, Christiane Schrader, Almuth Sellschopp, Ingrid Vallenas de Kimm-Friedenberg and others. We were joined by the international COWAP committee whenever needed. We are very thankful to have been supported by the Breuninger Stiftung. Thanks to the permissions of HarperCollinsPublishers (citations from "Wetlands"), the Museum of Modern Art Villeneuve d'Asqu ("Eloise"), John Riddy (Lucian-Freud-pictures) and others this book is able to have this outstanding appearance. I am very grateful to my co-editor Frances Thomson Salo, COWAP overall chair, who accompanied our project with enormous interest, knowledge and female wisdom. This book is the fruit thanks to all those involved. May it be another source helping to enlighten the "dark continent".

Ingrid Moeslein-Teising

INDEX